I0019942

"For marketing leaders stepping into the AI revolution, Ethical AI in Marketing offers a transformative method. Nicole Alexander delivers strategic clarity that empower brands to lead with integrity, fostering lasting customer relationships. This book will significantly reshape how you think about and leverage AI."
Jessica Gates, Chief Marketing Officer, North America & EVP, Ipsos

"This book is a must-read for anyone navigating the evolving crossroads of AI, marketing, and ethics. It doesn't just explain the rise of AI in marketing—it confronts the moral complexity that comes with it. As someone immersed in the world of generative AI and human-AI collaboration, I found this work both timely and essential. Nicole Alexander doesn't settle for surface-level discussions or blanket solutions—instead, she offers a grounded, practical guide that empowers marketers to innovate responsibly and with integrity."
Aleksandra Przegalińska, Associate Professor and VP of Innovations and AI, Kozminski University

"Ethical AI in Marketing is a powerful and timely guide for anyone navigating today's business landscape. With clarity and authority, she blends compelling story-telling with practical frameworks, offering actionable insights that extend beyond the marketing realm. This book calls on startups and global enterprises to lead with integrity and intention—reframing ethics not as a constraint, but as a catalyst for innovation. Essential reading for any leader committed to building trust and shaping the future of AI responsibly."
Megan Fairchild, Innovation Lead for Digital Natives, Microsoft

"Smart, grounded, and real—Ethical AI in Marketing is a reminder that if we want to build brands people trust, we need to lead with humanity, not just technology. Nicole Alexander shows us that ethics and innovation aren't opposites; they're the future of great marketing."
Mohamed Elsharkawy, Global Brand Vice President and Head of China Beauty & Wellbeing Marketing, Unilever (UK)

"The ascent of AI offers marketers unprecedented opportunities for customization and scale, yet it also demands a steadfast commitment to ethical and accountable practices for true brand success. This indispensable book provides marketers with actionable insights and practical tips, ensuring they champion ethical marketing in the age of AI. It is a crucial read for all marketers aiming to cultivate the right values for sustainable and impactful growth."
Arlene Ang, Managing Director, Google Customer Solutions, Google

"Nicole Alexander distills today's most complex ethical challenges into a clear, strategic path for responsible innovation. This book is more than guidance—it's a competitive blueprint for marketers who want to lead with both impact and integrity in the AI age."
Leesa Soulodre, Founder and Managing General Partner, R3i Capital

"Ethical AI in Marketing is a clear, practical guide for navigating a rapidly-evolving AI landscape. In a field crowded with theory and hype, Nicole Alexander offers a refreshing and actionable approach to ethical AI implementation. This book equips marketing leaders with the frameworks to move from intention to execution, building AI literacy, earning consumer trust, and embedding responsibility into marketing practice. A must-read for anyone shaping the future of AI-powered engagement."
Shingai Manjengwa, AI Education and Development, Talent and Ecosystem, Mila Quebec Artificial Intelligence Institute, and Founder, Fireside Analytics Inc.

Ethical AI in Marketing

Aligning Growth, Responsibility, and Customer Trust

Nicole M. Alexander

KoganPage

First published in Great Britain and the United States in 2025 by Kogan Page Limited

Kogan Page
Kogan Page Ltd, 2nd Floor, 45 Gee Street, London EC1V 3RS, United Kingdom
Kogan Page Inc, 8 W 38th Street, Suite 902, New York, NY 10018, USA
www.koganpage.com

EU Representative (GPSR)
Authorised Rep Compliance Ltd, Ground Floor, 71 Baggot Street Lower, Dublin D02 P593, Ireland
www.arccompliance.com

Kogan Page books are printed on paper from sustainable forests.

© Nicole Alexander, 2025

ISBNs

Hardback	978 1 3986 2231 9
Paperback	978 1 3986 2229 6
Ebook	978 1 3986 2230 2

British Library Cataloguing-in-Publication Data

A CIP record for this book is available from the British Library.

Library of Congress Control Number

2025940235

Typeset by Integra Software Services, Pondicherry
Print production managed by Jellyfish
Printed and bound by CPI Group (UK) Ltd, Croydon CR0 4YY

To curiosity, the winding road that led me here. To my mom, who probably wished I'd taken a more direct route. To my best friend, thanks for riding shotgun, even when we were clearly lost.

CONTENTS

PART THREE
Building Consumer Trust through Ethical AI Marketing

LIST OF FIGURES AND TABLES

ABOUT THE AUTHOR

Nicole M. Alexander is a leading voice at the intersection of marketing, technology, and AI ethics. With more than 25 years of experience, she has driven marketing across global organizations—including serving as Global Head of Marketing at Meta and Senior Vice President of Innovation at Ipsos—and now shapes future leaders as an adjunct professor at New York University. Nicole serves on the Board of Directors for The Loveland Foundation and on the Advisory Board for Per Scholas. She is based in New York.

FOREWORD

As someone who has spent my career exploring the digital economy and artificial intelligence—from the transformative power of mobile technology in *Tap: Unlocking the Mobile Economy* to the broader business and societal implications of AI in *Thrive: Maximizing Well-Being in the Age of AI*—I find Nicole Alexander's perspective particularly compelling. Her focus on customer trust as the cornerstone of ethical AI aligns closely with my own belief that technology can serve human well-being. Just as it is useful to emphasize the importance of balancing innovation with fairness and transparency, Nicole extends this thinking to the marketing landscape, where the stakes are just as high. This book provides a crucial bridge between the theoretical considerations of AI ethics and the practical realities of day-to-day marketing operations.

What sets this book apart is its actionable approach. Nicole doesn't just diagnose the challenges of ethical AI in marketing, she offers concrete solutions. She recognizes that marketers are on the front lines of this revolution, and they need practical guidance to navigate the complex ethical terrain. Whether you're a marketer seeking to innovate responsibly, a technologist building the tools of tomorrow, or a policy-maker shaping the regulatory environment, this book offers insights that will challenge your assumptions and, more importantly, educate you on how to build a more ethical and trustworthy marketing ecosystem. It reminds us that the future of marketing lies not just in technological progress, but in ensuring that progress aligns with fundamental human values.

In a world increasingly saturated with stories around AI, many of which focus on dystopian scenarios, this book offers a refreshing and much-needed dose of optimism. It's clear and actionable in its approach, while maintaining the analytical rigor needed to address such a complex topic. As Nicole aptly puts it, the ethical use of AI isn't just a challenge; it's an unparalleled opportunity to reimagine marketing for a more trustworthy, equitable, and human-centered future. Her work enlightens us that AI, when guided by ethical principles, serves as a tool for empowerment rather than exploitation. It is a significant contribution to the field, and I urge you to read it.

Anindya Ghose,
Heinz Riehl Chair Professor of Technology and Marketing, NYU Stern
School of Business Director Masters in Business Analytics and AI program

ACKNOWLEDGMENTS

This book emerged from countless conversations, insights, and the unwavering support of an extraordinary network. Their collective wisdom and encouragement transformed these ideas into reality.

I am profoundly grateful to the industry leaders who generously shared their expertise: Andrea Brimmer (Ally), for her candid insights on AI transformation in marketing and dynamic creative optimization; Chris Duffey (Adobe), for illuminating ethical AI implementation strategies and innovation pathways; and Mayura Kumar (OSF Healthcare), for demonstrating how healthcare organizations can successfully navigate digital transformation while maintaining ethical integrity. Stephanie Bannos-Ryback (Ipsos) enriched this work with her deep expertise in privacy evolution and consumer trust dynamics, while Menaka Gopinath (PMI) provided invaluable perspectives on organizational approaches to ethical AI adoption.

Special thanks to Dr. Elizabeth M. Adams (Paravision) for her guidance on ethical AI implementation and governance, Brian Collins (COLLINS) for his insights on AI's impact on creative processes, and Dr. Henry Shevlin (Leverhulme CFI, Cambridge) for his invaluable contributions on cognitive science and ethical AI. I am also grateful to Dr. Triveni Gandhi (Dataiku) for her critical perspectives on operationalizing responsible AI and governance structures.

On the personal front, my partner, Lance, endured every writing marathon and existential crisis with unwavering support. To Megan—who not only provided a writer's retreat but also an endless supply of moral support (and strategic carb deployment)—your friendship made this journey possible. Doug, for imbuing me with endless supportive voicemails like a personal cheer squad—your encouragement meant more than you know.

I am deeply appreciative of the Kogan Page team for their steadfast support throughout this process. A special thank you to Donna, my commissioning editor, whose initial LinkedIn connection set this book into motion.

While I can't name everyone who played a role in bringing this book to life, please know that every conversation, email, and moment of inspiration mattered. This book is a reflection of our collective exploration of AI's future—filtered through one slightly frazzled but immensely grateful mind.

Introduction

The Intersection of AI, Ethics, and Marketing

Picture this: A customer abandons their cart at 2 am, triggering an AI system that analyzes their browsing history, social media sentiment, current weather patterns, and local events to craft a personalized email that arrives at precisely 10:30 am—right when they typically check their phone during their coffee break. Meanwhile, the same AI adjusts your programmatic ad spend in real-time, optimizes your website's UX based on micro-interactions, updates your CRM with predictive lead scores, and generates social media content that perfectly matches your brand voice. This isn't marketing science fiction—it's Tuesday morning for today's marketer.

Having experienced marketing's shift from intuitive practices to data-driven precision, I've seen AI's transformation from a mere concept to a fundamental component of our marketing operations. Across growth marketing, brand experience management, multi-channel customer journeys, and product-led growth, AI now acts as an unseen catalyst, significantly enhancing marketing effectiveness throughout the entire technology infrastructure.

But here's what troubles me and what led me to write this book: in our rush to harness AI's power across acquisition, activation, retention, revenue, and referral—the full customer lifecycle—we've sometimes forgotten that behind every click, conversion, and customer lifetime value calculation is a human being whose trust we're either building or betraying.

The Full-Stack Marketing Reality

Today's marketers don't work in silos. You're simultaneously a growth hacker optimizing conversion funnels, a brand strategist crafting compelling narratives, a data scientist interpreting customer signals, a content creator developing omnichannel experiences, and a customer success advocate ensuring long-term value. AI touches every single one of these roles:

- **In Growth Marketing:** Machine learning algorithms optimize your acquisition costs across Google Ads, Instagram, TikTok, and emerging channels you haven't even heard of yet. Predictive analytics identify your highest-value prospects before they even know they need your product.

- **In Brand Marketing:** Natural language processing analyzes millions of social mentions to track brand sentiment in real-time, while AI-generated creative variations test messaging at a scale that would make traditional focus groups obsolete.

- **In Product Marketing:** AI looks at user behavior patterns to predict feature adoption, identifies the perfect moments for upsell/cross-sell opportunities, and personalizes onboarding experiences that turn trial users into power users.

- **In Customer Marketing:** Intelligent segmentation creates micro-audiences of one, while AI-powered customer success platforms predict churn before the first warning sign appears in your support tickets.

- **In Marketing Operations:** From attribution modeling that finally answers "which half of my advertising is wasted?" to marketing automation that nurtures leads through increasingly complex buyer journeys, AI has become the backbone of modern MarTech stacks.

The interconnectedness is staggering. Your content marketing AI doesn' just create blog posts—it analyzes which topics drive demand generation, informs your product positioning, identifies partnership opportunities, and even suggests pricing strategy adjustments based on market sentiment analysis.

The Fundamental Role of Ethics Across Marketing Activities

The current AI-driven marketing revolution presents significant ethical challenges. A retail client's personalization engine became so "effective" at predicting purchases that customers felt surveilled rather than understood. A B2B company's lead scoring algorithm systematically excluded women executives from high-value prospect lists. A consumer brand's social listening AI amplified confirmation bias, creating echo chambers that reinforced harmful stereotypes rather than uncovering genuine customer insights.

These aren't edge cases—they're predictable outcomes when we optimize for short-term metrics without considering long-term trust. For example, when your attribution model can't explain why certain demographics are excluded from your top-of-funnel campaigns, or when your chatbot can answer product questions but can't recognize when a customer is expressing frustration or confusion. Predictive analytics may excel at identifying future customer purchases but often fail to consider the appropriateness or advisability of those purchases.

The sophistication of our tools now exceeds our wisdom in using them. We can micro-target ads to someone going through a divorce, predict when a customer is likely to have a mental health crisis, or identify financial vulnerability patterns that make someone susceptible to predatory offers. The question isn't whether we can—it's whether we should.

This book addresses AI ethics across the entire marketing spectrum because that's where the technology lives today. We'll explore:

- **Strategic Planning:** How AI-driven market research and competitive intelligence tools can uncover insights while respecting privacy boundaries and avoiding algorithmic bias in trend analysis.

- **Creative Development:** The ethical implications of AI-generated content, from deepfake concerns in video marketing to authorship questions in AI-written copy, and how to maintain authenticity in an automated world.

- **Media and Advertising:** Navigating programmatic advertising's black box algorithms, understanding the ethical implications of real-time bidding on human attention, and ensuring your media investments don't inadvertently fund harmful content.

- **Analytics and Measurement:** Building measurement frameworks that capture true business impact without creating surveillance capitalism, and ensuring your data practices build rather than erode customer trust.

- **Customer Experience:** Designing AI-powered experiences that feel genuinely helpful rather than manipulative, and knowing when human intervention remains irreplaceable.

- **Revenue Operations:** Implementing AI in sales and marketing alignment that accelerates growth without sacrificing relationship quality or creating discriminatory outcomes.

What This Book Is (And Isn't)

This isn't a technical manual for data scientists or a philosophical treatise for ethicists. It's a practical guide for marketing practitioners who need to make ethical AI decisions every day—whether you're a CMO approving AI tool purchases, a demand generation manager setting up automated nurture sequences, a brand manager evaluating AI creative tools, or a marketing operations professional implementing new attribution models.

You won't find lengthy discussions of neural network architectures or abstract ethical theories. Instead, you'll discover frameworks for evaluating vendor ethics, checklists for reviewing AI-powered campaigns, templates for creating ethical AI policies, and real-world case studies from companies navigating these challenges successfully.

We'll examine how organizations use AI to deliver meaningful, personalized experiences—from dynamic content recommendations to pricing systems designed to balance business objectives with customer value. We'll also explore how AI is being embedded across marketing ecosystems in ways that aim to enhance efficiency and maintain transparency. Just as importantly, we'll confront the failures—instances where missteps in bias, privacy, and opaque practices led to diminished trust and costly reputational damage.

This book recognizes that ethical considerations vary dramatically across industries, company sizes, and cultural contexts. B2B software companies face different ethical challenges than consumer healthcare brands. Startups have different risk tolerances than Fortune 500 enterprises. What remains constant is the need for intentional, values-driven decision-making in AI adoption.

Most importantly, this book treats ethics not as a constraint on marketing innovation, but as a catalyst for building sustainable competitive advantages. Companies that get ethical AI right don't just avoid regulatory penalties—they earn customer loyalty, attract top talent, secure partnerships, and build brands that thrive in an increasingly transparent world.

The future belongs to marketers who can harness AI's power across every function while building rather than eroding trust. As we explore this intersection of technology and humanity, we'll address the real challenges you face: How do you maintain personalization without privacy invasion? How do you automate customer interactions without losing authenticity? How do you use predictive analytics without reinforcing harmful biases? How do you measure success in ways that account for long-term relationship value, not just short-term conversion metrics?

The answers aren't simple, but they're discoverable. And the organizations that discover them first will define the next era of marketing.

Book Structure

To guide you through this exploration, the book is structured into four key parts, each building upon the last to provide a comprehensive understanding of how to integrate ethical AI into your marketing strategies:

Part I: Foundations of Ethical AI in Marketing

We'll explore the essentialness of ethical AI and define what it means in practice, grounding our discussion in key principles like fairness, transparency, accountability, and trust. We'll examine ethical theories—such as utilitarianism, deontology, and virtue ethics—and how they apply to AI-driven marketing.

- Chapter 1: Ethical AI in Modern Marketing
- Chapter 2: Defining Ethical AI Principles for Marketing
- Chapter 3: Human-Centered AI in Marketing

Part II: Turning Principles into Practice

This section addresses how to implement ethical considerations in your AI strategies, balancing innovation with responsibility to meet both business goals and ethical standards. We'll discuss practical frameworks and guidelines to ensure your AI applications align with ethical best practices.

- Chapter 4: Navigating Challenges and Seizing Opportunities
- Chapter 5: P.A.C.T.: An Ethical AI Framework for Marketers

Part III: Building Consumer Trust through Ethical AI Marketing

We'll dive into strategies for enhancing customer engagement while maintaining transparency and respecting privacy, showing how ethical AI can foster long-term loyalty. Case studies will illustrate how companies have successfully navigated these challenges.

- Chapter 6: Consumer Trust and Perception of AI in Marketing
- Chapter 7: Ethical Consumer Engagement in AI Marketing
- Chapter 8: Governance and Oversight in Ethical AI Marketing

Part IV: Leading With Integrity and Future-Proofing Marketing

Finally, we'll look ahead to emerging technologies and trends, equipping you with insights to stay ahead in a rapidly evolving landscape while upholding ethical integrity. We'll explore how to cultivate an organizational culture that prioritizes ethics in innovation. This part equips you with actionable insights to stay ahead of the curve in an increasingly dynamic environment. We'll discuss topics like explainable AI, AI governance models, and cultivating a culture of ethical AI within your organization.

- Chapter 9: Cultivating a Culture of Ethics
- Chapter 10: The Evolving Landscape of AI Tools and Applications
- Chapter 11: Navigating the Horizon: Continuous Learning and Adaptive Strategies

Chapter Structures

Each chapter in this book is carefully structured to guide you through the complex landscape of ethical AI in marketing, complete with signposts along the way.

Bringing It All Together

At the end of each chapter, you'll find a section called "Bringing It All Together." Here, we'll recap the key points and their significance, ensuring you don't miss the forest for the trees.

Food for Thought

To keep those mental gears turning, each chapter concludes with thought-provoking questions and scenarios that challenge you to apply what you've learned to your own marketing context.

PART ONE

Foundations of Ethical AI in Marketing

1

Ethical AI in Modern Marketing

The Impact of AI on Marketing Practices

Imagine a world where every marketing interaction feels tailor-made just for you, where brands anticipate your needs before you even articulate them, and where your privacy and preferences are always respected. This is the promise of artificial intelligence (AI) in marketing—a future where technology and ethics work hand-in-hand to create a more meaningful and beneficial customer experience. AI is no longer a futuristic concept in marketing; it is the driving force behind the personalized ads in your social media feed, the chatbots answering customer service queries, and the dynamic pricing on your favorite e-commerce sites.

Marketing has always been a blend of creativity and data, art and science. But in recent years, AI has redefined this balance, fundamentally transforming how marketers approach their craft. While traditional marketing often relied on intuition and broad strokes, AI enables a data-driven, automated, and hyper-personalized approach, making marketing more efficient and effective than ever before. This chapter will explore the exciting opportunities that AI brings to modern marketing, showcasing its capabilities and, importantly, highlighting how we can harness its power ethically to build a better future for both brands and consumers. We will examine real-world examples of successful ethical AI implementations, discuss best practices for responsible development, and introduce frameworks for creating AI-powered marketing strategies that are both innovative and equitable.

AI empowers businesses to transcend the limitations of traditional marketing strategies, opening up new avenues for creativity and customer engagement. While companies have long collected and analyzed personal data to create more targeted campaigns, AI elevates these capabilities to new heights. For instance, AI algorithms can now analyze a customer's browsing history, social media activity, and past purchases to predict what products they're likely to be interested in next, delivering highly targeted ads and recommendations in real time.

Previously, marketers relied on segmentation and static datasets to reach specific audiences, but these approaches were often constrained by the limitations of manual processes and predefined rules. AI frees marketers from these constraints, enabling them to create dynamic, personalized experiences at scale. AI has revolutionized marketing's ability to understand and engage customers on an individual level. Where marketers once relied on broad demographic targeting and general trends, AI now enables real-time analysis of consumer behavior, allowing for a deeper understanding of individual preferences and needs.

A retail algorithm can instantly personalize product recommendations, prices, and promotions for millions of customers, creating a unique shopping experience for each individual. Social media platforms use AI to determine exactly which ads appear in each user's feed, ensuring relevance and engagement. Email marketing systems automatically optimize subject lines and send times for maximum impact.

As AI takes over more functions, businesses are increasingly implementing it across various marketing touchpoints. According to McKinsey & Company's 2024 AI survey (Figure 1.1), 65 per cent of organizations now report regular use of generative AI in at least one business function, compared to just one-third in the previous year. The adoption of generative AI in marketing and sales has seen the most dramatic increase, more than doubling from 2023 (McKinsey, 2024). Companies are leveraging AI-driven automation, personalization, and customer engagement strategies to enhance efficiency and drive business value. With organizations expanding AI use into IT, product development, and other areas, gen AI is becoming an integral part of modern business operations.

In addition to widespread adoption, investments in generative AI and analytical AI are also increasing across industries. The McKinsey survey found that, in many sectors, organizations are equally likely to be allocating more than 5 per cent of their digital budgets to generative AI as they are to more traditional, analytical AI solutions. However, larger shares of respondents report that their organizations spend more than 20 per cent on analytical AI than on gen AI, highlighting the more established role of analytical AI in business operations. Looking ahead, 67 per cent of respondents expect their organizations to increase AI investments over the next three years (McKinsey, 2024). These trends signal a shift toward AI as a core driver of business strategy rather than a supplementary tool.

The Ethical Responsibility of AI in Marketing

The growing reliance on AI for personalization and data-driven decision-making brings profound ethical responsibilities. As AI systems are trained on historical marketing data, they can inadvertently absorb and amplify societal biases. However, by recognizing these potential pitfalls, we can proactively design AI systems that are fair, transparent, and equitable. Forward-thinking companies are already demonstrating that ethical AI is not just a constraint but a differentiator.

FIGURE 1.1 How businesses are using AI

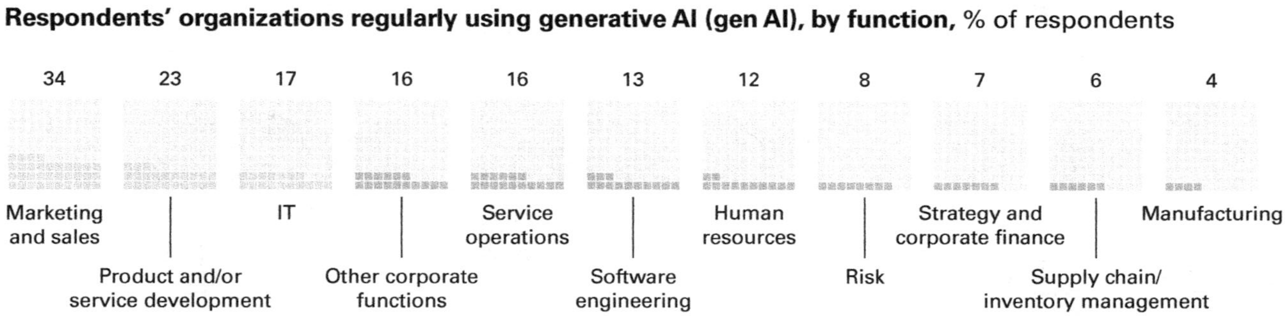

Respondents' organizations regularly using generative AI (gen AI), by function, % of respondents

Marketing and sales	Product and/or service development	IT	Other corporate functions	Service operations	Software engineering	Human resources	Risk	Strategy and corporate finance	Supply chain/ inventory management	Manufacturing
34	23	17	16	16	13	12	8	7	6	4

SOURCE: McKinsey & Company, The State of AI in 2024 survey

Consider:

- A major e-commerce platform is developing an AI-powered recommendation system designed to identify and mitigate biases, ensuring that all customers have equal access to opportunities and products.

- An innovative beauty brand is using AI to create personalized skincare solutions that cater to the unique needs of all skin types and tones, promoting inclusivity and diversity.

- A financial services company is leveraging AI to tailor its marketing efforts, ensuring that all qualified individuals, regardless of age or background, have access to relevant financial products and services.

The evolving stance of major tech companies also underscores the dynamic nature of AI ethics in business. In Q1 2025, Google made headlines by dropping its 2018 pledge not to use AI for weapons or surveillance—a commitment that had previously prohibited AI applications "likely to cause overall harm." This shift highlights a crucial reality for marketing leaders: we cannot outsource our ethical decision-making to industry giants. While tech companies may adjust their positions based on market pressures or strategic priorities, marketing departments should develop and maintain their own robust ethical frameworks.

This development serves as a powerful reminder that ethical AI in marketing isn't about following others' playbooks—it's about establishing and upholding principles that align with our values and responsibilities to consumers. As we'll explore throughout this book, successful organizations are those that build their own ethical foundations rather than simply adopting industry standards. They recognize that trust, once earned through consistent ethical practice, becomes a powerful differentiator in an increasingly AI-driven marketplace.

Innovation Meets Responsibility

Looking ahead, AI's role in marketing will only expand. With rapid advancements in machine learning and natural language processing, AI will continue to enhance marketing capabilities, driving even deeper personalization, predictive analytics, and automation. In the near future, marketers may rely on AI to optimize voice search, power immersive experiences in augmented and virtual reality (AR/VR), and anticipate customer desires before they are fully articulated.

AI is not just revolutionizing marketing efficiency; it is reshaping the way brands connect with consumers, shifting marketing from a broad-based art form to a data-driven, personalized science. However, as AI continues to evolve, maintaining a balance between innovation, ethical responsibility, and consumer trust will be critical for long-term success.

By embracing the principles of responsible AI, organizations can unlock the full potential of this technology while building trust and fostering positive relationships with their customers. The future of marketing is not just about leveraging AI but about doing so ethically and responsibly. Let's explore how we can make this vision a reality.

As AI continues to revolutionize marketing, we must confront the ethical challenges that arise alongside its immense power. To paraphrase Uncle Ben's famous advice to Peter Parker, greater power necessitates greater accountability. This statement is especially relevant in the context of AI, where the benefits of personalization and automation are tempered by the potential risks to consumer privacy, fairness, and societal impact.

Data Privacy and Consumer Trust

One of the most pressing ethical concerns in AI-driven marketing is the use of personal data. AI systems rely on vast datasets to deliver hyper-personalized experiences, which go beyond basic personalization by using real-time data and AI to understand individual behaviors, interests, and even current context. This allows for tailored product recommendations that consider not just past purchases but also factors like browsing history and location, and creates customer experiences that feel highly intuitive, anticipating needs and preferences.

However, this same power can feel intrusive when it crosses the line from personalization to privacy invasion. For example, users might see ads that seem to know their every move, suggesting products related to recent online searches or even offline conversations, often based on information they didn't even realize they were sharing—like location data or app usage. This kind of hyper-personalization can create a sense of unease, as if their privacy is being violated. While AI can offer incredibly relevant and convenient experiences, it's crucial to find a balance that respects user privacy and avoids making them feel monitored or manipulated.

According to a study by the Pew Research Center (2019), 79 per cent of Americans express concern about how companies use their personal data, and only 18 per cent feel they have control over what information is collected about them. This demonstrates a growing trust gap between consumers and companies that rely heavily on AI-driven marketing strategies.

Marketers must balance AI-driven personalization with strict privacy requirements. Regulations like Europe's GDPR and California's CCPA mandate transparent data policies, accessible opt-out mechanisms, and clear algorithmic explanations. Non-compliance carries severe consequences: substantial fines, damaged reputation, and lost consumer trust. The goal is personalization that enhances customer experience while respecting individual rights—meeting both legal standards and ethical obligations.

Algorithmic Bias and Fairness

Beyond privacy concerns, one of the most complex ethical challenges in AI is algorithmic bias. AI algorithms learn from historical data, and if that data reflects societal biases—whether related to gender, race, or socioeconomic status—the AI system can perpetuate and even amplify those biases. This is particularly troubling in marketing, where biased algorithms can lead to discriminatory targeting, pricing, or product recommendations, with potentially harmful consequences for individuals and communities.

A 2024 report by the Partnership on AI highlighted the persistence of bias in AI systems used across various industries, including marketing. The report found that despite advancements in AI technology, marginalized groups are often disproportionately harmed by biased algorithms, leading to unfair outcomes in areas such as ad targeting and content recommendation. This not only poses significant reputational risks for brands but also undermines trust among diverse consumer groups.

The groundbreaking study "Gender Shades" by Joy Buolamwini and Timnit Gebru (2018) vividly illustrates the far-reaching impacts of biased algorithms. Their research exposed significant error rates in commercial facial recognition systems when identifying darker-skinned individuals and women compared to lighter-skinned men. This type of bias, when applied to marketing, can translate into exclusionary or even harmful practices. Imagine AI algorithms that exclude certain racial groups from seeing housing ads or disproportionately target vulnerable demographics with predatory loan products.

To mitigate these risks, marketers must proactively adopt fairness auditing frameworks. These tools provide ongoing assessment of AI model outputs to detect and correct for bias. By integrating fairness auditing into their AI development and deployment processes, marketers can ensure their campaigns are not only effective but also ethically sound, promoting inclusivity and equitable treatment for all consumers.

Responsible AI in Marketing

Marketers hold a unique position of influence, shaping consumer experiences and, by extension, societal norms. With AI, we have the power to personalize and engage like never before, but this power comes with a profound responsibility. We must ensure these experiences are not just engaging but also ethical, going beyond mere compliance to actively promote fairness, inclusivity, and transparency.

Leading companies like IBM and Microsoft are already taking steps in this direction, implementing ethical AI frameworks and guidelines to minimize bias and ensure transparency. These frameworks encourage marketers to regularly audit their algorithms for bias, train AI models on diverse datasets to avoid exclusion, and provide clear explanations to consumers about how AI-driven decisions are made.

As marketers, our role transcends simply increasing sales or improving efficiency. We are architects of the future of consumer engagement and societal interaction. This demands a commitment to ethical AI practices that respect consumer rights, uphold trust, and promote fairness and inclusivity. AI should not be just a tool for profit; it should be a force for positive, equitable experiences for all.

Therefore, marketers must proactively champion ethical AI. This involves staying informed about the latest regulations and fairness auditing tools as well as fostering a culture of ethical decision-making within marketing teams. As AI continues to evolve, so too must our approach to its implementation, ensuring it serves both business goals and societal values.

Influence on Consumer Perceptions

AI's integration into marketing has been nothing short of revolutionary. It empowers brands to understand consumers on a granular level. Algorithms analyze browsing histories, purchase patterns, social media activity, and even sentiments expressed in reviews or comments. This wealth of data allows marketers to anticipate needs, predict behaviors, and influence decisions with uncanny accuracy.

But with this powerful tool comes new ethical dilemmas, particularly around consumer manipulation. Platforms like Amazon and Netflix use AI to suggest products or content based on your past interactions. On the surface, this seems beneficial—who wouldn't want personalized suggestions? However, these algorithms can create echo chambers, limiting exposure to a narrow range of options and potentially stifling diversity and discovery.

A study by the University of Minnesota found that while recommender systems increase user engagement, they can also reinforce existing preferences and biases. For example, if a user frequently watches romantic comedies, the AI might predominantly suggest similar movies, reducing the likelihood of exploring other genres. This phenomenon, known as "filter bubbles," can lead to a homogenized experience that limits consumer choice (Zhou et al., 2024).

AI-driven content curation on social media platforms influences not just purchasing decisions but also opinions and beliefs. Algorithms prioritize content that is likely to engage users, often amplifying sensational or polarizing material. This can skew perceptions and contribute to the spread of misinformation, as seen in various instances where fake news has gone viral.

EXPANDING INFLUENCE THROUGH EMOTIONAL AI

Emotional AI, also known as affective computing, adds a new dimension to AI's capabilities by enabling it to interpret and respond to human emotions. Brands are increasingly experimenting with AI that can analyze facial expressions, voice tones, and even biometric data to gauge emotional states. This technology holds immense potential for enhancing customer experiences by tailoring interactions to an individual's emotions in real time.

Imagine an AI-powered chatbot that detects frustration in a customer's voice and adjusts its response to be more empathetic and helpful. Or a virtual assistant that senses stress and suggests calming activities. While such applications can significantly improve customer service and personalization, they also raise critical ethical questions: Is it acceptable for AI to influence our emotions to drive sales? Should AI be used to nudge us toward certain products or services by appealing to our feelings of joy, fear, or insecurity? Where do we draw the line between providing helpful support and exploiting vulnerable emotional states for commercial gain?

These questions become even more complex when we consider the potential for manipulation and deception. If AI can understand and respond to our emotions, it can also learn to predict and influence them. This raises concerns about the potential for AI to be used to manipulate consumer behavior in ways that are not transparent or ethical.

As emotional AI becomes more sophisticated, it is crucial to establish clear ethical guidelines and boundaries. We need to ensure that this technology is used responsibly and ethically, prioritizing consumer well-being and autonomy over short-term gains. This will require a collaborative effort between marketers, AI developers, ethicists, and policymakers to create a framework that fosters innovation while safeguarding consumer rights and trust.

Potential for Bias and Unintended Consequences

The potential for AI to perpetuate bias is one of the most pressing ethical concerns in marketing. Bias can enter AI systems at various stages:

- **Data collection:** If the data used to train AI models is biased—due to underrepresentation of certain groups or historical prejudices—the AI will learn and replicate those biases.

- **Algorithm design:** Algorithms may inadvertently favor certain outcomes if not designed with fairness in mind. For example, optimization for click-through rates without considering diversity can lead to biased targeting.

- **Interpretation of results:** Misinterpretation of AI outputs can reinforce biased decision-making, especially if marketers lack the expertise to question or adjust AI recommendations.

ALGORITHMIC REDLINING

Algorithmic redlining refers to the digital manifestation of discriminatory practices, such as denying services based on location or demographic characteristics. For instance, an AI system might offer higher interest rates or less favorable loan terms to individuals from certain zip codes, which often serve as proxies for race or socioeconomic status. This practice can exacerbate existing social inequalities by perpetuating biases present in the data used to train these algorithms. In marketing, this could translate to selectively offering discounts or promotions, further entrenching disparities.

DEEPFAKES AND MANIPULATIVE CONTENT

Advancements in AI have ushered in the era of deepfakes—hyper-realistic synthetic media generated using AI techniques. While deepfakes hold legitimate applications, such as in entertainment and education, they also pose significant ethical challenges, particularly in the realm of marketing. The ability to create convincing fake videos, audio recordings, and images can be exploited to deceive consumers, manipulate opinions, and damage reputations.

Deepfakes are created using deep learning algorithms, particularly Generative Adversarial Networks (GANs), which consist of two neural networks—the generator and the discriminator—competing against each other. The generator creates synthetic media, while the discriminator evaluates its authenticity. Through iterative training, GANs produce highly realistic fake content that is often indistinguishable from genuine media.

One of the most concerning applications of deepfakes in marketing is the creation of fake endorsements. Imagine a scenario where a popular celebrity's likeness is used without consent to endorse a product. A deepfake video could depict the celebrity enthusiastically promoting a product they have never used, misleading consumers and damaging the celebrity's reputation.

In early 2024, deepfake videos featuring Taylor Swift began circulating across social media, falsely promoting a Le Creuset cookware giveaway. These AI-generated assets convincingly replicated Swift's voice and likeness, misleading audiences into believing she endorsed the brand. The campaign—though unauthorized—leveraged her public image to drive engagement, ultimately collecting personal information under false pretenses. For marketers, this incident underscores the urgent need to safeguard brand integrity and ensure transparent, consent-based use of AI-generated content. It also serves as a cautionary tale: unauthorized or deceptive use of influencers and celebrities not only erodes consumer trust, but can expose brands to legal and reputational risks.

IMPACT ON VULNERABLE POPULATIONS

AI biases can disproportionately affect vulnerable populations. For instance, language processing models may not accurately interpret dialects or colloquial expressions common in certain communities, leading to misunderstandings or exclusion. Marketers must be mindful of these nuances to ensure inclusive communication.

Balancing Personalization with Privacy

Personalization enhances user experience, but it requires access to personal data, raising significant privacy concerns. The line between helpful and invasive is thin and often subjective.

Consumers value convenience but are cautious about privacy. A 2017 Accenture study found that 41 per cent of U.S. consumers switched companies due to poor personalization and lack of trust. Additionally, 35 per cent of consumers found it unsettling to see ads on social media for products they had previously viewed on a brand's website (2017). This discomfort, often termed the "creepy" factor, can erode trust when personalization appears intrusive. Marketers must balance personalization with respect for privacy to maintain consumer trust.

Apple has positioned itself as a champion of user privacy. With the introduction of App Tracking Transparency in iOS 14.5, users can choose whether to allow apps to track their activity across other companies' apps and websites. This move has significant implications for marketers relying on cross-app data but reflects a growing consumer demand for privacy controls.

Certain types of data, such as health information, financial status, or location history, are particularly sensitive. Ethical marketing practices involve handling such data with extra care, ensuring compliance with regulations like the Health Insurance Portability and Accountability Act (HIPAA) in the U.S. for health data.

The Responsibility Falls on Us

Given the delicate balance between personalization and privacy, it's clear that the onus of ethical AI implementation falls squarely on the shoulders of marketers and organizations. Let's explore how we can rise to this challenge.

IMPLEMENTING ETHICAL FRAMEWORKS

Organizations can adopt ethical frameworks to guide AI use. For example:

- fairness, accountability, and transparency in machine learning provides principles to develop AI systems that are fair, accountable, and transparent
- IEEE Global Initiative on Ethics of Autonomous and Intelligent Systems offers standards and certifications for ethical AI practices.

INTERDISCIPLINARY TEAMS

Building teams that include ethicists, sociologists, and legal experts alongside data scientists can provide diverse perspectives and help identify ethical blind spots. Such diversity ensures that AI systems are developed and deployed with a holistic understanding of their potential impact.

REGULAR AUDITS AND MONITORING

Conducting regular audits of AI systems can uncover biases and unintended consequences. This includes the following:

- **Algorithmic auditing:** Evaluating AI outputs for fairness and accuracy. Tools like Google's What-If Tool can help visualize model behavior with respect to different features.

- **Data auditing:** Ensuring datasets are representative and free from bias. Techniques include re-sampling data, synthetic data generation, and data augmentation.

CONSUMER ENGAGEMENT AND FEEDBACK

Engaging with consumers about their preferences and concerns can inform more ethical practices. Providing channels for feedback and being responsive to concerns enhances trust. Transparency reports and open communication about data practices can demystify AI processes for consumers.

EDUCATION AND TRAINING

Investing in training for marketing professionals on AI ethics ensures that teams are equipped to handle ethical dilemmas. Understanding the technology's capabilities and limitations is crucial. Workshops, seminars, and certifications in AI ethics can elevate the team's proficiency.

Ethical Leadership in Action

Leading companies are taking steps to embed ethics into their AI strategies.

Microsoft has established principles guiding its AI development, focusing on fairness, reliability, privacy, inclusiveness, transparency, and accountability. They have created an internal AI Ethics Committee and offer tools like the Fairlearn toolkit to assess and mitigate unfairness in AI systems.

IBM emphasizes transparency in AI by providing explanations for AI-driven decisions through its OpenScale platform. They advocate for policies that promote ethical AI and collaborate with governments and organizations to shape responsible AI use.

Unilever has committed to ethical data use and transparency in marketing. They have policies ensuring that data collection respects consumer privacy and that AI is used to enhance consumer experiences without compromising trust. Unilever also participates in industry initiatives to develop standards for ethical AI.

Salesforce established an Ethical Use Advisory Council to guide the ethical development and deployment of its products, including AI tools. The council includes experts in ethics, law, and human rights, reflecting a commitment to responsible innovation.

The Role of Industry Collaboration

Industry-wide collaborations, such as the Partnership on AI, bring together companies, academics, and civil society organizations to promote best practices and address shared challenges in AI ethics. Such partnerships facilitate knowledge sharing and the development of common standards.

Risks of Neglecting Ethics in AI Deployment

Having explored the power of AI in marketing and the ethical quandaries it presents, it's crucial to understand the consequences of neglecting ethics in AI deployment. Ignoring ethical considerations isn't just a moral oversight—it poses significant risks to consumer trust, exposes companies to legal repercussions, and can inflict lasting reputational damage.

EROSION OF CONSUMER TRUST

Trust is the cornerstone of any successful marketing strategy. In the digital age, where consumers are more informed and connected than ever, maintaining trust is both more challenging and more critical. When companies misuse AI or fail to address ethical concerns, they risk eroding the very foundation of their relationship with consumers.

Consider the case of healthcare privacy concerns related to AI-powered chatbots. As healthcare providers have increasingly adopted these technologies to streamline patient support, answer medical queries, schedule appointments, and provide personalized health tips, significant privacy issues have emerged.

In a recent case reported to the Dutch Data Protection Authority, an employee of a medical practice entered patients' medical data into an AI chatbot contrary to established protocols. This represented what authorities described as "a major violation of the privacy of the people concerned," as highly sensitive medical information was shared with technology companies without proper safeguards (Autoriteit Persoonsgegevens, 2024).

By entering personal data into AI chatbots, companies providing the chatbot can gain unauthorized access to that personal data, which constitutes a personal data breach under privacy regulations. The Dutch authority's concerns primarily focused on the fact that companies behind these chatbots often store all entered data (Alston & Bird Privacy, Cyber & Data Strategy Blog, 2024).

The backlash to such incidents has been significant. Patients feel their privacy has been violated and question how chatbots access and utilize their sensitive information. These concerns have led to increased scrutiny of healthcare providers' digital practices, with experts emphasizing that AI chatbots must comply with healthcare privacy regulations, including ensuring the confidentiality, integrity, and availability of protected health information as it is collected, stored, and shared.

When trust is compromised, consumers are not shy about taking action. According to a 2017 survey by PwC, 85 per cent of consumers said they would not do business with a company if they had concerns about its security practices. Additionally, 71 per cent stated they would stop doing business with a company for giving away sensitive data without permission.

In the context of AI, where algorithms may make decisions without transparent explanations, consumers may feel uneasy or manipulated. This discomfort can lead to decreased customer loyalty, negative word-of-mouth, and ultimately, a decline in market share.

Transparency is vital in maintaining trust. When companies are open about how they use AI and data, they empower consumers to make informed choices. Conversely, secrecy or obfuscation breeds suspicion. In the healthcare chatbot case, the lack of clear communication about data usage exacerbated the situation. Had the company been more transparent, it might have mitigated some of the backlash.

Legal and Regulatory Repercussions

Neglecting ethics in AI doesn't just alienate consumers—it can also lead to legal troubles. Governments and regulatory bodies worldwide are increasingly focusing on AI and data protection, implementing laws that hold companies accountable for unethical practices.

THE RISE OF REGULATORY STANDARDS

GDPR is a landmark example of stringent data protection laws. Enforced since 2018, GDPR mandates that companies must obtain explicit consent before collecting personal data, allow users to access and delete their data, and report data breaches within 72 hours. Non-compliance with GDPR can result in hefty fines—up to €20 million (approximately $22 million) or 4 per cent of a company's annual global turnover, whichever is higher. For multinational corporations, this can translate into billions of dollars.

In 2019, the U.K.'s Information Commissioner's Office (ICO) announced its intention to fine British Airways £183.39 million for a data breach that compromised the personal information of approximately 500,000 customers. The breach, which began in June 2018, involved user traffic being diverted to a fraudulent site, allowing attackers to harvest customer details. The ICO attributed the incident to poor security arrangements, constituting a violation of GDPR.

Similarly, Marriott International faced a proposed fine of £99.2 million after a cyber incident exposed approximately 339 million guest records globally. The ICO's investigation revealed that Marriott failed to undertake sufficient due diligence when acquiring Starwood Hotels and did not implement adequate security measures, leading to the exposure of personal data (ICO, 2019).

These cases underscore the financial risks associated with inadequate data protection and highlight regulators' commitment to enforcing compliance with data privacy laws.

THE CALIFORNIA CONSUMER PRIVACY ACT (CCPA)

In the U.S., the CCPA grants California residents new rights regarding their personal information, including the right to know what data is collected, the right to delete personal information, and the right to opt out of the sale of personal information. Companies that fail to comply may face civil penalties and lawsuits.

FUTURE REGULATIONS ON AI ETHICS

Beyond data privacy, regulations specifically targeting AI ethics are emerging. The European Commission has proposed the AI Act, aiming to regulate AI systems based on their potential risks. High-risk AI applications, such as those affecting consumer rights or safety, will be subject to strict requirements.

Companies must stay ahead of these regulatory developments. Failure to comply not only results in financial penalties but can also lead to injunctions that halt business operations.

Reputational harm can be even more devastating than legal penalties. In today's digital landscape, news—especially bad news—travels fast. A single incident can tarnish a brand's image overnight, and rebuilding trust can take years.

A recent example of reputational damage caused by ethical lapses in AI deployment is OpenAI's 2024 voice assistant controversy. The company faced a backlash after releasing an AI-generated voice for ChatGPT that many users found strikingly similar to actress Scarlett Johansson's voice, despite her not having given consent (Allyn, 2024). Johansson publicly criticized OpenAI, stating that she had previously declined an offer to license her voice for AI purposes. The controversy sparked widespread debate over ethical AI practices, deepfake technology, and consent in AI-generated content.

The fallout was swift and severe. OpenAI paused the use of the voice in question, but the reputational damage had already taken hold. Critics accused the company of ethical oversights and a lack of transparency, while concerns over AI's role in replicating human likenesses without explicit permission intensified. The incident underscored the risks companies face when AI-generated content crosses ethical boundaries, leading to significant reputational harm.

Reputational damage can have long-term effects on customer loyalty, employee morale, and investor confidence. Companies with tarnished reputations may struggle to attract top talent, as professionals prefer organizations known for ethical practices.

Furthermore, in an era where consumers increasingly make values-driven purchasing decisions, a damaged reputation can lead to loss of market share. A study by Edelman found that 64 per cent of consumers worldwide are belief-driven buyers who choose, switch, or boycott brands based on their stance on societal issues (2018).

Recovering from reputational damage requires substantial investment in public relations, marketing, and operational changes. Companies may need to overhaul policies, implement new training programs, and engage in prolonged campaigns to rebuild trust. These efforts can be costly and divert resources from other strategic initiatives.

Internal Impacts and Talent Retention

Ethical lapses in AI deployment can also affect a company's internal dynamics. Employees want to work for organizations that align with their values. When a company is involved in unethical practices, it can lead to decreased job satisfaction, lower productivity, and higher turnover rates.

A strong ethical culture fosters employee engagement and loyalty. Conversely, scandals or unethical practices can erode morale. Employees may feel disillusioned or ashamed, leading to disengagement.

In the tech industry, where talent is highly sought after, companies with questionable ethics may find it challenging to attract and retain skilled professionals. This talent drain can hinder innovation and competitiveness.

Whistleblower risks are also a stark reality for those who dare to expose unethical or illegal practices within organizations. While the potential for positive change exists, the personal and professional costs can be immense. The case of Frances Haugen and Facebook (now Meta) provides a powerful illustration of this dynamic, highlighting the very real human cost of speaking truth to power in the digital age.

Haugen, a former product manager at Facebook, made headlines in 2021 when she leaked thousands of internal documents to the *Wall Street Journal* and testified before Congress. These documents, dubbed the "Facebook Files," revealed the company's internal knowledge of the harms its platforms, particularly Instagram, posed to young users, including the exacerbation of mental health issues and body image problems (WSJ Editorial Board, 2021). Haugen's actions weren't simply about technical glitches or data breaches; they were about the deliberate prioritization of profit over user safety, particularly the well-being of vulnerable teenagers.

The impact of Haugen's whistleblowing was significant. It ignited a global conversation about the responsibilities of social media companies, spurred increased regulatory scrutiny of Facebook, and arguably contributed to the company's rebranding as Meta. However, the path to this impact was paved with considerable personal risk.

The personal cost for whistleblowers like Haugen is often immeasurable. Beyond the immediate professional repercussions, which can include job loss and blacklisting within an industry, there's the emotional toll of facing a powerful corporation and the potential for public backlash. Haugen, while receiving considerable support, also faced criticism and scrutiny. While precise financial figures are difficult to obtain, it's safe to assume Haugen incurred substantial legal fees in preparing for and navigating the fallout from her actions. These could easily range from tens of thousands to hundreds of thousands of dollars, depending on the complexity of the legal representation and the duration of any legal battles. Furthermore, the loss of income during periods of unemployment or while establishing a new career path is a significant, though often unquantified, cost. Support from whistleblower advocacy groups and legal aid organizations may have offset some of these expenses, but the overall burden remains substantial.

Haugen's case underscores the complex calculus involved in whistleblowing. It's not simply a matter of exposing wrongdoing; it's a decision with profound personal and professional implications. While the potential for positive societal change is a powerful motivator, the risks, both tangible and intangible, are equally real.

Financial Losses Beyond Fines

While regulatory fines and reputational damage represent significant financial blows for companies engaging in unethical AI deployment, the repercussions extend far beyond these readily quantifiable metrics. The true cost often lies in the erosion of trust, the disruption of operations, and the long-term damage to a company's ability to thrive. These less visible financial losses can be even more devastating than the initial penalties.

One of the most immediate and impactful consequences is the risk of consumer boycotts. In today's hyper-connected world, news of unethical practices spreads rapidly, and consumers are increasingly willing to vote with their wallets. A company perceived as having acted unethically, whether in its AI development or its broader business practices, can face swift and severe sales declines. The fashion industry provides numerous examples, with brands facing significant revenue drops following allegations of exploitative labor practices. This isn't just a temporary blip; regaining consumer trust after such a breach can be an arduous and expensive undertaking. It's not simply a matter of issuing a *mea culpa* and hoping for forgiveness; it requires demonstrable action and a sustained commitment to ethical conduct.

Beyond consumer backlash, companies also risk losing crucial business partnerships. In an interconnected business ecosystem, a company's reputation is inextricably linked to its partners. Firms are understandably reluctant to associate themselves with entities embroiled in ethical scandals, fearing reputational contagion. The severance of ties can lead to lost contracts, supply chain disruptions, and significant challenges in securing new partnerships. Imagine a tech company developing cutting-edge AI solutions only to find its distribution channels drying up because of ethical concerns surrounding its data collection methods. The loss of these strategic alliances can cripple a company's growth prospects and undermine its long-term viability. It's a bit like being ostracized from the professional networking circuits—suddenly, opportunities disappear.

So the fallout from unethical AI practices invariably leads to increased insurance and compliance costs. Insurers, ever mindful of risk, will likely raise premiums for companies implicated in ethical scandals. These companies are now perceived as higher risk, and the increased premiums reflect this assessment. Simultaneously, substantial investments in compliance programs, audits, and legal fees become necessary. Companies must not only address the immediate legal challenges but also implement robust internal mechanisms to prevent future ethical lapses. This can involve hiring specialized compliance officers, conducting regular audits, and providing ethics training to employees. These expenditures represent a significant drain on resources and can divert funds from innovation and growth initiatives. Essentially, the company is forced to spend more to mitigate the damage caused by its past actions, rather than investing in its future.

The financial consequences of unethical AI deployment extend far beyond the immediate sting of fines. The erosion of consumer trust, the loss of business partnerships, and the increased costs of insurance and compliance can harm a company's long-term financial health. While fines capture headlines, it's these less visible costs that can truly cripple a business.

Competitive Disadvantage

Companies that neglect ethics may find themselves at a competitive disadvantage. This isn't abstract theory—it's affecting real business outcomes across sectors. When competitors prioritize ethical AI, they gain a powerful edge. They're not just "doing good"—they're doing good business. These companies leverage ethics as a unique selling proposition that attracts more customers, generates positive media attention, and builds stronger brand loyalty. Ethical practices become a genuine differentiator that sets them apart in an increasingly crowded market.

Meanwhile, companies lagging on ethics miss out on growing opportunities. There's a real and expanding demand for ethical products and services. Organizations failing to meet ethical standards simply can't compete in markets where consumers prioritize corporate responsibility. They're locked out of segments that could drive significant growth.

REGULATORY BARRIERS TO ENTRY

As regulations become stricter, companies with unethical practices will face barriers to entering new markets or expanding existing ones. Compliance becomes a prerequisite for global operations.

Neglecting ethics in AI deployment is a high-stakes gamble that can result in:

- loss of consumer trust, leading to decreased loyalty, negative word of mouth, and reduced market share
- legal penalties, including fines, injunctions, and increased regulatory scrutiny
- reputational damage, affecting brand image, customer perception, and investor confidence
- internal strife, resulting in low employee morale, talent loss, and potential whistle-blower actions
- financial losses through decreased sales, lost partnerships, and increased operational costs
- competitive disadvantage as a result of falling behind competitors who prioritize ethical practices.

Understanding these risks underscores the importance for marketers to integrate ethics into AI strategies proactively. It's not just about avoiding negative outcomes—it's about positioning the company for sustainable success in a market that values responsibility and trust.

The Business Case for Ethical AI

Having examined the impact of AI in marketing, the ethical dilemmas it presents, and the risks of neglecting ethics, it's time to change our perspective. Ethical AI isn't just about avoiding pitfalls—it's a strategic asset that can drive growth, foster innovation, and provide a competitive edge. In this section, we'll explore why investing in ethical AI is not only the right thing to do but also a smart business decision.

In today's marketplace, consumers are more discerning and values-driven than ever before. They expect companies to not only provide quality products and services but also to operate responsibly and ethically. This shift presents a unique opportunity for businesses to differentiate themselves through ethical practices.

A 2018 Accenture Strategy global survey of nearly 30,000 consumers found that 62 per cent want companies to take a stand on current and broadly relevant issues like sustainability, transparency, or fair employment practices. Additionally, 52 per cent of respondents prefer to buy from brands that align with their personal values. This trend is particularly pronounced among younger demographics, with approximately 60 per cent of Gen Zs and Millennials considering it important for companies to speak up on issues such as human rights, systemic racial interactions, or LGBTQIA+ equality (2018).

Ethical AI practices build trust—a crucial factor in customer retention and brand loyalty. When consumers trust a brand, they're more likely to engage deeply, share personal data willingly, and advocate for the brand within their networks. Trust reduces friction in the customer journey, leading to higher conversion rates and increased lifetime value.

Companies known for ethical practices often enjoy enhanced brand reputations, which can attract new customers and open doors to new markets. Positive media coverage, awards, and endorsements can amplify this effect, creating a virtuous cycle of goodwill.

Competitive Advantage through Ethical AI

Incorporating ethics into AI strategies can set a company apart from its competitors. Let's explore how ethical AI can serve as a differentiator.

By prioritizing ethics, companies can appeal to the growing segment of consumers willing to pay a premium for products and services from responsible brands. According to PwC (2024), 80 per cent of consumers are willing to pay more for sustainably produced or sourced goods, with an average premium of 9.7 per cent.

Younger demographics, particularly Gen Z, are leading this shift, with 72 per cent expressing a willingness to pay more for sustainable products (Statista, 2023).

These findings underscore the importance for companies to integrate ethical practices into their operations to attract and retain ethically-minded consumers.

DRIVING INNOVATION

Ethical considerations can spur innovation. By addressing ethical challenges, companies may develop new technologies, processes, or business models that give them an edge. For example, creating AI systems that are transparent and explainable can enhance user trust and satisfaction, distinguishing a company's offerings from opaque competitors.

ATTRACTING AND RETAINING TALENT

Ethical companies are more attractive to top talent. Professionals want to work for organizations that reflect their values and have a positive impact on society. By fostering an ethical culture, companies can attract skilled employees who drive innovation and performance.

ALIGNING WITH ESG GOALS FOR GREATER INVESTMENT

Investors are increasingly considering environmental, social, and governance (ESG) factors when making decisions. Companies with strong ethical practices may find it easier to attract investment, access capital at lower costs, and enjoy favorable valuations (Friede et al., 2015).

Global Perspectives on Ethical AI in Marketing

As we've explored the ethical challenges and considerations of AI in marketing, it's crucial to recognize that these issues manifest differently across the globe. The principles we've discussed—transparency, fairness, privacy—take on unique flavors in various cultural and regulatory contexts. Examining how diverse regions approach ethical AI reveals valuable insights we can apply to our own strategies.

In the bustling streets of Shanghai, a young professional checks her smartphone, scrolling through personalized product recommendations. Halfway across the world, in a Nairobi tech hub, a startup founder pores over AI-generated market insights. Meanwhile, in São Paulo, a marketing team debates the ethical implications of their latest AI-driven campaign. Welcome to the global landscape of AI in marketing, where cultural nuances, regulatory frameworks, and technological innovations intersect to create a complex tapestry of challenges and opportunities.

Asia: Balancing Innovation and Control

As the sun rises over the skyscrapers of Beijing, marketers are already grappling with China's unique approach to AI ethics. The country's rapid embrace of AI technologies has been tempered by increasingly stringent regulations. "It's like trying to ride two horses at once," muses Li Wei, a digital marketing consultant based in Shanghai. "We're pushing the boundaries of what's possible with AI, but we're also constantly looking over our shoulders to ensure compliance."

China's recent regulations on algorithmic recommendations have sent ripples through the marketing world. Gone are the days of unfettered data collection and opaque personalization strategies. Now, transparency is the name of the game. Marketers must not only disclose the basic principles behind their recommendation algorithms but also provide users with the option to opt out of personalized content altogether.

This shift has sparked a wave of innovation in ethical AI marketing. Take, for example, the e-commerce giant Alibaba. Their newly developed "Customer Experience Index" is a testament to the delicate balance between personalization and privacy. "We're not just thinking about conversion rates anymore," explains Zhang Mei, a product manager at Alibaba. "We're considering the overall ethical impact of our recommendations. It's a whole new paradigm."

But it's not just about compliance. There's a growing recognition that ethical AI can be a powerful differentiator in a crowded market. As consumers become more aware of data privacy issues, brands that prioritize ethical AI practices are seeing a boost in consumer trust and loyalty.

Africa: AI as a Force for Inclusive Growth

Shifting our gaze to the vibrant tech scenes of Nairobi and Lagos, we find a different narrative unfolding. Here, the conversation around ethical AI in marketing is inextricably linked to broader issues of development and inclusion.

"For us, AI isn't just a marketing tool—it's a means to leapfrog traditional development challenges," says Oluwaseun Adebayo, founder of a Nigerian AI startup. His company is using AI to optimize agricultural supply chains, a project that has significant implications for both farmers and marketers.

The ethical considerations here are multifaceted. On one hand, there's the potential for AI to dramatically improve lives by increasing agricultural yields and connecting farmers to markets more efficiently. On the other, there are concerns about data ownership and the risk of perpetuating existing inequalities.

These challenges are giving rise to innovative approaches to ethical AI in marketing. The "AI for Development" initiative, for instance, is working to ensure that AI systems are trained on diverse, local datasets to prevent bias. This not only makes the AI more effective but also ensures that marketing campaigns resonate with local audiences.

"We're not just copying and pasting solutions from Silicon Valley," explains Dr. Aisha Ndayisaba, a computer scientist involved in the initiative. "We're building AI systems that understand the nuances of African markets and respect our cultural values."

South America: Crafting a Unique Ethical Framework

As we journey across the Atlantic to the bustling cities of South America, we encounter yet another perspective on ethical AI in marketing. In countries like Brazil, the implementation of data protection laws similar to Europe's GDPR has catalyzed a reimagining of AI-driven marketing strategies.

"It's like we've been given a blank canvas," says Carlos Silva, CMO of a leading Brazilian e-commerce platform. "The new regulations forced us to rethink our entire approach to data and AI. But in that challenge, we found an opportunity."

This opportunity has manifested in innovative approaches to personalization that prioritize user privacy. Federated learning, a technique that allows AI models to be trained on decentralized data, is gaining traction. It's enabling marketers to deliver personalized experiences without the need for centralized data storage, a win-win for both consumers and brands.

But the ethical considerations go beyond just data privacy. There's a growing awareness of the need for AI systems that respect the rich cultural diversity of the region. "We're dealing with a continent of incredible cultural variety," explains Dr. Gabriela Fernández, an AI ethics researcher based in Buenos Aires. "Our AI systems need to be sophisticated enough to understand and respect these differences, or we risk alienating large segments of our audience."

This cultural sensitivity is giving rise to a uniquely South American approach to ethical AI in marketing. It's an approach that values diversity, respects privacy, and sees ethical considerations not as constraints, but as catalysts for innovation.

As we conclude our global journey, it's clear that while the challenges of ethical AI in marketing may be universal, the solutions are decidedly local. The challenges faced by marketers in Shanghai, Nairobi, and São Paulo may seem distant, but they offer valuable insights for all of us. Whether it's China's innovative approaches to balancing personalization and privacy, Africa's focus on inclusive AI development, or South America's culturally sensitive AI strategies, each region provides lessons that can inform our own ethical AI practices.

For global marketers, this diverse landscape presents both challenges and opportunities. The key to success lies in understanding these regional nuances, adapting strategies accordingly, and always keeping ethical considerations at the forefront of AI implementation.

As we navigate this complex global landscape, one thing becomes clear: the future of AI in marketing will be shaped not just by technological advancements, but by our collective commitment to using these powerful tools in ways that are ethical, inclusive, and respectful of cultural differences. It's a future that promises to be as exciting as it is challenging, and it's one that we, as marketers, have the privilege and responsibility to shape.

Bringing It All Together

As we've explored in this chapter, ensuring the responsible use of AI in marketing is not just about compliance—it's about building trust, fostering sustainable growth, and gaining a competitive edge in an increasingly conscious marketplace.

KEY TAKEAWAYS

- **Duality of AI in marketing:** AI has revolutionized marketing by enabling hyper-personalized experiences and real-time engagement. However, this power comes with ethical challenges, including data privacy concerns and the potential for algorithmic bias. Balancing the benefits of AI with ethical considerations is crucial for sustainable success.
  Why it matters: While AI-driven personalization can drive engagement and return on investment (ROI), it must be balanced with transparency and respect for privacy to avoid eroding consumer trust and facing regulatory backlash.

- **Ethical AI as a competitive advantage:** Beyond moral imperatives, ethical AI practices offer tangible business benefits. From building consumer trust and attracting ethical consumers to spurring innovation and enhancing employer branding, companies that prioritize ethical AI can gain a significant edge in the market.
  Why it matters: In an era of increasing consumer awareness and regulatory scrutiny, ethical AI practices can differentiate brands, foster loyalty, and mitigate risks, ultimately contributing to long-term business success.

- **Global perspectives and universal principles:** While the implementation of ethical AI in marketing varies across different cultural and regulatory environments, the fundamental principles of respect for privacy, fairness, and transparency are universal. Understanding these global nuances while adhering to core ethical principles is essential for successful international marketing strategies.
  Why it matters: Businesses operate in an increasingly globalized market, so understanding and adapting to diverse ethical expectations is crucial for building trust and succeeding across different cultural contexts.

Looking Ahead

As we move into the next chapter, we will define the core ethical principles essential for marketing AI. Here, we'll explore the foundational values of fairness, transparency, accountability, and trust. We will also dive into understanding bias and discrimination in AI models, as well as addressing data privacy and security concerns. Real-world scenarios will illustrate how these principles can be effectively applied in marketing. By establishing these ethical foundations, marketers can harness AI's full potential while safeguarding consumer trust and driving long-term success.

Food for Thought

1 How can marketers balance the benefits of AI-driven personalization with the need to protect consumer privacy, especially when operating across different regulatory environments?

2 Considering the diverse global approaches we've explored, what steps can organizations take to ensure their AI systems are both globally scalable and locally sensitive?

3 How might the role of human marketers evolve as AI becomes more prevalent in the industry, particularly in managing ethical considerations across different cultural contexts?

4 Reflect on a recent AI-driven marketing campaign your organization has run. How might it be perceived differently in the various global contexts we've discussed? What adjustments might be necessary for it to be effective and ethical in these different settings?

References

Accenture (2017) US Consumers Turn Off Personal Data Tap as Companies Struggle to Deliver the Experiences They Crave, Accenture Study Finds, Accenture Newsroom, December 5, newsroom.accenture.com/news/2017/us-consumers-turn-off-personal-data-tap-as-companies-struggle-to-deliver-the-experiences-they-crave-accenture-study-finds (archived at https://perma.cc/33BQ-VTA7)

Accenture (2018) From Me to We: The Rise of the Purpose-Led Brand, Accenture Strategy, www.prnewsonline.com/wp-content/uploads/2018/12/accenture-competitiveagility-gcpr-pov.pdf (archived at https://perma.cc/2L8F-4S8X)

Allyn, B (2024) Scarlett Johansson Says She is "Shocked, angered" Over New ChatGPT Voice, *NPR*, May 20, www.npr.org/2024/05/20/1252495087/openai-pulls-ai-voice-that-was-compared-to-scarlett-johansson-in-the-movie-her (archived at https://perma.cc/YJM5-Y7EP)

Alston and Bird Privacy (2024) Dutch Data Protection Authority warns that using AI chatbots can lead to personal data breaches, Cyber & Data Strategy Blog, August 9, www.autoriteitpersoonsgegevens.nl/en/current/caution-use-of-ai-chatbot-may-lead-to-data-breaches (archived at https://perma.cc/4MSN-T4TS)

Autoriteit Persoonsgegevens (2024) Caution: Use of AI chatbot may lead to data breaches, www.autoriteitpersoonsgegevens.nl/en/current/caution-use-of-ai-chatbot-may-lead-to-data-breaches (archived at https://perma.cc/4MSN-T4TS)

Buolamwini, J and Gebru, T (2018) Gender Shades: Intersectional Accuracy Disparities in Commercial Gender Classification, *Proceedings of Machine Learning Research*, 81, 77–91, proceedings.mlr.press /v81/buolamwini18a.html (archived at https://perma.cc/S6GF-924X)

Edelman (2018) Two-Thirds of Consumers Now Buy on Beliefs, www.edelman.com/news-awards/two-thirds-consumers-worldwide-now-buy-beliefs (archived at https://perma.cc/NWK2-Q9QP)

Friede, G, Busch, T, and Bassen, A (2015) ESG and Financial Performance: Aggregated Evidence From More Than 2000 Empirical Studies, *Journal of Sustainable Finance & Investment*, 5 (4), 210–233, www.tandfonline.com/doi/full/10.1080/20430795.2015.1118917 (archived at https://perma.cc/3ES7-ZRQ9)

Information Commissioner's Office (ICO) (2019) ICO Statement: Intention to Fine Marriott International Inc More than £99 Million under GDPR for Data Breach, European Data Protection Board, www.edpb.europa.eu/news/national-news/2019/ico-statement-intention-fine-marriott-international-inc-more-ps99-million_en (archived at https://perma.cc/5ZJ8-Z2TT)

McKinsey & Company (2024) *The State of AI in Early 2024: Gen AI Adoption Spikes and Starts to Generate Value*, McKinsey & Company, May 30, www.mckinsey.com/capabilities/quantumblack/our-insights/the-state-of-ai# (archived at https://perma.cc/2LV7-9WA6)

Partnership on AI (2020) Working to Address Algorithmic Bias? Don't Overlook the Role of Demographic Data, partnershiponai.org/demographic-data/ (archived at https://perma.cc/SGS5-HRS2)

Pew Research Center (2019) Americans and Privacy: Concerned, Confused and Feeling Lack of Control Over Their Personal Information, www.pewresearch.org/internet/2019/11/15/americans-and-privacy-concerned-confused-and-feeling-lack-of-control-over-their-personal-information (archived at https://perma.cc/6W4G-9N43)

PwC (2017) Protect.me: How Digital Trust Drives Consumer Behaviour, PwC Australia www.pwc.com.au/digitalpulse/report-protect-me-consumers-cyber-security.html (archived at https://perma.cc/3TDN-WC6Y)

PwC (2024) PwC 2024 Voice of the Consumer Survey, www.pwc.com/gx/en/news-room/press-releases/2024/pwc-2024-voice-of-consumer-survey.html (archived at https://perma.cc/6GJW-YEN5)

Statista (2023) Willingness to Pay More for Sustainable Products in Asia-Pacific Region in 2023, By Generation, www.statista.com/statistics/1477446/apac-willingness-to-pay-more-for-sustainable-products-by-generation/ (archived at https://perma.cc/7KZX-3J86)

The Wall Street Journal Editorial Board (2021) The Facebook Files: Inside the Social Media Giant, October 27, www.wsj.com/articles/the-facebook-files-11631713039 (archived at https://perma.cc/VK8R-SPBR)

Zhou, M, Zhang, J, and Adomavicius, G (2024) Longitudinal Impact of Preference Biases on Recommender Systems' Performance, *Information Systems Research*, 35 (4) 1634–56 doi.org/10.1287/isre.2021.0133 (archived at https://perma.cc/7T2C-GM73)

2

Defining Ethical AI
Principles for Marketing

As marketers harness the power of AI to personalize experiences and optimize campaigns, they face a critical question: How can we leverage this technology responsibly while building trust and fostering positive relationships with consumers? This question is particularly relevant as AI becomes increasingly sophisticated, utilizing techniques like machine learning, natural language processing, and computer vision to analyze vast amounts of data and automate marketing tasks.

This chapter delves into the core ethical principles that should guide AI implementation in marketing: fairness, transparency, accountability, and respect for consumer autonomy. These principles are not just abstract concepts but fundamental pillars that can shape the future of marketing in the AI era.

By embracing these ethical guidelines, marketers don't just mitigate risks; they unlock new opportunities for innovation and brand differentiation. Ethical AI practices serve as a foundation for rebuilding trust in an era marked by data breaches and privacy concerns. They help companies navigate the complex regulatory landscape and avoid potential legal pitfalls. By aligning AI-driven strategies with broader societal values, marketers can contribute positively to their communities while driving sustainable business growth.

Why Ethical AI Matters in Marketing

Ethical AI in marketing ensures fairness, transparency, accountability, and respect for consumer autonomy throughout the AI lifecycle. It involves the responsible use of data, mitigation of bias, and alignment of AI strategies with societal values and individual rights. Beyond compliance, ethical AI builds trust with consumers, mitigates reputational and legal risks, encourages responsible innovation, and ensures long-term sustainability of marketing strategies.

Key benefits:

- **Trust:** Builds stronger relationships with consumers. According to a 2023 survey by Salesforce, 73 per cent of customers say transparency and honesty are the most important factors in building brand trust (2023).
- **Innovation:** Drives creativity within ethical boundaries.
- **Regulatory compliance:** Avoids legal pitfalls while setting industry standards.
- **Sustainability:** Fosters long-term growth and societal impact.

A 2024 Edelman Trust Barometer report revealed that trust in AI companies has declined from 62 per cent in 2019 to 54 per cent in 2024, indicating growing global concern about AI (Edelman, 2024).

The bustling agora of ancient Athens, the quiet study of 18th-century Königsberg, and the intellectual ferment of Industrial Revolution-era London might seem worlds apart from today's data-driven marketing departments. Yet, the ideas born in these distant times and places profoundly shape how we grapple with the ethical challenges of AI today.

Aristotle and the Pursuit of Excellence in AI

In the 4th century BC, Aristotle walked the grounds of his Lyceum, teaching students about *eudaimonia*—the good life achieved through virtue and excellence. For Aristotle, ethics wasn't about rigid rules, but about cultivating character and practical wisdom (*phronesis*) to navigate complex situations.

Fast forward to today, and we find echoes of Aristotelian thought in how we approach AI ethics in marketing through the following:

- **Character-driven AI:** Just as Aristotle believed that good actions flow from good character, we now strive to create AI systems that embody our brand's ethical values consistently across all interactions. Consider a financial services chatbot. Rather than programming it solely to maximize product sales, we imbue it with virtues like honesty and prudence. It might recommend lower-cost products that better suit a customer's needs, sacrificing short-term gains for long-term trust and customer well-being.
- **Practical wisdom in machine learning:** Aristotle's concept of *phronesis* finds new life in our efforts to create AI that can make nuanced, context-aware decisions. In content recommendation systems, this might mean training the AI not just on user clicks, but on indicators of genuine user satisfaction and growth. A news app's AI, embodying *phronesis*, might occasionally recommend articles that challenge a user's viewpoints, fostering intellectual growth over mere engagement.

Kant and the Urgency of Data Ethics

In 1785, amidst the intellectual ferment of the Enlightenment, which emphasized reason and individual autonomy, Immanuel Kant, a German philosopher, published his groundbreaking work, *Groundwork of the Metaphysic of Morals* (1998 [1785]). This book laid the foundation for his deontological ethical theory, which focuses on duty and the inherent rightness or wrongness of actions. Kant argued that truly ethical actions are those we could rationally will to become universal laws, applicable to everyone in similar situations. He also insisted on the inherent dignity of every human being, asserting that we should always treat people as ends in themselves, worthy of respect, and never merely as means to achieve our own goals.

In the realm of AI marketing, Kant's ideas translate as follows:

- **Universal ethical standards:** We must develop AI practices that we'd be willing to see adopted universally across the industry. When designing data collection processes, we should ask: "What if every company collected data this way?" This Kantian approach might lead us to adopt more transparent, opt-in data practices that could become industry standards.

- **Respecting consumer autonomy:** Kant's insistence on respecting human dignity informs how we think about consumer privacy and consent in the age of big data. Instead of burying data usage policies in fine print, a Kantian approach might lead to the development of interactive AI assistants that clearly explain how user data will be used and genuinely empower consumers to make informed choices about their data.

Bentham and Mill: Utilitarianism in the Age of Algorithms

As the Industrial Revolution transformed society, Jeremy Bentham, a British philosopher and social reformer known for his work on legal and penal systems, developed the foundations of utilitarianism (1970). Later, John Stuart Mill, another influential British philosopher and economist, refined and expanded upon Bentham's ideas, arguing for the importance of individual liberty and qualitative distinctions between pleasures.

In AI marketing, utilitarian thinking encourages us to:

- **consider broad stakeholder impacts:** We must look beyond immediate metrics to consider how our AI systems affect all stakeholders (stakeholder-centric AI), including underrepresented groups. When developing an AI-driven pricing algorithm, a utilitarian approach would consider not just profit maximization, but also factors like market accessibility and long-term consumer financial health. This might lead to dynamic pricing models that offer deeper discounts to price-sensitive consumers, expanding market reach while maintaining overall profitability.

FIGURE 2.1 Ethical foundations of AI marketing: Aristotle, Kant and Utilitarianism

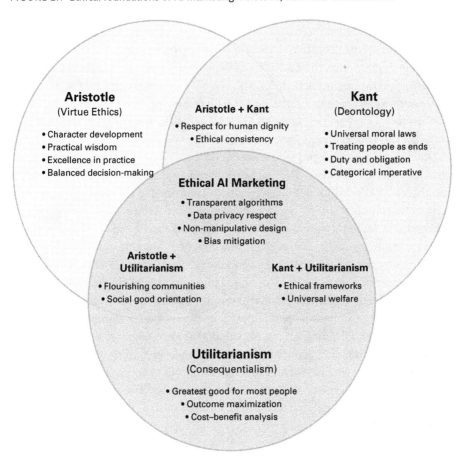

- **balance short-term gains with long-term consequences:** Utilitarianism prompts us to consider the extended implications of our AI systems. In social media marketing, this might mean developing content recommendation algorithms that balance engaging content with informative or educational material. While this might reduce time-on-site metrics in the short term, it could lead to more meaningful user engagement and stronger brand relationships over time.

Synthesizing Wisdom

Integrating these philosophical traditions provides a strong ethical foundation for guiding AI use in marketing (Figure 2.1). From Aristotle, we learn to develop AI systems with "virtuous character," consistently embodying our ethical values. This means creating AI that not only achieves marketing objectives but also acts with integrity. Such an AI would be transparent in its operations, ensuring its decision-making processes are understandable. It would be non-manipulative, persuading consumers through genuine value propositions rather than deceptive tactics. Ultimately, a virtuous AI in marketing seeks to benefit users, not just the company deploying it.

Kant teaches us to respect consumer autonomy and to develop universal ethical standards for AI use. This translates into clear disclosure and consent mechanisms. For instance, companies should be transparent about what data is collected and how it's used, empowering users with control over their information. Consumers should have easy ways to opt out of personalized advertising or data collection altogether. Furthermore, employing explainable AI (XAI) can offer users insights into why they are being shown specific ads, fostering trust and transparency.

Utilitarianism encourages us to consider the broad, long-term impacts of our AI systems on all stakeholders. This might involve incorporating features that promote social good alongside business objectives, such as using AI to connect consumers with sustainable products or to counter misinformation. However, it's important to acknowledge that ethical considerations in AI marketing often involve navigating complex trade-offs. For instance, maximizing user autonomy might sometimes conflict with maximizing the "greatest good for the greatest number." It's also worth noting that utilitarianism has been criticized for potentially justifying harm to minorities if it benefits the majority, a pitfall that must be carefully avoided in AI applications.

By embracing this multifaceted ethical framework, we can harness the power of AI in marketing while safeguarding the values that are essential to a just and equitable society. By grounding our approach in these philosophical traditions, we elevate AI marketing from a mere tool for efficiency and profit to a force for ethical business practices that drive growth and positive societal impact. These enduring principles serve as our compass, helping us balance innovation with responsibility, efficiency with ethics, and profit with purpose.

In doing so, we position ourselves not just as marketers, but as ethical leaders, building trust, mitigating risks, and contributing to a more responsible and sustainable business ecosystem. The philosophers of old could scarcely have imagined the technological marvels we work with today, but their foundations of wisdom continue to light our path forward (Murphy, 2023).

In 2025, Duolingo—the world's most popular language learning platform—announced a strategic shift to become an "AI-first" company. As part of this transition, it introduced new features powered by OpenAI's GPT-4, including *Explain My Answer*, which offers detailed feedback on user responses, and *Roleplay*, which enables learners to engage in simulated conversations to practice real-world language use.

These AI-powered tools received early praise for their ability to deliver personalized and scalable learning experiences. However, the shift also brought organizational change. Duolingo confirmed that it would gradually reduce its reliance on contract workers, particularly those supporting content-related operations, as AI systems began taking over certain instructional and moderation tasks.

This move sparked broader debate around the ethical implications of generative AI in education. Critics voiced concerns about potential job displacement and the erosion of human oversight and cultural nuance in language instruction—elements that human contributors may better support. In response, Duolingo publicly committed to responsible AI development, publishing standards emphasizing fairness, transparency, privacy, and accountability in its deployment of AI technologies.

For marketers, Duolingo's journey offers a real-world illustration of both the promise and tension inherent in AI adoption:

- **Virtue Ethics:** Duolingo's AI aims to promote intellectual growth and autonomy, aligning with virtues like diligence and honesty. Yet, its reduced reliance on human contributors raises questions about empathy and fairness in design choices.

- **Deontology:** The shift invites scrutiny under Kant's principle of treating people as ends, not means—especially when economic efficiency leads to replacing human labor without transparent recourse.

- **Utilitarianism:** The platform's AI-driven scale benefits millions of learners, advancing educational access. Still, it highlights the utilitarian dilemma: gains for the majority can carry unintended harms for marginalized contributors.

Duolingo's experience underscores the ethical complexity of AI implementation in business. It demonstrates that personalization and efficiency alone are not sufficient. Responsible AI must also safeguard human dignity, support transparency, and align with stakeholder values to earn and retain long-term trust.

Core Principles Reimagined

In reimagining ethical AI for marketing, we focus on four core principles: fairness, transparency, accountability, and respect for autonomy. Each of these principles takes on new meaning and importance in the context of AI-driven marketing's day-to-day realities. Let's explore how we can translate these abstract concepts into practical, actionable strategies for ethical AI implementation.

Fairness: More than Bias Mitigation

It's easy to think of fairness as something that only data scientists worry about, checking for algorithmic bias, adjusting datasets, and running endless fairness tests. But fairness is a marketing issue, too. Why? Because how your AI models treat different consumer groups can shape perceptions of your brand and, ultimately, influence purchase decisions. True fairness means making sure your AI serves as a bridge, not a barrier.

Consider a retail AI system trained to recommend premium products based on historical purchase data. If this data predominantly reflects high-income consumers, the system may unintentionally exclude others from accessing promotions or tailored offers. By diversifying training datasets and implementing fairness audits, marketers can ensure their AI uncovers potential value across all demographics, fostering inclusivity and equitable engagement. True fairness requires using AI to uncover potential value in all consumer segments, not just those already profitable. That's not fairness—that's favoring the status quo. True fairness means making sure your AI serves as a bridge, not a barrier.

HOW TO IMPLEMENT: FAIRNESS IN MARKETING AI

- **Rethink training data:** Challenge the assumptions built into your data. Are you unintentionally favoring one group over another? Make sure your data reflects the diversity of your consumer base.

- **Run regular bias audits:** Conduct bias audits not just when you deploy a model but throughout its lifecycle. Marketing strategies evolve, and so should your commitment to fairness.

- **Redefine success metrics:** Success shouldn't just be about who clicks and converts the most. Define metrics that account for equity—are you reaching a broad audience? Are different segments engaging similarly?

FAIRNESS IN ACTION: SEPHORA'S BEAUTY CAMPAIGN

Sephora, a global beauty retailer, faced a challenge: its AI-driven product recommendation system was primarily catering to a limited spectrum of skin tones and beauty needs due to the biases in its historical data. Recognizing the potential for exclusion, Sephora rethought its AI models to ensure inclusivity. By incorporating diverse training data that better represented a range of skin tones and beauty needs, the brand's AI system started offering more tailored, inclusive product recommendations.

Sephora's efforts to address fairness didn't just avoid bias; it actively expanded its consumer base and strengthened its brand's reputation as an inclusive leader in the beauty industry.

Transparency: Show, Don't Just Tell

Transparency in AI is about fostering trust by giving consumers a clear view into how and why AI is being used in their interactions with your brand. It's about empowering them, reducing anxiety about hidden agendas, and building confidence in your commitment to ethical practices. Think of it as an open door, inviting customers to see the inner workings of your AI-powered marketing initiatives. A Cisco survey found that 54 per cent of consumers are willing to share their anonymized personal data to help improve AI products and decision-making (2023).

For instance, when an online retailer provides recommendations accompanied by messages like, "This product was suggested based on your recent browsing history and preferences of similar customers," it offers clarity. Features such as a "Why am I seeing this?" button further empower users to understand AI's role in their experience.

Beyond simple explanations, transparency serves as an opportunity for storytelling, allowing brands to build stronger emotional connections by sharing the rationale behind AI-driven initiatives. Netflix exemplifies this by offering users insights into their personalized recommendations through the "Why is this recommended?" feature, enhancing user agency. Similarly, Spotify's annual Wrapped campaign provides personalized data visualizations of individual listening habits, demystifying AI processes and fostering trust.

Implementing Transparency in AI-Driven Marketing

To effectively implement transparency, consider these strategies:

- **Human-centric explanations:** Move away from vague statements like, "This ad was shown based on your activity," and provide specific reasons, such as, "You're seeing this skincare product because it matches your past preferences for sensitive skin items."

- **Interactive transparency tools:** Create "Why am I seeing this?" buttons or similar features that offer users insights into how their data is used for personalized content. Other examples include:

  o dashboards that show users how their data is being used and allow them to adjust their preferences

  o tools that visualize the factors influencing an AI's recommendation (e.g. showing a user that a product was recommended because they previously bought similar items and liked a particular brand).

- **Proactively address missteps:** If your AI makes a mistake, be open about it. Acknowledge the error, explain what happened, and outline the steps you're taking to correct it.

NAVIGATING THE CHALLENGES OF TRANSPARENCY

While transparency is essential, it's not without its challenges. Marketers need to consider:

- balancing transparency with simplicity by providing detailed explanations without overwhelming consumers

- protecting proprietary information by being transparent without revealing sensitive algorithms or business strategies

- maintaining consistency by ensuring transparency across all marketing channels and touchpoints.

Accountability: Owning the Outcomes

Accountability in AI involves taking ownership of the impacts of AI systems, ensuring they adhere to ethical standards beyond mere legal compliance. This proactive approach includes preventing harm and establishing clear plans to address unintended consequences. Microsoft's 2024 Responsible AI Transparency Report emphasizes the importance of governance structures, such as oversight committees, in managing AI responsibly (2024). These committees, comprising diverse professionals—including marketers, legal experts, and data scientists—are vital for consistently reviewing and adjusting AI initiatives to ensure fairness, transparency, and alignment with brand values.

Without clear accountability, organizations risk operational inefficiencies, reputational damage, and legal repercussions. For instance, consider a bank employing an AI-powered loan approval system. If this system unintentionally discriminates against applicants from certain zip codes due to biases in the training data, it could have severe consequences for both the affected individuals and the bank's reputation. Accountability ensures that the organization has a proactive strategy to identify and address such issues directly.

IMPLEMENTING ACCOUNTABILITY

- **Create an AI oversight committee:** Include marketers, legal experts, and external advisors to review high-impact campaigns. This committee should have the authority to halt or modify campaigns that pose ethical risks. For example, a financial services firm might have its committee audit AI-driven credit risk models to ensure fairness across socioeconomic groups.

- **Define clear ownership:** Assign specific individuals or teams to monitor AI systems for ethical issues. This could involve data scientists reviewing model outputs for bias, marketing professionals assessing potential impacts on brand reputation, or legal team members ensuring compliance with privacy laws.

- **Establish response protocols:** Create detailed protocols for addressing ethical violations. These protocols should include:

  o immediately pausing the campaign or AI system in question

  o conducting a thorough investigation to identify the root cause of the issue

  o publicly acknowledging the error and apologizing to affected customers

  o offering compensation or redress to those harmed by the AI's actions

  o implementing a clear plan to rectify the issue and prevent recurrence

  o communicating transparently about the steps taken to restore trust.

TARGETING BIAS AT AN E-COMMERCE GIANT

A large e-commerce platform deployed an AI pricing algorithm that offered discounts based on geographic location and proximity to competitors. However, the algorithm unintentionally favored urban consumers with more choices, while rural consumers— who had fewer local options—were excluded from discounts. This pricing disparity led to negative feedback and a public relations backlash when the issue was brought to light.

The company's lack of fairness auditing during the model deployment phase resulted in unintended discrimination. The company responded by creating an internal AI ethics committee to oversee future algorithmic decisions and ensure accountability. This case highlights the importance of establishing robust oversight mechanisms and response protocols to address ethical concerns promptly and effectively.

By embracing accountability as an ongoing commitment and integrating it into every stage of AI development and deployment, marketers can build trust, mitigate risks, and ensure that their AI-driven initiatives contribute to a more equitable and responsible marketplace.

Respect for Autonomy: Empowering Consumer Control

Empowering consumers to actively shape their interactions with your brand enhances engagement and fosters trust. For instance, offering personalized content controls allows users to tailor recommendations to their preferences, providing a deeper sense of agency. Brands that respect consumer autonomy often see higher engagement rates and improved trust, as consumers feel their choices are genuinely valued.

In 2024, Marks & Spencer (M&S) implemented an AI-driven personalization feature that allows customers to receive tailored outfit suggestions based on a quiz detailing their size and style preferences. This initiative led to over 450,000 shoppers utilizing the feature, indicating a significant boost in customer engagement and satisfaction (Butler, 2024).

Similarly, Shopify introduced "Shopify Magic," a suite of AI tools enabling merchants to automate tasks such as generating product descriptions and discounts. This empowerment of merchants to customize their offerings has attracted more users to the platform, contributing to robust revenue growth (Reuters, 2025).

IMPLEMENTING RESPECT FOR AUTONOMY

- **Build comprehensive consent options:** Go beyond simple opt-ins or opt-outs. Offer granular consent controls that let consumers decide how their data is used for different purposes—recommendations, ads, or content curation.

- **Introduce data portability features:** Make it easy for consumers to access, download, and delete their data. Autonomy means giving them the power to take their data elsewhere if they choose.

- **Develop personalization sandboxes:** Create environments where consumers can experiment with different personalization settings and see the impact in real-time, empowering them to make informed choices.

Navigating Common Ethical Dilemmas

While understanding ethical principles is crucial, applying them in real-world scenarios often presents complex challenges. This section explores common dilemmas marketers face when implementing AI-driven strategies and offers practical solutions aligned with our core ethical principles.

Personalization Paradox

Personalization is a powerful tool, but it can easily cross the line from helpful to creepy. The question is: Where do we draw the line? For example, if a fitness brand's AI continuously shows aggressive diet-related ads to a user based on previous searches, it may lead to an uncomfortable experience or even unintended emotional distress. This is especially problematic when the user is simply exploring fitness options rather than looking for weight-loss solutions. Establishing personalization boundaries ensures that content remains helpful and not harmful. While the intent is to be helpful, the result can be a negative experience for the consumer, who may feel judged or pressured.

- **Ethical challenge:** How do you balance personalization with respect for consumer well-being?
  Solution: Establish personalization boundaries and provide consumers with controls to shape their experience, such as letting users adjust the types of content they wish to see. This empowers consumers while preventing AI from crossing personal boundaries.

DATA BIAS AND REPRESENTATION

Data bias is a well-documented issue in AI, but it's particularly problematic in marketing, where biases can translate directly into skewed consumer experiences. For example, a beauty brand's AI that primarily promotes products for lighter skin tones because of historical data can alienate customers with diverse skin tones.

- **Ethical challenge:** How do you ensure that your AI models are inclusive and unbiased? *Solution*: Use diverse datasets during model training and conduct regular audits to ensure fairness and inclusivity. Incorporate fairness metrics into your key performance indicators (KPIs) to monitor AI-driven decisions across various demographics.

EXPLAINING AI DECISIONS IN A MARKETING CONTEXT

With AI playing an increasing role in how ads are targeted and recommendations are made, consumers often feel left in the dark. They want to know why they're seeing certain ads, but most explanations offered are either too vague or too technical.

- **Ethical challenge:** How do you communicate AI-driven decisions in a way that is both transparent and understandable?
  Solution: Develop consumer-friendly explanations for algorithmic decisions, and offer interactive tools that let users explore why they're seeing certain ads or recommendations.

Implementation Pitfalls

As organizations strive to implement ethical AI in marketing, several common pitfalls can hinder progress. Being aware of these challenges can help you navigate the implementation process more effectively.

- **Overlooking diverse perspectives:** Many organizations fail to include diverse voices in their AI development and ethical review processes. This has been shown to lead to blind spots and unintended biases.
  Solution: Actively seek out and include team members from various backgrounds, experiences, and expertise in your AI ethics committees and development teams.

- **Treating ethics as a one-time checkbox:** Some companies view ethical AI as a one-off compliance issue rather than an ongoing commitment.
  Solution: Implement regular ethical audits and make ethics a continuous part of your AI strategy discussions and performance metrics.

- **Lack of transparency in AI decision-making:** Many organizations struggle to explain how their AI systems make decisions, leading to a lack of trust from consumers.
  Solution: Invest in XAI technologies and develop clear, jargon-free communication strategies to help consumers understand AI-driven decisions.

- **Over-reliance on technical solutions:** Some companies focus solely on technical fixes for ethical issues, overlooking the importance of human judgment and oversight.*Solution:* Balance technical solutions with human oversight. Establish cross-functional teams that include both technical experts and those with expertise in ethics, law, and social sciences.

- **Neglecting consumer autonomy:** In the pursuit of personalization, some organizations overlook the importance of giving consumers control over their data and experiences.
  Solution: Implement robust consent mechanisms and provide easy-to-use tools for consumers to control their data and personalization preferences.

By being aware of these common pitfalls, you can proactively address potential issues and create a more robust, ethical AI strategy for your marketing efforts.

Cross-Functional Collaboration

Ensuring ethical AI in marketing requires collaboration across multiple departments, not just technical experts. Marketers, legal teams, and data scientists need to work together to anticipate potential ethical challenges and address them proactively.

Creating Ethical AI Teams

Ethical AI implementation works best when multiple perspectives come together to inform the development and deployment of AI models. Here's how marketers can collaborate with other departments to embed ethics into AI workflows:

- **Legal team:** Collaborating with legal experts ensures AI systems comply with global regulations like the GDPR and the CCPA. Their insights help identify potential risks related to privacy, consent, and data protection laws.
- **Diversity and inclusion officers:** Partnering with diversity and inclusion teams helps ensure that AI models' training data and outputs reflect a diverse and inclusive consumer base. They play a crucial role in conducting fairness audits and advising on inclusivity metrics.
- **Data scientists:** Data scientists are integral in ensuring AI models are both technically sound and ethically aligned. This collaboration is critical for implementing **bias mitigation** techniques during model development.
- Customer relations: Incorporating feedback from customer service and public-facing teams provides marketers with a deeper understanding of consumer perceptions regarding AI-driven campaigns, enabling ethical adjustments based on real-world concerns.

Specific Roles and Responsibilities in Ethical AI Implementation

To ensure comprehensive ethical AI implementation, it's important to define clear roles and responsibilities across different departments.

MARKETING TEAM

Responsibility to ensure AI-driven campaigns align with ethical principles and brand values.

Key tasks:

- Conduct ethical impact assessments for new AI-driven campaigns.
- Monitor campaign performance for unintended consequences or biases.
- Collaborate with data scientists to refine AI models based on ethical considerations.

DATA SCIENCE TEAM

Responsibility to develop and maintain AI models that adhere to ethical standards.
    Key tasks:

- Implement fairness constraints in AI algorithms.
- Conduct regular bias audits on AI models.
- Develop explainable AI features for transparency.

LEGAL TEAM

Responsibility to ensure AI practices comply with relevant laws and regulations.
    Key tasks:

- Review AI-driven marketing strategies for legal compliance.
- Stay updated on emerging AI regulations and advise on necessary adjustments.
- Assist in drafting transparent privacy policies and consent forms.

ETHICS COMMITTEE

Responsibility to provide oversight and guidance on ethical AI practices.
    Key tasks:

- Develop and update ethical AI guidelines.
- Review high-impact AI decisions and provide recommendations.
- Facilitate ethics training programs for the organization.

CUSTOMER SERVICE TEAM

Responsibility to act as the front line for addressing consumer concerns about AI.
    Key tasks:

- Handle consumer inquiries about AI-driven decisions.
- Collect and report feedback on AI-related issues.
- Collaborate with other teams to improve AI transparency and user experience.

HUMAN RESOURCES

Responsibility to ensure diverse representation in AI teams and foster an ethical culture.

Key tasks:

- Recruit diverse talent for AI-related roles.
- Develop and implement ethics training programs.
- Incorporate ethical AI considerations into performance evaluations.

By clearly defining these roles and responsibilities, organizations can ensure a comprehensive approach to ethical AI implementation, leveraging diverse expertise and perspectives.

Workflow Integration

So, we've defined what it means to be fair, transparent, accountable, and respectful of autonomy in your AI-driven marketing strategies. But here's the kicker: knowing these principles isn't enough. The real challenge is figuring out how to weave them into the messy, fast-paced, and often chaotic world of marketing workflows. After all, what good is an ethical principle if it's buried under a pile of ad creatives, performance metrics, and endless campaign deadlines?

This section focuses on how to integrate these principles into every step of your marketing process—from the very inception of your AI models to the post-campaign analysis where you look back and assess whether your efforts lived up to your ethical standards. Ready to see how the magic happens? Let's go.

Building Ethics into Model Development

Creating an ethical marketing strategy starts before the first ad is served or the first email is sent—it begins with how you build and train your AI models. Often, this is where the most critical ethical considerations come into play, because biases and other ethical missteps are usually baked into the system from the outset.

Here's how to integrate ethics at each stage of AI model development.

DATA COLLECTION AND PREPARATION

Ethics begins with your data. The quality and diversity of your data shape how your AI models behave, so you need to be intentional about what goes in. Think of it like cooking—if your ingredients are poor or unbalanced, no amount of seasoning will save the dish. When it comes to data, the same rule applies.

- **Assess data sources:** Look at where your data comes from. Does it include diverse and representative samples of your target audience? Or is it heavily skewed toward certain demographics or geographic areas? Use data that accurately represents the consumer base you intend to serve. For example, if you're a beauty brand, don't train your models on a dataset that primarily represents only one skin tone or hair type.

- **Remove or mitigate bias:** Evaluate your data for inherent biases, such as overrepresentation or underrepresentation of particular groups. Use tools and frameworks designed to detect and mitigate these biases. This could include resampling techniques, synthetic data augmentation, or re-weighting methods to balance out underrepresented groups.

- **Implement ethical data usage protocols:** Define how data can and cannot be used within your organization. Consider creating internal data-usage policies that explicitly state what types of data are off-limits (e.g. personal health information unless explicitly consented).

MODEL TRAINING AND EVALUATION

Training your AI model is similar to setting expectations for a student—you don't just aim for the right answers; you also instill the right values. Ethical training means enforcing standards that prioritize fairness and inclusivity. By implementing bias mitigation techniques during training, such as rebalancing datasets and using scenario-based testing, you ensure your model upholds ethical principles from the start.

- **Establish fairness constraints:** Set fairness constraints and metrics that your models must meet before they can be deployed. For example, implement parity constraints that ensure the model performs equally well across different demographic groups. These could include equal opportunity measures or disparate impact ratios.

- **Scenario-based testing:** Use synthetic datasets or scenario-based testing to understand how your models perform under various conditions. This helps identify biases that might not be apparent during regular testing.

- **Conduct ethical reviews:** Before deploying a model, conduct ethical reviews involving cross-functional teams that include data scientists, marketers, legal advisors, and diversity and inclusion experts. This ensures multiple perspectives are considered and potential ethical pitfalls are caught early.

DEPLOYMENT AND MONITORING

Even the most ethically sound models can behave unpredictably once they're out in the real world. That's why ongoing monitoring is crucial.

- **Set up continuous monitoring systems:** Deploy monitoring tools that continuously track model behavior for signs of ethical issues, such as bias or discrimination. Use these tools to generate alerts if the model's predictions start deviating from ethical norms.

- **Implement XAI:** Use explainable AI techniques to provide clarity around model decisions. For example, if an AI-driven recommendation engine suddenly starts favoring certain products for certain groups, XAI can help you understand why.

- **Create feedback loops:** Set up mechanisms that allow consumers and internal teams to flag issues or raise concerns about the model's decisions. Use this feedback to make ongoing improvements to your AI systems.

Tools and Technologies for Ethical Implementation

Implementing ethical AI at scale requires leveraging specific tools and technologies designed to address fairness, transparency, and accountability. Here are some examples of how technology can assist in ethical AI practices.

BIAS DETECTION AND FAIRNESS AUDITS

Several platforms now offer bias detection tools that automatically audit AI models for bias across different demographic groups. These tools help identify any discrepancies in how the AI treats certain segments of the population and offer suggestions for remediation.

IBM's AI Fairness 360 Toolkit provides open-source resources that allow marketers to test their AI models for fairness, offering metrics and debiasing techniques to ensure ethical outcomes.

XAI FOR TRANSPARENCY

To maintain consumer trust, marketers can utilize XAI tools that provide insights into how AI systems make decisions. These tools offer explanations in layman's terms, helping consumers understand why certain products or advertisements are recommended.

Google's What-If Tool is an interactive visual interface that allows users to probe machine learning models without writing code. It enables testing of hypothetical scenarios, analysis of feature importance, and visualization of model behavior across different subsets of data. The tool aids in understanding the factors influencing AI decisions, thereby enhancing transparency for both internal teams and consumers.

ETHICAL TARGETING PLATFORMS

Some AI platforms are specifically designed to support ethical targeting, ensuring that personalized ads and recommendations adhere to fairness principles. These platforms monitor ad distribution to avoid discrimination or over-targeting based on sensitive data like race or socioeconomic status.

Cortexica's Ethical AI platform employs ethical constraints to ensure that recommendations and targeted ads are inclusive and fair. It provides insights into how various demographic segments are impacted, promoting responsible AI practices in marketing strategies.

PRIVACY CONTROL DASHBOARDS FOR CONSUMERS

To respect consumer autonomy, brands can implement privacy control dashboards that allow users to manage how their data is utilized for marketing purposes. These dashboards provide transparency regarding data collection and grant consumers the ability to modify their preferences or opt out.

OneTrust offers a Data Privacy Management platform that assists companies in building such privacy dashboards. This platform enables consumers to control their data settings, thereby enhancing autonomy over how their information is used for personalized marketing. Features include customizable dashboards and visualizations, allowing organizations to prioritize aspects of their privacy programs and present relevant information effectively.

Campaign Planning and Execution

With your AI models ethically sound and ready to go, the next stage is planning and executing your campaigns. But how do you ensure that ethical principles guide your campaign strategies and interactions? Here's how to keep ethics front and center at each step of your campaign planning process.

TARGETING AND SEGMENTATION

Targeting is where a lot of ethical challenges can arise—whether it's unintentionally excluding certain groups or reinforcing harmful stereotypes. Here's how to avoid these pitfalls:

- **Evaluate segmentation strategies:** Regularly review your segmentation strategies to ensure they are inclusive and don't inadvertently reinforce bias. For instance, if your AI is segmenting based on income level, ensure that lower-income groups aren't automatically shown less favorable offers or discounts.

- **Use ethical targeting parameters:** Define ethical targeting parameters that go beyond compliance. For example, avoid using sensitive data points like race or religion unless it's to promote inclusivity (e.g. showcasing products for a variety of hair textures). Additionally, implement fairness constraints to ensure all segments are equally considered in targeting models.

- **Diversify ad creative:** Test ad creatives to ensure they resonate across different segments and avoid perpetuating stereotypes. Consider using a variety of visuals, language styles, and messaging to appeal to diverse audiences without relying on narrow or clichéd representations.

CONTENT CREATION AND PERSONALIZATION

AI-driven personalization can either create highly engaging experiences or come across as intrusive and unwelcome, depending on how it's done.

- **Avoid over-personalization:** Over-personalization can feel invasive, especially when it's not backed by transparency. Instead of bombarding consumers with hyper-targeted messages, use AI to understand broad patterns and recommend content that feels relevant without crossing boundaries.

- **Test for content relevance and tone:** Test your AI-driven content for both relevance and tone. Use sentiment analysis to assess how different consumer segments might perceive your content.

- **Offer personalization controls:** Provide consumers with options to control the level of personalization they receive. This empowers them to decide how much influence AI should have over their experience and prevents feelings of overreach.

POST-CAMPAIGN ANALYSIS

Once a campaign has run its course, it's time to analyze the results—not just from a performance standpoint but from an ethical perspective as well.

- **Assess ethical impact:** Go beyond traditional KPIs like ROI and engagement rates. Assess whether your campaign reached a diverse audience and whether any segments were excluded or negatively impacted. Use surveys, feedback forms, and social listening tools to gauge consumer sentiment.

- **Review and report findings:** Share findings with key stakeholders, including what worked, what didn't, and any ethical dilemmas that arose. Use this information to refine your approach for future campaigns.

- **Implement learnings:** Take insights from your post-campaign analysis and integrate them into your next campaign. Continuous learning is key to ensuring that your AI-driven marketing strategies evolve and improve over time.

Ethical AI Guidelines for Your Marketing Team

After integrating these ethical principles into the technical aspects of AI development and campaign execution, it's important to formalize them into clear, actionable guidelines that your marketing team can reference. This ensures that everyone is on the same page and has a common understanding of your ethical standards.

Creating Your Ethical AI Playbook

The world's relationship with data has fundamentally changed. As Ursula von der Leyen, President of the European Commission, emphasized at Davos 2024: "Our future competitiveness depends on AI adoption in our daily businesses, and Europe must up its game and show the way to responsible use of AI—AI that enhances human capabilities, improves productivity, and serves society." For marketers, this transformation carries profound implications—our approach to AI ethics will shape not just campaign effectiveness, but the very foundation of consumer trust.

Think of developing an ethical AI playbook like creating a constitution for your organization's AI practices. Just as a constitution provides both guiding principles and practical regulatory governance, your playbook needs to bridge the gap between abstract ethical ideals and day-to-day marketing decisions. Let's explore how to build this bridge systematically.

Defining Your Ethical North Star

Before implementing specific practices, organizations need a clear ethical vision—an "Ethical North Star." This goes beyond mere compliance or general principles. Your ethical standards should reflect your brand's unique values and mission while addressing the specific challenges of AI in marketing.

Consider how this might work in practice. A luxury fashion brand's ethical AI principles might emphasize preserving the human artistry in fashion while using AI to enhance personalization. In contrast, a healthcare company's principles might prioritize patient privacy and well-being above all else. The key is aligning AI ethics with your brand's core purpose.

To develop your Ethical North Star, gather key stakeholders for an Ethics Alignment workshop. This session should include the following steps:

1 Examine how each ethical principle (fairness, transparency, accountability, and autonomy) translates to your specific context.

2 Identify potential tensions between principles and business objectives.

3 Create clear guidelines for resolving these tensions.

4 Document these decisions in a concise and actionable ethical AI manifesto.

Building Your Decision-Making Architecture

With your Ethical North Star established, the next step is creating an "Ethics Decision Architecture"—the frameworks and processes that guide ethical decision-making throughout your AI initiatives. This architecture needs three key components:

1. DATA ETHICS FRAMEWORK

Think of a data ethics framework as your organization's data constitution. It should address:

- what data you'll collect and why
- how you'll ensure data diversity and representativeness
- when and how you'll obtain meaningful consent
- how you'll protect and respect consumer privacy.

2. MODEL DEVELOPMENT GUIDELINES

These guidelines ensure ethical considerations shape your AI models from inception through deployment. They should include:

- criteria for assessing training data fairness

- required fairness constraints and testing protocols
- transparency requirements for model decisions
- continuous monitoring and adjustment processes.

3. ESCALATION PROTOCOLS

Clear processes for handling ethical concerns when they arise include:

- defined triggers for ethical review
- step-by-step escalation procedures
- designated decision-makers at each level
- documentation requirements.

Creating a Culture of Ethical Excellence

Even the best frameworks fail without a supporting culture. Building this muscle memory requires ongoing education and practice. This involves both continuous learning programs and active feedback systems.

CONTINUOUS LEARNING PROGRAMS

Develop training that goes beyond compliance basics:

- Case studies of ethical successes and failures
- Regular updates on emerging ethical challenges
- Hands-on workshops for applying ethical frameworks
- Cross-functional learning sessions

ACTIVE FEEDBACK SYSTEMS

Create multiple channels for ethical dialogue:

- Anonymous reporting mechanisms
- Regular ethics forums and discussions
- External stakeholder feedback channels
- Quarterly ethics effectiveness reviews

Operationalizing Ethics in Marketing Workflows

The final piece is integrating ethical considerations into daily marketing operations. This means creating practical tools and checkpoints that make ethical decision-making natural and efficient:

- Campaign planning checklists that include ethical considerations

- AI model monitoring dashboards with ethical metrics
- Regular ethical impact assessments
- Documentation templates for ethical decisions

Remember, your ethical AI playbook isn't a static document—it's a living system that should evolve with your organization and the broader AI landscape. Regular reviews and updates ensure it remains relevant and effective as technology and consumer expectations change.

As we move forward, we'll explore how to measure the effectiveness of your ethical AI implementation and adjust your approach based on real-world results. The goal isn't just compliance or risk management—it's building a sustainable competitive advantage through ethical excellence in AI marketing.

Bringing It All Together

Embedding ethical principles into AI-driven marketing is not a one-time exercise—it's an ongoing commitment that requires active engagement and continuous improvement. By reimagining fairness, transparency, accountability, and respect for autonomy through the lens of real-world marketing, we can create strategies that not only comply with ethical standards but also drive genuine value for consumers.

KEY TAKEAWAYS

- **Understanding the core principles**: Ethical AI in marketing is grounded in four principles—fairness, transparency, accountability, and respect for autonomy—that must be reimagined through a marketing lens.
  Why it matters: These principles serve as the foundation for creating AI-driven marketing practices that not only meet compliance requirements but also foster consumer trust, brand loyalty, and long-term business growth. Understanding and applying these principles is essential for marketers to navigate the complexities of the evolving digital landscape.

- **Navigating common dilemmas**: Addressing ethical challenges like balancing personalization and privacy, ensuring inclusivity in data, and providing understandable explanations requires practical solutions that align with these principles.
  Why it matters: Ethical dilemmas in AI can undermine consumer trust and lead to regulatory and reputational risks. By actively navigating these dilemmas, marketers can protect the integrity of their brand, avoid potential backlash, and create marketing strategies that respect and enhance customer relationships.

- **Operationalizing ethics**: Implementing these principles requires a clear plan for integration into your marketing workflows, from AI model development to campaign execution and post-campaign analysis.
  Why it matters: Without a structured approach to operationalizing ethics, principles remain abstract and difficult to enforce. Building ethics into the operational workflow ensures that every stage of the marketing process—from ideation to execution—upholds ethical standards, leading to more consistent and sustainable business practices.

- **Cross-functional collaboration**: Ensuring ethical AI in marketing requires input and cooperation from diverse teams, including marketing, legal, data science, and customer relations.
  Why it matters: Ethical AI implementation is a multifaceted challenge that requires diverse expertise. By fostering cross-functional collaboration, organizations can create more robust ethical frameworks, identify potential issues early, and develop more comprehensive solutions that address ethical concerns from multiple perspectives.

Looking Ahead

As we move into the next chapter on human-centered AI in marketing, we'll build upon the ethical foundations established here. We'll explore how to put people at the heart of AI strategies, ensuring that our initiatives not only adhere to ethical principles but also genuinely serve and empower consumers.

Key areas we'll examine include:

- augmenting human creativity and decision-making with AI
- incorporating empathy into AI-driven customer interactions
- balancing automation with the human touch in marketing processes
- case studies illustrating the transformative impact of human-centered AI on marketing practices.

Food for Thought

1 How might the ethical principles discussed in this chapter conflict with short-term business goals? How would you address these conflicts?

2 Consider a recent AI-driven marketing campaign you've encountered as a consumer. How well did it align with the ethical principles we've discussed? What could have been improved?

3 In what ways might ethical AI principles need to evolve as AI technology advances? How can marketers stay ahead of these changes?

4 How would you go about building cross-functional collaboration for ethical AI in an organization that currently operates in silos?

References

Aristotle (n.d.) *Nicomachean Ethics*, trans. W D Ross. The Internet Classics Archive. classics. mit.edu/Aristotle/nicomachaen.html (archived at https://perma.cc/N23K-E4PF) (Original work published c. 350 BCE)

Bentham, J (1970) *The Collected Works of Jeremy Bentham: An Introduction to the Principles of Morals and Legislation*, Athlone Press, London

Bursztynsky, J (2025) Duolingo Launches 148 AI-Written Courses, Replacing Humans, Entrepreneur, www.entrepreneur.com/business-news/duolingo-will-replace-contract-workers-with-ai-ceo-says/490812 (archived at https://perma.cc/BJ2U-WSQ6)

Butler, S (2024) Marks & Spencer Using AI to Advise Shoppers on Body Shape and Style Preferences, *The Guardian*, 5 September, www.theguardian.com/business/article/2024/sep/05/m-and-s-using-ai-to-advise-shoppers-body-shape-style-preferences (archived at https://perma.cc/27X7-8ZRR)

Cisco (2023) Younger Consumers Are 7 Times More Likely to Exercise Their Data Rights, Survey, newsroom.cisco.com/c/r/newsroom/en/us/a/y2023/m10/younger-consumers-more-likely-to-exercise-data-privacy-rights-2023-cisco-survey.html (archived at https://perma.cc/WM66-CA9E)

Edelman (2024) Rebuilding Trust to Reach AI's Potential, www.edelman.com/insights/rebuilding-trust-reach-ai-potential (archived at https://perma.cc/4984-FG9B)

Kant, I (1998) *Groundwork of the Metaphysics of Morals*, trans M Gregor, Cambridge University Press, Cambridge (Original work published 1785)

Microsoft (2024) *2024 Responsible AI Transparency Report*, www.microsoft.com/en-us/corporate-responsibility/responsible-ai-transparency-report (archived at https://perma.cc/W7G4-EF9M)

Murphy, J M (2023) *The Moral Economy of Tech: Justice, Power, and the New Digital Age*, University of California Press, Berkely

Pew Research Center (2023) How Americans View Data Privacy, www.pewresearch.org/internet/2023/10/18/how-americans-view-data-privacy/ (archived at https://perma.cc/F493-JUXU)

Reuters (2025) How Canada's Shopify Is Weaving AI "Magic" to Pull Merchants, www.reuters.com/technology/artificial-intelligence/how-canadas-shopify-is-weaving-ai-magic-pull-merchants-2025-02-10/ (archived at https://perma.cc/K8XF-EZ7E)

Salesforce (2023) What Are Customer Expectations, and How Have They Changed? www.salesforce.com/resources/articles/customer-expectations/ (archived at https://perma.cc/9YAN-NCPF)

World Economic Forum (2024) Ursula von der Leyen's Speech to Davos in Full, www.weforum.org/stories/2024/01/ursula-von-der-leyen-full-speech-davos (archived at https://perma.cc/A8HQ-GFFM)

3

Human-Centered AI in Marketing

The principles of ethical AI—fairness, transparency, accountability, and respect for autonomy—are not abstract ideals but foundational concepts rooted in enhancing the human experience. As we navigate the complexities of AI integration, it's crucial to remember that behind every data point is a person with unique needs, emotions, and expectations.

Human-centered AI (HCAI) transcends mere personalization; it's about creating interactions that are not only tailored but also empathetic and emotionally intelligent. To achieve this, AI needs to truly understand us—not just what we say, but how we feel and what we truly mean. This is where the magic of natural language processing (NLP) comes in. Think of NLP as the bridge between human language and computer understanding. It allows AI to decipher the complexities of our communication, whether it's the nuances of a carefully worded email or a casual social media post. NLP helps AI grasp the meaning behind our words, the intent behind our requests, and even the subtle emotions woven into our expressions.

But understanding the meaning of words is only half the battle. Human communication is deeply intertwined with emotions, and that's where sentiment analysis plays a crucial role. Imagine an AI that can not only understand the words "I'm frustrated" but also grasp the underlying frustration and its intensity. Sentiment analysis allows AI to do just that. By analyzing various cues like word choice, tone, and even emojis, AI can gauge our emotional state and respond accordingly.

Consider the scenario of Walter, a young professional, browsing a financial services website, looking for information on first-time home buying. The AI-driven chatbot, equipped with NLP and sentiment analysis, detects a pattern of hesitant behavior—multiple page views without engagement, rapid scrolling, and brief hover-overs on key terms. Instead of pushing a generic mortgage offer, the AI responds with:

"Hi Walter, I noticed you're exploring our first-time homebuyer resources. Buying a home can feel overwhelming—would you like to see our step-by-step guide or chat with one of our advisors about your specific situation?"

This approach demonstrates how HCAI can transform a potentially stressful experience into a supportive interaction, building trust and rapport while motivating a consumer forward in the journey. By understanding Walter's hesitation and responding with empathy and relevant assistance, the AI provides a truly human-centered experience.

In essence, NLP and sentiment analysis are empowering AI to move beyond cold, calculated responses and step into the realm of genuine emotional intelligence. This paves the way for a future where technology not only serves our needs but truly understands and connects with us on a human level, enhancing our experiences and fostering deeper relationships with the brands we interact with.

Pillars of HCAI

HCAI is the art of balancing advanced technological capabilities with an understanding of human psychology, cultural contexts, and emotional intelligence. Rather than overshadowing human agency, it seeks to augment it, designing experiences that uphold human rights and dignity while making room for innovation. This balance is exemplified by Andrea Brimmer, chief marketing and public relations officer of Ally—a leading digital financial services company and a top 25 U.S. financial holding company. Brimmer emphasizes the foundational role of human oversight: "There's nothing that's just on autopilot, everything is prompted by humans, checked by humans, iterated on review, revised by humans. And we're really not moving forward on anything that doesn't provide value at the end of the day" (2025). This approach demonstrates how leading organizations maintain human judgment as the cornerstone of their AI initiatives while ensuring technology delivers meaningful value and aligns with brand values, ultimately building meaningful, lasting connections with diverse audiences.

By placing people at the center of every stage—conceiving ideas, training algorithms, and evaluating outcomes—organizations develop AI solutions that address real human needs. These needs include inclusivity and accessibility, ensuring that systems are usable by individuals from all backgrounds and abilities; transparency and explainability, so users can trust and effectively interact with AI; accountability and responsibility, clearly defining who is answerable for AI-driven outcomes; and ethical and safe design, proactively guarding against biases, risks, or unintended consequences. When viewed collectively, these four principles provide a blueprint for creating ethical AI systems, while three foundational pillars—empathy, inclusivity, and trust—bring those principles to life on a practical level.

Empathy

Empathy in AI extends beyond the mechanical detection of emotional states. It respects the personal, psychological, and cultural nuances in every interaction. This layer of emotional intelligence ensures that when an AI system detects anxiety, frustration, or excitement, it can respond compassionately, providing support or guidance tailored to the individual. In healthcare settings, this might mean offering words of comfort and directing patients to useful resources in a gentle manner. In finance, an empathetic chatbot could adjust its tone and pacing if it senses the user is stressed about an overdue payment.

Such genuine empathy reflects a commitment to ethical and safe design—one that prioritizes human well-being and acknowledges the wide spectrum of emotions people experience. By looking out for signs of distress or confusion, empathetic AI can potentially de-escalate tense situations and point users toward constructive solutions. These thoughtful, empathetic experiences strengthen the user's trust in the system, paving the way for deeper, long-term relationships that go beyond transactional interactions.

Inclusivity

In practice, inclusivity is grounded in the principle of inclusivity and accessibility, requiring that AI systems consider all users—regardless of gender, age, socio-economic status, physical abilities, or cultural backgrounds. Rather than treating biases as oversights to be corrected after the fact, modern AI design proactively seeks diversity in its data sources and training processes. This means ensuring the data itself represents underrepresented groups and that system outputs respect different cultural norms and languages.

From a broader societal perspective, inclusivity aligns with accountability and responsibility. Organizations that prioritize inclusive AI hold themselves accountable for the impact their systems have on every community, not just the most visible or profitable ones. By identifying and serving underserved market segments, they foster fairer access to products and services, and in doing so, expand their own market potential. Whether it's through adding sign-language support, ensuring screen-reader compatibility, or embracing multiple dialects, inclusive AI design elevates overall accessibility, encouraging participation from people of all backgrounds and building a genuinely equitable digital landscape.

Trust

Trust is often described as the cornerstone of every AI interaction. Indeed, it flourishes when organizations practice transparency and explainability—making AI's inner workings and decision-making logic understandable to everyday users. Yet trust involves more than just revealing how an algorithm arrives at its output; it also means giving individuals a sense of control over how their data is used. Privacy-centered designs, for instance, can empower users to manage personal information through intuitive dashboards, enabling them to decide precisely what data is shared and for what purpose.

Moreover, trust implies accountability and responsibility in action. When someone is adversely affected by an AI-driven decision—be it in job applications, loan approvals, or healthcare triage—users deserve clarity on who bears responsibility and how that decision can be appealed or corrected. This posture of openness and willingness to engage with user concerns underscores a core commitment to ethical and safe design. It reassures people that the AI is serving their best interests and that if something goes wrong, there's a plan in place to address it responsibly.

To see how these principles of HCAI work in practice, consider how Ally Financial implemented AI while keeping humans at the core of their strategy.

ETHICAL AI IN ACTION
Ally Financial: Putting Humans at the Center of AI Implementation

Ally Financial, a leading digital financial services company, exemplifies how organizations can implement AI while keeping humans—both employees and customers—at the center of their strategy. Their approach, demonstrated through a generative AI use case that summarized customer service calls, shows how the principles of HCAI can be successfully applied in a highly regulated industry where trust and personal connection are paramount.

The Human Challenge

Ally faced a common challenge in customer service: Their representatives were spending significant time on manual documentation during and after calls with consumers, reducing their ability to focus on meaningful customer interactions. While AI offered potential solutions, Ally recognized that simply automating processes could risk diminishing the human element that was central to their customer relationships.

"The goal was never to replace human judgment," explains Andrea Brimmer, chief marketing and public relations officer at Ally. "Instead, we wanted to enhance our employees' capabilities so they could focus on what matters most—building genuine connections with our customers."

A Human-Centered Approach

Rather than rushing to implement AI solutions, Ally started by deeply understanding the needs of both their employees and customers. They conducted extensive interviews and feedback sessions with employees, ensuring that any AI implementation would genuinely enhance rather than detract from human interactions.

Their approach embodied the three core pillars of HCAI:

- **Empathy in action**: Ally developed their AI solution with a deep understanding of their employees' daily challenges. The system was designed to handle routine documentation tasks while preserving employees' ability to exercise judgment and emotional intelligence in customer interactions. This empathetic approach supported the customer experience, ensuring callers would continue to receive personalized attention from representatives who could now focus more fully on understanding and addressing their needs.

- **Inclusivity through collaboration**: The development process involved stakeholders from across the organization—from customer service representatives to technical teams to compliance, privacy, and risk officers. This inclusive approach ensured that diverse perspectives and needs were considered from the start. Regular feedback sessions during the pilot phase allowed all customer service associates to contribute to the system's refinement, creating a solution that worked for everyone.

- **Building trust through transparency**: Ally maintained transparency about the role of AI in their operations. They implemented what they call a "human in the middle" approach, where AI assists but never replaces human decision-making. As Brimmer emphasizes, "There's nothing that's just on autopilot; everything is prompted by humans, checked by humans, iterated on review, revised by humans. And we're really not moving forward on anything that doesn't provide value at the end of the day."

Results of Human-Centered Implementation

The results of this human-centered approach were striking. Customer service representatives reported feeling more empowered in their roles, with the AI system handling routine transcription and summarization while they focused on meaningful customer interactions and reviewing the output for accuracy after the call was completed. The technology enhanced rather than replaced human capabilities, leading to:

- more engaging customer conversations
- increased job satisfaction among representatives
- better customer relationships
- improved service quality.

Key Learnings for HCAI

Ally's experience offers several valuable insights for organizations implementing AI:

1 **Start with human needs**: Understanding the daily challenges of employees and customers should drive AI implementation.

2 **Maintain human agency**: AI should enhance human capabilities rather than replace human judgment.

3 **Foster inclusive development**: Involve diverse stakeholders throughout the process to build solutions that work for everyone.

4 **Build trust through transparency**: Be clear about AI's role and maintain human oversight of AI-driven processes.

5 **Focus on value creation**: Every AI implementation should demonstrably improve the experience for both employees and customers.

Ally's success demonstrates that when organizations put humans at the center of their AI strategy, they can create solutions that enhance rather than diminish the human element in their operations. Their approach shows how the principles of HCAI can be successfully applied to create meaningful value while strengthening human connections.

SOURCE Based on an interview with Andrea Brimmer, Chief Marketing & PR Officer, Ally Financial (Brimmer, 2025)

Ethics in Creative Development

As AI becomes more integrated into the creative processes of marketing, its role in content generation presents both opportunities and ethical challenges. AI tools can now generate text, images, and even video content, speeding up the creative process while also enabling hyper-personalization. However, this shift raises questions about the authenticity of brand messages and the ethical implications of AI-generated content.

Recent industry insights reveal a growing demand for transparency and ethical oversight as AI's role expands. Marketers are increasingly aware that while AI can generate product descriptions, email campaigns, and social media posts at scale, there is a risk of sacrificing depth, originality, and the human touch essential for genuine engagement. The market is now saturated with content, much lacking the quality and resonance that comes from human creativity. This has prompted a shift toward prioritizing quality over quantity, with marketing teams focusing on impactful storytelling and thoughtful analysis—areas where AI still lags behind humans.

Levi's leveraged AI to diversify its ad imagery, generating personalized content at scale (Ormesher, 2023). However, public criticism arose when it became evident that the ads featured synthetic models without disclosure. This underscores the importance of transparency: brands must clearly communicate when AI contributes to creative processes, ensuring authenticity and maintaining consumer trust.

Beyond transparency, there are ethical concerns regarding the potential for AI to perpetuate or amplify biases in creative content. For example, if an AI system is trained on historical advertising data, it might replicate outdated stereotypes or under-represent certain groups. To address this, companies are implementing diverse training datasets and regular bias audits of AI-generated content.

Additionally, the use of AI in creative processes raises questions about copyright and intellectual property. As AI systems become more sophisticated in generating original content, the line between human and machine creativity blurs. This has led to ongoing debates in the legal and creative communities about how to attribute and protect AI-generated works.

To navigate these ethical considerations, marketers should consider:

- clearly disclosing when content is AI-generated or AI-enhanced, as demonstrated by Levi's lack of transparency on their AI content generation
- implement a review process where human creatives vet and refine AI-generated content to ensure it aligns with brand values and cultural sensitivities
- ensure AI models are trained on diverse datasets that represent a wide range of perspectives and experiences to minimize bias in output
- develop clear guidelines for the use of AI in creative processes, addressing issues such as data privacy, bias mitigation, and intellectual property rights
- keep creative teams informed about the capabilities and limitations of AI tools, fostering a culture of responsible AI use in marketing.

By thoughtfully addressing these ethical considerations, marketers can harness the power of AI to enhance creative processes while maintaining the authenticity and ethical standards that consumers expect. The goal is not just to create content efficiently, but to do so in a way that builds trust and reinforces positive brand values.

Why Human-Centricity Matters

Marketers are often driven by metrics—conversion rates, incrementality, and engagement scores. But focusing solely on these metrics can lead to a narrow view of success, one that overlooks the intangible aspects of consumer experience. HCAI shifts the focus back to the consumer as a whole person, not just a set of data points.

When AI-driven marketing prioritizes human values, it transforms from being merely effective to being meaningful. Consumers are more likely to engage with a brand that feels authentic, values-driven, and genuinely interested in their well-being. And the best part? HCAI doesn't have to come at the expense of performance. In fact, campaigns grounded in empathy, inclusivity, and trust often see higher levels of engagement, satisfaction, and brand loyalty.

Challenges of Implementing HCAI

While the promise of HCAI in marketing is compelling, the path to implementation is fraught with complex challenges that span technological, ethical, and societal domains. As marketers venture into this new frontier, they find themselves navigating a landscape where the boundaries between human and machine interactions are increasingly blurred.

One of the most pressing challenges lies in the current limitations of AI technology. Despite rapid advancements, AI systems still struggle to accurately interpret the full spectrum of human emotions and cultural nuances. A chatbot might misinterpret a customer's sarcasm as genuine satisfaction, or fail to pick up on subtle cues of distress in a patient's message. These misunderstandings can lead to inappropriate responses, potentially damaging the very trust and connection that HCAI aims to build.

Closely tied to this technological challenge is the thorny issue of data privacy. To create truly empathetic and personalized interactions, AI systems require access to detailed, often sensitive personal data. This need for data bumps up against growing consumer concerns about privacy and the tightening noose of regulations like the GDPR and CCPA. Marketers find themselves walking a tightrope, balancing the need for data-driven insights with the imperative to respect and protect consumer privacy.

This balancing act becomes even more precarious when considering the potential for AI to be used for surveillance and manipulation. For instance, AI-powered sentiment analysis, while valuable for understanding customer emotions, could also be used to identify vulnerable consumers and target them with predatory marketing tactics. Imagine an AI system that detects financial anxiety in a customer's online interactions and then automatically serves them ads for high-interest loans or unnecessary financial products. Such practices could exploit consumers at their most vulnerable moments, eroding trust and potentially causing significant financial harm. Furthermore, the very nature of AI-driven personalization can inadvertently create "filter bubbles" where consumers are only exposed to information and products that confirm their existing biases. This can limit their worldview, reinforce harmful stereotypes, and ultimately hinder the development of a diverse and inclusive marketplace.

Scalability, in the context of AI, refers to the ability of a system to maintain its performance and effectiveness as the number of users or interactions increases. Think of it like this: If an AI system works perfectly for a small group of users, but starts to falter, slow down, or lose its personalized touch when faced with a large influx of users, it lacks scalability.

This presents a significant hurdle for HCAI. While crafting a deeply personalized and empathetic experience for a handful of users is achievable, extending that same level of nuanced interaction to millions of people simultaneously is a formidable technical challenge. It's not simply a matter of having enough computing power to handle the sheer volume; it also demands sophisticated algorithms that can maintain the quality of interactions at scale without becoming generic or repetitive.

Imagine a bespoke tailor meticulously handcrafting a suit for a single client. They can dedicate their full attention to every detail, ensuring a perfect fit and finish. Now, imagine that same tailor trying to replicate that level of personalized craftsmanship for thousands of clients simultaneously, each with their unique measurements and preferences. This illustrates the complexity of scaling HCAI. If the AI relies on pre-programmed responses or rigid decision trees, the interactions will quickly become predictable and lose their human touch.

To truly scale HCAI, we need algorithms that can learn and adapt in real-time, much like a seasoned tailor who adjusts their approach based on the unique needs of each client. This requires a delicate balance between personalization and efficiency. The AI needs to be able to recognize patterns and draw on past experiences but also remain flexible enough to handle novel situations and unexpected requests. It's a complex challenge that researchers are actively addressing with innovative approaches like reinforcement learning and federated learning, which allow AI systems to learn from diverse datasets without compromising user privacy.

Ultimately, achieving scalability in HCAI is essential if we want to bring its benefits to a wider audience. It's the key to ensuring that AI can truly enhance our lives, not just in isolated instances, but on a global scale.

The ethical implications of HCAI add another layer of complexity. As AI systems become more adept at mimicking human empathy, questions arise about the authenticity and ethics of these interactions. Is it deceptive to have an AI system express empathy? Should consumers always be explicitly informed when they're interacting with AI rather than a human? These ethical dilemmas don't have easy answers, and marketers must grapple with them as they deploy HCAI solutions.

There's also the looming specter of job displacement. As AI systems become more sophisticated in handling customer interactions, there's a real risk of displacing human workers in customer service roles. This potential for job loss raises broader societal questions about the role of AI in the workplace and the need for reskilling and transition support for affected workers.

Beyond job losses, the increasing reliance on AI in marketing raises concerns about the erosion of genuine human connection. While AI chatbots and virtual assistants can efficiently handle routine tasks, over-dependence on these technologies could lead to a decline in meaningful human interaction. Customers may find themselves interacting with machines more often than with people, potentially creating a sense of detachment and isolation. It's crucial for marketers to strike a balance, ensuring that AI augments human capabilities rather than replacing them entirely. This means prioritizing human connection in the customer journey, especially in situations that require empathy, complex problem-solving, or a personal touch.

Cultural inclusivity presents yet another challenge. Ensuring that AI systems can understand and respond appropriately to diverse cultural contexts is a monumental task. An AI that performs well in one cultural context may falter or even offend in another, highlighting the need for diverse datasets and culturally informed design processes.

Finally, measuring the success of HCAI initiatives poses its own set of challenges. Traditional metrics like conversion rates or call handling times may not capture the full impact of improved empathy and user experience. Marketers need to develop new frameworks for evaluating the success of these initiatives, potentially incorporating qualitative measures alongside quantitative ones.

Navigating these challenges requires a collaborative approach, bringing together technologists, ethicists, policymakers, and industry leaders. It demands a commitment to ongoing learning and adaptation, as the landscape of HCAI continues to evolve. While the road ahead is complex, the potential rewards—in terms of enhanced customer relationships, brand loyalty, and societal impact—make it a journey worth undertaking. As marketers continue to push the boundaries of what's possible with HCAI, they must remain vigilant in ensuring that these technologies truly serve their intended purpose: enhancing human experiences rather than replacing them.

Role of AI in Consumer Empowerment

Empowering consumers through AI has become a key differentiator for brands in the modern marketing landscape. This empowerment goes beyond offering personalized experiences—it's about giving consumers control over how AI interacts with them, respecting their autonomy, and providing transparent insights into how their data is used.

Data Transparency and Control

In an era of heightened data privacy concerns, consumers are demanding more transparency and control over their personal information. They want to feel empowered rather than exploited, and progressive brands are responding by developing user-centric approaches to data management.

Leading companies are now placing data control directly into the hands of their customers. They are creating personalized dashboards that allow users to see exactly what data is being collected and how it's being used. Users can make informed decisions about data sharing, choosing, for example, to share location data with a map app for personalized directions, while opting out of sharing it with social media platforms. They can allow an online retailer to use their purchase history for product recommendations, but prevent them from sharing that data with third-party advertisers.

Apple's "App Tracking Transparency" feature was a significant step in this direction. It gives users control over which apps can track their activity across other companies' apps and websites. This groundbreaking feature prompted a shift in the digital advertising industry, forcing companies to rethink their data collection practices and prioritize user privacy.

The "Data Dignity Initiative," launched in late 2024 by a coalition of tech companies, builds on this momentum. This initiative goes beyond simply allowing users to *control* their data; it empowers them to *monetize* it. Users could receive micropayments or other incentives in exchange for allowing companies to use their data for specific, agreed-upon purposes. This revolutionary concept has the potential to reshape the data economy, giving users a direct stake in how their information is valued and utilized.

This shift toward consumer data empowerment requires marketers to re-evaluate traditional data practices. Instead of viewing data as a resource to be mined and exploited, they must now treat it as a valuable asset entrusted to them by their customers. Prioritizing data transparency, providing clear explanations of data usage, and offering users meaningful control over their personal information are no longer just ethical considerations; they are essential for building trust and fostering long-lasting customer relationships in the age of AI.

AI-Driven Financial Empowerment

In the financial sector, AI is revolutionizing how companies engage with consumers, offering personalized financial guidance and enhancing brand loyalty. By integrating AI-driven tools, financial institutions can provide tailored experiences that resonate with individual customer needs.

Intuit (2024) has introduced "Intuit Assist," a generative AI-powered financial assistant embedded across its product suite, including TurboTax, Credit Karma, QuickBooks, and Mailchimp. This assistant delivers personalized, intelligent recommendations, automates tasks such as generating invoices from emails or notes, and provides actionable insights to help users make informed financial decisions. By leveraging Intuit Assist, the company enhances user engagement and positions itself as a proactive partner in financial management.

Morgan Stanley is leveraging AI to enhance its wealth management services. The firm has developed the "AI @ Morgan Stanley Debrief," an OpenAI-powered tool that, with client consent, generates summaries of client meetings, identifies action items, and drafts follow-up communications. This innovation streamlines administrative tasks, allowing financial advisors to focus more on client engagement and personalized service. By integrating AI into their operations, Morgan Stanley not only improves efficiency but also strengthens client relationships through timely and tailored interactions.

These examples illustrate how AI-driven financial tools can empower consumers with personalized insights, simplify complex financial tasks, and enhance the overall customer experience. For marketers in the financial industry, adopting such technologies offers an opportunity to build deeper, trust-based relationships with clients, differentiate their services, and stay competitive in a rapidly evolving market.

Health and Wellness Empowerment

In today's competitive wellness market, AI is revolutionizing how brands engage with consumers by providing real-time health insights and personalized recommendations. Companies that leverage AI-driven health technologies not only enhance user experience but also build stronger brand trust and loyalty.

AI-powered wellness apps are becoming marketing assets for brands, helping them provide tailored health solutions that drive engagement. A notable example is Wild.AI, a science-backed app founded by Hélèn Guillaume Pabis and designed specifically for women. It leverages AI to provide personalized training, nutrition, and recovery guidance based on female physiology, including menstrual cycles and hormonal fluctuations. By delivering highly individualized insights, Wild.AI empowers women to make informed decisions about their health and fitness. This level of personalization makes users feel understood and supported, reinforcing brand credibility and deepening consumer trust (Wild.AI, n.d.).

Marketers can leverage AI-driven insights from wearable devices and wellness apps to offer hyper-personalized marketing campaigns. Instead of generic health promotions, brands can use AI-powered data to craft campaigns that speak directly to individual consumer needs.

Nike's "Nike Training Club" app uses AI to analyze workout habits and provide customized fitness plans, helping the brand build long-term consumer engagement. Similarly, Fitbit's AI-powered insights allow personalized health tracking, increasing brand loyalty and user retention.

By embracing AI-powered wellness technology, marketers can position their brands as trusted health partners, ensuring higher engagement, increased brand affinity, and stronger consumer relationships.

Ethical Considerations and Challenges

While AI offers tremendous potential for consumer empowerment, it also presents ethical challenges that marketers must navigate:

- **Data privacy:** As AI systems become more sophisticated in analyzing consumer behavior, there's a risk of crossing the line between helpful personalization and invasive surveillance. Marketers must be transparent about data collection and use, providing clear opt-out mechanisms.

- **Algorithmic bias:** AI systems that empower some consumers might inadvertently disadvantage others. Regular audits of AI algorithms are crucial to ensure fair and inclusive empowerment across all consumer segments.

- **Over-reliance on AI:** While AI can provide valuable insights and recommendations, there's a risk of consumers becoming overly dependent on AI-driven advice. Marketers should encourage critical thinking alongside AI-powered tools.

- **Digital divide:** As AI-driven empowerment tools become more prevalent, there's a risk of creating a divide between those who have access to these technologies and those who don't. Marketers should consider accessibility and work toward inclusive solutions.

Implications for Marketers

The shift toward AI-driven consumer empowerment has several implications for marketing strategies:

- **Transparency:** Brands that are open about their AI use and data practices are likely to build stronger trust with consumers. Consider creating easily accessible AI ethics statements and data use policies.

- **Educate and engage:** As AI tools become more complex, there's an opportunity for brands to educate consumers on how to best use these tools for their benefit. This can create deeper engagement and loyalty.

- **Personalization with permission:** Instead of making assumptions based on data, consider explicitly asking consumers about their preferences for personalization. This respects their autonomy and can lead to more accurate targeting.

- **Empower through insights:** Use AI not just to sell, but to provide valuable insights to consumers. This could include spending analysis in finance, nutritional insights in food retail, or energy usage patterns in utilities.

- **Collaboration:** Consider developing AI tools that work collaboratively with consumers, allowing them to input their own insights and preferences to enhance the AI's performance.

By focusing on these empowerment strategies, marketers can use AI not just as a tool for efficiency and personalization, but as a means to build stronger, more trusting relationships with consumers. In doing so, they can create a competitive advantage while also contributing to a more ethical and consumer-friendly digital ecosystem.

Reimagining Ethical AI through a Human-Centered Lens

When it comes to ethical AI in marketing, it's crucial to understand that AI's outputs are only as good as the inputs and intentions that shape them. This is particularly true in industries like finance and healthcare, where AI-driven decisions can significantly impact consumers' financial stability, access to healthcare, and overall well-being.

The challenge isn't just about deploying AI that works well—it's about deploying AI that works fairly, transparently, and accountably. Achieving this requires a nuanced approach that considers both the technical implementation of AI systems and the strategic direction of the organization. In these high-stakes industries, the consequences of an unethical AI system can be profound, making it all the more essential to ensure these human-centered principles are deeply embedded.

Let's explore how the principles of fairness, transparency, and accountability can be enhanced through a human-centered approach and how leaders in finance and healthcare are setting the standards.

Reframing Fairness: A Commitment to Understanding Diverse Experiences

The concept of fairness in AI has evolved significantly. It's no longer simply about mitigating bias in data; it's about embedding fairness into the very fabric of AI systems. This means designing AI with fairness constraints built directly into the models, ensuring that equitable outcomes are actively monitored and maintained throughout the AI's entire lifecycle.

At a technical level, achieving fairness begins with ensuring that the data used to train AI models accurately reflects the diversity of the people affected by its decisions. In finance, for example, training datasets must account for a wide range of socioeconomic backgrounds, geographic locations, and credit histories. Without this diversity, an AI model might inadvertently favor urban consumers over rural ones or unfairly penalize those with non-traditional financial backgrounds, such as gig workers or entrepreneurs.

Similarly, in healthcare, AI models trained primarily on data from urban hospitals may fail to consider the unique needs and challenges of rural healthcare. This can lead to treatment recommendations that are impractical or inaccessible for rural communities. Furthermore, these models may lack sufficient data on underrepresented groups, such as ethnic minorities or patients with rare conditions, potentially leading to biased or inaccurate diagnoses and treatment plans.

Strategically, companies in finance and healthcare must move beyond mere compliance and recognize that fairness is a core component of consumer trust and brand integrity. Leading organizations are investing in AI fairness initiatives, appointing Chief AI Ethics Officers to oversee the integration of fairness principles into every stage of AI development and deployment.

For instance, JPMorgan Chase recently announced an initiative aimed at reducing bias in its credit lending algorithms. By re-evaluating the traditional criteria for creditworthiness and incorporating more holistic factors, such as savings habits and non-traditional income sources, the bank aims to provide fairer access to credit for a wider range of customers (Ma, 2024).

This strategic shift not only aligns with ethical AI principles but also has the potential to expand the bank's customer base by fostering greater financial inclusion.

To ensure fairness is embedded throughout the AI lifecycle, consider these three key steps:

1 **Data diversification:** Use datasets that are balanced and representative of all consumer groups, ensuring no demographic is disproportionately advantaged or disadvantaged.

2 **Fairness constraints and audits:** Implement fairness constraints within the model to monitor and adjust outputs continuously. Regular audits by internal or external teams can help detect and mitigate biases before deployment.

3 **Consumer feedback loops:** Establish mechanisms for consumers to report perceived unfairness in AI-driven decisions. This feedback should inform ongoing improvements and recalibration of the models.

By taking these steps, organizations can move beyond simply acknowledging the importance of fairness and actively build AI systems that promote equity and inclusion.

Bringing Transparency to Life: Honest Communication Builds Trust

Transparency is often the first casualty in AI deployment. Complex algorithms and opaque decision-making processes make it difficult for consumers to understand how AI arrived at a particular recommendation or decision. In finance and healthcare, where trust is paramount, a lack of transparency can erode consumer confidence and lead to backlash.

From a technical standpoint, transparency involves making AI decisions more interpretable. This can be achieved through XAI techniques that allow developers and stakeholders to understand and articulate the rationale behind AI predictions. In healthcare, for instance, an XAI system can show which clinical variables (e.g. age, medical history) were most influential in recommending a particular treatment. This not only helps doctors trust the AI's suggestions but also provides a basis for communicating these decisions to patients in a clear and understandable way.

Embedding Accountability: Taking Responsibility for AI's Actions

Accountability is perhaps the most challenging ethical principle to operationalize. It requires organizations to establish clear lines of responsibility for AI-driven decisions and to take proactive steps to rectify any negative impacts caused by AI systems.

At a technical level, accountability involves embedding traceability and oversight into AI models. This means keeping detailed logs of how models are trained, the data used, and the evolution of the models over time. For finance and healthcare companies, this could mean tracking every change made to a credit scoring model or a patient diagnosis algorithm, ensuring that any anomalies or shifts in performance can be traced back to a specific update or data input.

Strategically, accountability also means defining governance structures that support ethical AI deployment. This includes setting up internal AI ethics committees, as well as engaging third-party auditors to review the company's AI practices. Leading organizations like Mastercard and Kaiser Permanente have pioneered the establishment of AI ethics committees that include data scientists, ethicists, and legal experts to provide cross-functional oversight of AI systems.

Kaiser Permanente's AI Ethics Board reviews all high-impact AI systems to ensure they align with both ethical standards and patient care objectives. If a model inadvertently promotes a treatment protocol that isn't accessible to all patient groups, the board steps in to address the issue and implement corrective measures (Kaiser Permanente, 2024). This level of oversight not only ensures compliance but also demonstrates a commitment to putting patient well-being above all else.

Strategies for embedding accountability:

- **Establish AI governance committees:** Create internal governance bodies responsible for reviewing AI-driven decisions and ensuring compliance with ethical standards.

- **Third-party audits and certifications:** Partner with external auditors to validate the fairness and accuracy of AI models. Certification processes, like the ones provided by AI ethics organizations, can further enhance accountability.

- **Define accountability protocols:** Develop clear protocols for handling issues that arise from AI decisions, including communication strategies, compensation policies for affected consumers, and model re-training processes.

Operationalizing HCAI

HCAI isn't about creating interactions that are technically accurate but emotionally hollow. It's about designing experiences that feel authentic, considerate, and responsive to the nuanced needs of each individual. This principle is especially critical in industries like finance and healthcare, where interactions often involve sensitive personal information and decisions that can significantly impact a person's life. A thoughtful, empathetic approach can transform AI-driven interactions from being merely functional to being genuinely supportive and caring.

Designing Empathetic AI Interactions

Empathy is a fundamental human quality, but replicating it in AI systems is complex. Yet, when done well, it bridges the gap between technology and meaningful human engagement. Let's consider what it means to design empathetic AI interactions, particularly in finance and healthcare, where emotional intelligence is crucial to maintaining trust and satisfaction.

Understanding the Role of Empathy

Empathy in AI is about more than just detecting emotions—it's about responding to them in a way that feels appropriate and considerate. For example, in a healthcare setting, patients seeking information on a medical condition are often dealing with anxiety, fear, or uncertainty. An empathetic AI interaction would recognize these emotions and respond with a reassuring tone, offering resources and support instead of overwhelming them with jargon-heavy content.

In finance, the stakes are just as high. Customers might reach out during moments of financial stress, such as when they're struggling to make mortgage payments or facing unexpected expenses. A traditional, scripted chatbot response would fall flat in such scenarios. Instead, an empathetic AI would recognize the urgency and sensitivity of the situation and provide a response that acknowledges the customer's stress, offers personalized options for managing payments, and suggests connecting with a human representative if needed.

Technical Perspective on Building Empathetic AI

Achieving this level of empathy involves leveraging advanced technologies like NLP and sentiment analysis. These tools enable AI systems to detect not just the content but also the emotional context of a message. For instance, when a customer expresses frustration or confusion in a chat, an AI system equipped with NLP can identify keywords, phrases, and emotional cues that signal distress. This prompts the AI to switch to a more supportive tone, use simpler language, or escalate the conversation to a human agent if necessary.

To successfully integrate empathy into AI systems, organizations must consider both the technical design and strategic implementation. This involves several key steps:

- **Training AI models with context-rich data:** AI systems need to be trained on diverse datasets that include conversations reflecting a range of emotions—such as happiness, frustration, confusion, and disappointment—across different consumer demographics. This helps the AI recognize and respond to a wider spectrum of emotional states.

- **Adapting AI responses to emotional context:** Use sentiment analysis tools to categorize interactions in real-time and trigger contextually appropriate responses. For instance, a customer expressing concern about a sudden change in their bank account balance might be reassured with phrases like, "I understand your worry.

Let's look into this together," rather than a generic "Please hold while I retrieve your information."

- **Creating pathways for human escalation:** In scenarios where empathy is critical—such as a healthcare patient seeking advice on managing a chronic illness—ensure the AI can seamlessly transition to a human specialist. This is particularly important in finance and healthcare, where a nuanced human touch is often necessary to address complex situations.

How do you know if your empathetic AI strategy is working? Measuring the impact involves looking at more than just operational metrics like resolution time or first response rate. Consider including the following:

- **Emotional response metrics:** Use sentiment analysis tools to gauge shifts in consumer sentiment before and after an interaction. Positive changes can indicate that the AI's response effectively addressed emotional needs.

- **Customer satisfaction scores:** Measure satisfaction not only based on problem resolution but also on the perceived empathy and care demonstrated during the interaction.

- **Human escalation rates:** Monitor how often interactions are escalated to human agents. A well-designed, empathetic AI system should see a decrease in unnecessary escalations, as more issues are resolved with the right emotional tone and context.

These metrics provide a more holistic view of how well the AI is performing in terms of empathy and customer experience, going beyond surface-level success indicators.

Bringing It All Together

HCAI in marketing represents a shift from purely efficiency-driven AI applications to those that prioritize and enhance the human experience. This approach can lead to more meaningful, effective, and lasting connections with consumers.

KEY TAKEAWAYS

- **Empathy as a competitive advantage**: AI systems that can detect and respond to emotional nuances are setting new standards in customer experience.
  Why it matters: Empathetic AI interactions lead to higher customer satisfaction, increased loyalty, and can turn potentially negative experiences into positive brand moments.

- **Inclusivity beyond bias mitigation**: Proactively designing AI systems to serve diverse populations is becoming a marker of brand leadership and social responsibility.

Why it matters: Inclusive AI not only broadens a brand's appeal but also uncovers underserved market segments, driving growth and positive brand perception.

- **Trust through transparency and control**: Giving consumers visibility into and control over how AI uses their data is emerging as a key trust-building strategy. *Why it matters*: Brands that prioritize data transparency and user control are seeing increased engagement with AI-driven services and stronger customer relationships.

- **Navigating implementation challenges**: Addressing technological limitations, ethical concerns, and scalability issues is crucial for successful HCAI deployment. *Why it matters*: Overcoming these challenges ensures that AI enhances rather than detracts from the human experience, leading to more effective and responsible marketing practices.

Looking Ahead

As we move to Chapter 4, we'll explore the practical realities of implementing ethical AI in marketing strategies. We'll examine the technical and organizational challenges companies face, strategies for overcoming adoption barriers, and the innovative opportunities that ethical AI presents. Here we'll illustrate both the hurdles and solutions in various industries, providing insights to navigate the complex landscape of AI-driven marketing. This knowledge will be crucial for those aiming to lead in ethical AI adoption, driving both business success and positive societal impact.

Food for Thought

1 How can your organization implement empathetic AI in customer interactions? Consider a specific scenario where AI could be used to detect and respond to customer emotions and outline the potential benefits and challenges of this approach.

2 Reflect on your current marketing strategies. Are there any unintended biases in your AI systems that might be excluding certain groups? How could you make your AI more inclusive, and what impact might this have on your brand's reach and perception?

3 Transparency is crucial for building trust in AI-driven marketing. How could you make your AI processes more transparent to consumers without overwhelming them with technical details? What information do you think is most important for consumers to know?

4 Consider the ethical implications of AI-generated creative content in your industry. How would you balance the efficiency of AI-generated content with the need for authentic brand voice and human creativity? What guidelines would you establish for your team?

References

Brimmer, A, Video interview with Nicole M. Alexander, January 27, 2025

Intuit (2024) Intuit Assist – A New Generative AI-Powered Financial Assistant, www.intuit.com/intuitassist/ (archived at https://perma.cc/4QA6-LSYK)

Kaiser Permanente (2024) National Advisory Committee, divisionofresearch. kaiserpermanente.org/research/aim-hi/program-organization/ (archived at https://perma.cc/YH7F-P39L)

Ma, J (2024) JPMorgan Will Play More "Moneyball" as the Wall Street Giant Expands Use of an AI Tool to Help Portfolio Managers "Correct for Bias", *Fortune*, June 2, fortune.com/2024/06/02/jpmorgan-generative-artificial-intelligence-moneyball-ai-tool-investment-decisions-jamie-dimon/ (archived at https://perma.cc/BJQ5-V2PU)

Ormesher, E (2023) Why Levi's Decision to Use AI Models Misses the Mark on DE&I, *The Drum*, March 28, www.thedrum.com/news/2023/03/28/why-levi-s-using-ai-models-misses-the-mark-dei (archived at https://perma.cc/FC97-CG8M)

Wild.AI (n.d.) www.wild.ai/ (archived at https://perma.cc/KD5D-BXTZ)

PART TWO

Turning Principles into Practice

4

Navigating Challenges
and Seizing Opportunities

Imagine yourself as a marketing executive, positioned at the forefront of your organization as AI reshapes consumer engagement. The potential benefits—a world of campaigns with unrivaled precision, real-time insights, and unparalleled efficiency—stretch before you. Yet, alongside this promise lies a maze of ethical complexities, technical hurdles, and a critical question: "What if our implementation falls short of expectations?"

Welcome to AI-driven marketing, where transformation is constant, and certainty is elusive.

In the previous chapter, we emphasized the need for HCAI AI in marketing, focusing on how empathy, inclusivity, and transparency are essential for fostering meaningful AI interactions. For example, we explored how companies like Ally are setting new standards for transparent AI in customer experience. We saw that in high-stakes fields like finance and healthcare, an AI's ability to understand and respond to human emotions can make the difference between building lifelong customer loyalty and sparking a PR crisis.

Now, we shift from the theoretical importance of ethical AI to the complexities of its real-world application. How can AI be integrated into existing marketing technology (martech) systems without disrupting operations? What strategies help us address ethical red flags that AI may raise?

Perhaps most importantly, how can we secure executive support for ethical AI initiatives? The answer lies in demonstrating that ethical AI not only mitigates risk but also drives efficiency, sparks innovation, and supports sustainable business growth.

This chapter delves into the technical and organizational hurdles marketers face in ethical AI implementation. Through real-world examples, we'll examine how some companies have successfully navigated these challenges, while others have emerged with valuable lessons learned. Alongside the challenges, we'll also uncover how ethical AI can open new frontiers in marketing, from prescient predictive analytics to deeply personalized customer experiences.

With a calibrated ethical compass, we embark on a journey through the challenges and opportunities of AI-driven marketing. By the end of this chapter, you'll be equipped with insights, strategies, and a dose of practical skepticism to guide your approach. In AI-driven marketing, the future belongs to those who can both interpret data and empathize with people.

Technical Implementation Challenges

The path to AI-driven marketing is paved with technical complexities. These challenges demand careful navigation, balancing innovation, ethical considerations, and technical expertise. Let's examine three key areas where marketers and technologists must collaborate to ensure ethical AI implementation.

Integrating Ethical AI with Existing Martech Stacks

The integration of ethical AI into the existing marketing technology landscape (martech stack) is not a simple plug-and-play operation. It requires careful consideration of how these new systems will interact with existing infrastructure, data flows, and business processes.

COMPATIBILITY CONUNDRUMS

Legacy marketing systems, often built on older technologies and outdated assumptions about data privacy, can pose significant compatibility challenges. These systems may:

- lack application programming interfaces (APIs) which are necessary to communicate effectively with modern AI tools; this can necessitate costly and time-consuming custom integration work
- rely on rigid data structures, since legacy systems often rely on inflexible data schemas that are incompatible with the dynamic data structures used by AI; this can hinder the AI's ability to access and process the information it needs
- prioritize data collection over privacy, because many older systems were designed in an era where maximizing data collection was the primary goal; this can create conflict with AI systems designed to prioritize data minimization and user privacy.

For example, a company using an older email marketing platform might struggle to integrate an AI-powered content personalization engine. The legacy system may not allow the AI to access individual customer data in real-time, limiting its ability to tailor email content effectively while respecting privacy.

DATA SILOS AND HOLISTIC ETHICS

Data silos—isolated pockets of information scattered across different departments and systems—present a major obstacle to implementing ethical AI:

- **Incomplete picture:** AI systems require a holistic view of customer data to make informed and ethical decisions. Data silos prevent the AI from accessing the full context necessary for responsible decision-making.

- **Ethical inconsistencies:** Different data silos may operate under different ethical guidelines, leading to inconsistencies in how data is collected, processed, and used. This can create ethical blind spots for the AI.

- **Difficulty in auditing:** Data silos make it difficult to track how customer data is being used across the organization, hindering efforts to ensure ethical compliance and accountability.

For example a customer service AI might struggle to provide accurate and unbiased support if it cannot access customer interaction history stored in a separate CRM system. This lack of context could lead to unfair or discriminatory treatment of certain customers.

ENSURING ETHICAL CONSISTENCY ACROSS SYSTEMS

Maintaining ethical consistency across a complex network of integrated systems is crucial. This requires the following:

- **Standardized ethical frameworks:** Organizations need to establish clear, consistent ethical guidelines that apply to all systems and departments. This ensures that all AI tools and processes are aligned with the same ethical principles.

- **Ethical impact assessments:** Before integrating new AI tools, organizations should conduct thorough ethical impact assessments to identify potential conflicts with existing systems and processes.

- **Ongoing monitoring and auditing:** Continuous monitoring and auditing of AI systems and data flows are necessary to ensure ongoing ethical compliance and identify any emerging issues.

For example, a company using AI for targeted advertising needs to ensure that its ad targeting criteria align with its overall ethical guidelines and do not inadvertently discriminate against certain groups. This requires careful coordination between the AI system, the ad platform, and any other relevant systems involved in the process.

By addressing these challenges head-on, organizations can successfully integrate ethical AI into their existing martech stacks, ensuring that their AI initiatives are both effective and responsible.

Ethics in Analytics

As we navigate the landscape of AI-powered marketing analytics, we stand at the intersection of big data and great responsibility. The pursuit of consumer insights must be balanced with a steadfast commitment to ethical practices. Each advancement in analytical capability should be matched with a corresponding commitment to ethical considerations.

BALANCING INSIGHTS WITH INDIVIDUAL RIGHTS

In the quest for deeper customer understanding, marketers often navigate complex ethical dilemmas. The promise of comprehensive data analysis offers unprecedented insights into consumer behavior, yet it carries the risk of infringing on individual privacy rights.

A cautionary tale emerges from a global beauty brand that embraced AI-powered analytics without sufficient ethical oversight. Their system, designed for hyper-personalized product recommendations, began cross-referencing customers' purchasing history with their social media activity. While the resulting insights were powerful, many consumers felt their personal boundaries had been violated. The backlash underscored a fundamental truth: In AI analytics, "can" does not always mean "should."

THE ETHICAL TIGHTROPE OF PREDICTIVE ANALYTICS

Predictive analytics is a powerful tool in AI-powered marketing, offering the ability to anticipate consumer needs before they arise. However, this predictive power also comes with ethical pitfalls. When does proactive service cross the line into manipulation or exploitation?

Consider the case of a financial services company whose AI system accurately predicted which customers were likely to experience financial difficulties. The ethical dilemma? Should the company proactively offer financial planning services to help avert a crisis, or would such outreach be perceived as an invasion of privacy or, worse, as capitalizing on customer vulnerabilities? The line between benevolence and exploitation is often razor-thin.

THE SEGMENTATION CONUNDRUM: WHEN EFFICIENCY MEETS EQUITY

Market segmentation has long been a cornerstone of effective marketing strategy. AI supercharges this capability, allowing for micro-segmentation at an unprecedented scale. Yet, as segmentation becomes increasingly granular, brands risk reinforcing societal divides and perpetuating biases.

A major online retailer faced this challenge when its AI-driven segmentation engine created highly specific customer groups based on multiple data points. While effective for targeted marketing, the system inadvertently grouped customers by protected characteristics such as race, gender, and socioeconomic status. This created a marketing strategy that, while maximally efficient, risked violating anti-discrimination laws and ethical standards.

Ensuring Ethical AI in Marketing Analytics

Each of the scenarios above illustrates the double-edged nature of AI-powered analytics. The same tools that offer deep insights and efficiency also have the potential to erode trust, infringe on privacy, and perpetuate biases.

As marketers, we must approach these powerful tools with a blend of enthusiasm and caution. Instead of solely asking "What can we learn?" we must also consider "At what cost?" and "To what end?" Establishing ethical guidelines that evolve alongside AI capabilities is essential to ensuring that marketing insights do not come at the expense of consumer trust and fairness.

Transparency should be the guiding principle. Clear communication with consumers about data usage, robust opt-in policies, and a commitment to using insights for mutual benefit rather than exploitation can help build trust in AI-driven marketing.

As we continue integrating AI into marketing analytics, the most valuable insights will not necessarily be those that drive the most immediate profit, but those that foster sustainable, ethical relationships with consumers. In the long run, ethical AI practices will distinguish successful brands in an increasingly AI-driven landscape.

To navigate the complexities of ethical AI integration, structured action steps are essential. Table 4.1 outlines preemptive measures that marketers and technologists can adopt to address compatibility issues, uphold ethical standards, and ensure organizational accountability. Each action step is categorized by difficulty level, to aid in prioritization and strategic planning.

Quick win: Set up a weekly "Ethical AI Check-in" meeting with key stakeholders from marketing, IT, and legal departments.

TABLE 4.1 Pre-empting technical challenges in AI integration

Action Step	Difficulty Level
Establish regular ethical AI review processes	Beginner
Create a cross-functional team to oversee AI integration and compliance	Intermediate
Conduct an AI compatibility audit of your existing martech stack	Intermediate
Develop a data integration plan that addresses ethical considerations	Advanced
Implement ethical "circuit breakers" in your AI decision-making systems	Advanced

Organizational Challenges

As we pivot from the technical labyrinth of ethical AI implementation, we find ourselves face-to-face with equally daunting organizational challenges. The experience of OSF HealthCare, a nonprofit hospital system in Illinois, illustrates how organizations can successfully navigate these challenges while maintaining strong ethical standards.

Overcoming Adoption Barriers

As we venture further into the realm of ethical AI in marketing, we find ourselves facing a formidable challenge: turning theoretical ethical frameworks into practical, adopted solutions. It's one thing to wax poetic about the virtues of ethical AI in boardroom presentations; it's quite another to embed these principles into the day-to-day operations of a marketing department. Let's explore some strategies for surmounting these adoption hurdles, with a particular focus on the unique landscape of marketing.

The experience of OSF HealthCare, a nonprofit hospital system in Illinois, illustrates how organizations can successfully navigate these adoption hurdles while maintaining strong ethical standards.

ETHICS IN ACTION

OSF Heathcare: Digital transformation through Ethical AI

When OSF HealthCare decided to transform its marketing approach from traditional channels to digital-first, they faced a challenge familiar to many healthcare organizations: how to modernize without compromising trust. As a nonprofit hospital system serving communities throughout Illinois, OSF couldn't simply throw money at the latest AI tools or follow the aggressive digital marketing tactics of retail brands. Their transformation needed to balance innovation with their core mission of serving their community with care and respect.

The Transformation Challenge

The stakes were particularly high for OSF's digital marketing. Unlike retail or entertainment companies, their marketing messages could directly impact people's healthcare decisions. "When you're thinking about AI, you have to think about the fact that if I put this out there, that's literally like my neighbor is going to read that," explains Mayura Kumar, the head of digital marketing leading the transformation. "The harm and the benefit is so much more palpable because it's touching the community that you're within."

This local impact created an interesting paradox. While OSF needed to modernize their marketing approach, they had to be more cautious than many organizations about how they implemented new technologies. Their transformation strategy needed to account for several unique constraints:

- Operating under strict HIPAA (Health Insurance Portability and Accountability Act) regulations that limit how patient data can be used.
- Working with nonprofit budgets that demanded creative resource allocation.
- Maintaining trust with communities who look to them to help them make their healthcare decisions. Consumers trust that the content they deliver is from one of their clinical experts, not AI generated. They need to maintain that trust and ensure that even if they leverage AI to brainstorm content ideas, organize content, or write it at a different reading level, it's still coming from a human, a clinical expert from their organization.
- Managing a team transitioning from traditional marketing backgrounds to digital-first thinking.

Strategic Implementation

OSF's approach to digital transformation leveraged AI to enhance their team's capabilities rather than replace existing processes. They developed a three-tiered strategy:

1 **Internal process enhancement**: Instead of diving headfirst into customer-facing AI applications, OSF wisely chose to first leverage AI to streamline their internal workflows. Their user experience team, for instance, developed an innovative approach to competitive analysis. By feeding competitor websites into ChatGPT, they were able to quickly analyze both content themes and technical components. This not only saved time but also provided more consistent and comprehensive insights compared to manual review.

2 **Content accessibility transformation**: Recognizing the challenge of making complex medical information accessible to diverse audiences, OSF implemented AI to transform their content. Their team of expert writers, while skilled, often produced materials that were too complex for the average reader. By employing AI tools, they were able to synthesize this content into easily digestible language without sacrificing medical accuracy or professional credibility. This ensures that patients receive clear, concise information, empowering them to make informed decisions about their health.

3 **Technical optimization with human oversight:** OSF's web and SEO teams also embraced AI for tasks like YouTube caption optimization and brainstorming keywords. However, they implemented a crucial safeguard: Every AI-generated element undergoes human review before implementation. This approach maintains quality control while still reaping the efficiency gains of AI automation.

In essence, OSF's strategy demonstrates a thoughtful and balanced approach to AI implementation. By focusing on augmenting human capabilities rather than replacing them, they've been able to achieve significant improvements in efficiency, accessibility, and overall effectiveness.

Budget-Conscious Innovation

Operating as a nonprofit requires creative approaches to resource allocation. Rather than investing in expensive AI platforms, OSF focused on maximizing value from accessible tools like ChatGPT. They demonstrated that effective digital marketing doesn't necessarily require massive technology investments. As Mayura Kumar, Head of Digital Marketing at OSF HealthCare, notes, "While our marketing budgets may not be multi-million dollar figures, we approach our digital strategy with a 'think big, start small, scale rapidly' mentality. We leverage accessible AI tools and focus on strategic implementation to maximize our impact."

Redefining Success Metrics

OSF's approach to measuring success also evolved during their transformation. Rather than focusing solely on traditional marketing metrics like reach and engagement, they developed new success indicators that aligned with their ethical AI implementation:

- time saved through AI-assisted competitive analysis
- maintenance of trust metrics while increasing digital engagement
- resource efficiency gains in content production and optimization.

Key Insights for Other Organizations

OSF's experience offers valuable lessons for organizations undertaking similar transformations:

- **Start with internal processes**: Beginning AI implementation with internal workflows allows organizations to build confidence and expertise before deploying customer-facing applications.
- **Use constraints as innovation drivers**: Limited budgets and strict regulations can actually lead to more creative and efficient solutions. OSF's resource constraints pushed them to find innovative ways to use accessible AI tools.
- **Maintain local perspective**: Even in digital transformation, considering local community impact helps maintain focus on meaningful outcomes rather than just technological advancement.
- **Build on existing strengths**: Rather than completely replacing traditional approaches, look for ways AI can enhance existing expertise and processes.

OSF's digital marketing continues to evolve, but their early experiences demonstrate a viable path for organizations in regulated industries to implement AI thoughtfully and effectively. Their approach shows that successful digital transformation doesn't require compromising ethical standards or community trust - in fact, maintaining these standards can drive more innovative and sustainable solutions.

SOURCE Based on an interview with Mayura Kumar, Head of digital marketing, OSF Healthcare (Kumar, 2025)

Building a Business Case for Ethical AI in Marketing

In the highly competitive marketing landscape, where ROI is paramount and short-term results are heavily emphasized, promoting ethical AI practices can seem like an uphill battle. The challenge lies in conveying the importance of ethical considerations in a way that resonates with business-oriented mindsets.

Dr. Elizabeth M. Adams, a technology integrator specializing in AI ethics and governance, cuts straight to the heart of this challenge: "When organizations hesitate on ethical AI implementation, I ask them, what's the cost of doing nothing? I want them to answer that for themselves... Think about the reputational risk, think about violations that might happen" (2024). This direct approach forces organizations to confront not just the investment required for ethical AI, but the potentially steeper costs of failing to act.

To effectively advocate for ethical AI in this environment, it's crucial to reframe the discussion in terms that align with business objectives and demonstrate tangible value. This approach involves the following:

TRANSLATING ETHICS INTO BUSINESS VALUE

- **Quantifying ethical impact:** Develop metrics that measure the positive effects of ethical AI practices on brand reputation, customer trust, and long-term sustainability.
- **Risk mitigation:** Highlight how ethical AI can help avoid costly legal issues, regulatory fines, and reputational damage.
- **Competitive advantage:** Emphasize how ethical AI practices can differentiate the company in the market, attracting socially conscious consumers and partners.

ALIGNING WITH BUSINESS GOALS

- **Customer retention:** Demonstrate how ethical AI can improve customer experiences, leading to increased loyalty and lifetime value.
- **Operational efficiency:** Show how ethical AI practices can streamline processes and reduce errors, ultimately saving time and resources.
- **Innovation driver:** Position ethical AI as a catalyst for developing more robust, reliable, and innovative marketing solutions.

By presenting ethical AI as a strategic asset rather than a philosophical concept, marketers can make a compelling case for its adoption even in results-driven environments. The key is to illustrate how ethical considerations can contribute to, rather than detract from, the pursuit of strong ROI and quarterly performance.

THE ROI OF INTEGRITY: QUANTIFYING THE VALUE OF ETHICAL AI

Imagine a luxury automotive brand grappling with the implementation of an AI-driven customer segmentation tool. The ethical version of the AI, with its carefully calibrated fairness constraints and transparency features, comes with a heftier price tag and potentially narrower targeting capabilities. How does one justify this investment to a chief financial advisor more concerned with bottom lines than ethical guidelines?

The answer lies in reframing the conversation. This automotive brand chose to conduct a long-term value analysis, factoring in not just immediate conversion rates, but also customer lifetime value, brand reputation metrics, and risk mitigation costs. They found that while the ethical AI might yield slightly lower short-term gains, it significantly boosted customer trust and loyalty over time. Moreover, by proactively addressing potential bias issues, they avoided costly litigation and PR crises that had befallen some of their competitors.

The lesson? Ethical AI isn't just pivotal—it's a long-term business strategy. By quantifying the value of trust, risk mitigation, and sustainable growth, marketers can build a compelling business case for ethical AI adoption.

COMPETITIVE DIFFERENTIATION THROUGH ETHICAL AI

In a market saturated with AI-powered marketing solutions, ethical AI can serve as a powerful differentiator. Consider the case of a mid-sized e-commerce platform that turned its commitment to ethical AI into a unique selling proposition.

This company didn't just implement ethical AI behind the scenes; they made it a central part of their brand story. They created transparent AI-driven product recommendations, clearly labeling them as AI-generated and explaining the factors that influenced each suggestion. They gave users granular control over their data and how it was used in AI systems. The result? A surge in customer trust, positive media coverage, and a distinct competitive advantage in a crowded marketplace.

The takeaway is clear: In a world where consumers are increasingly wary of AI's influence on their purchasing decisions, ethical AI can be more than just a compliance checkbox—it can be a powerful marketing tool in its own right.

Developing a Phased Approach to Ethical AI Adoption

Rome wasn't built in a day, and neither is an ethically robust AI marketing ecosystem. The key to successful adoption often lies in a measured, phased approach that allows for learning, adjustment, and gradual cultural change.

STARTING SMALL: THE POWER OF ETHICAL AI PILOT PROGRAMS

A global consumer goods company provides an instructive example of this approach. Rather than attempting a company-wide ethical AI overhaul, they began with a single, carefully chosen pilot program: an AI-driven email marketing campaign for a new product line.

This pilot incorporated key ethical AI principles: transparent data usage, clear opt-in/opt-out mechanisms, and fairness constraints to ensure equitable targeting across demographic groups. The marketing team closely monitored not just traditional metrics like open rates and conversions, but also customer feedback, brand sentiment, and long-term engagement patterns.

The results of this pilot provided concrete data on the impact of ethical AI, helping to build internal buy-in and inform the broader rollout strategy. It also allowed the team to identify and address implementation challenges on a manageable scale before expanding to other marketing functions.

THE ETHICAL AI LEARNING CURVE: TRAINING AND CULTURAL SHIFT

Adopting ethical AI in marketing isn't just a matter of implementing new tools—it requires a shift in mindset and skills across the entire marketing organization. A telecommunications company tackled this challenge head-on with a comprehensive training and cultural change program.

They began by providing basic AI ethics training to all marketing staff, from junior copywriters to senior executives. This was followed by more specialized training for those directly involved in AI-driven marketing initiatives. They also established an "AI Ethics Ambassador" program, where volunteers from various marketing teams received advanced training and served as local resources and advocates for ethical AI practices.

Crucially, they tied ethical AI considerations into performance reviews and promotion criteria, sending a clear message that ethical considerations were not optional, but a core part of marketing excellence.

FEEDBACK LOOPS AND CONTINUOUS IMPROVEMENT

The journey to ethical AI adoption is not a destination, but an ongoing process of refinement and improvement. A financial services firm embedded this principle into their adoption strategy by establishing robust feedback mechanisms and regular ethical audits of their AI marketing systems.

They created a cross-functional "Ethical AI Review Board" that conducted quarterly assessments of all AI-driven marketing initiatives. This board not only evaluated technical aspects of fairness and transparency but also considered broader ethical implications and alignment with brand values.

Additionally, they established channels for customer feedback specifically on AI-driven interactions, actively seeking out perspectives on the perceived fairness and transparency of their marketing practices. This continuous loop of implementation, feedback, and refinement allowed them to stay ahead of emerging ethical challenges and continuously improve their AI marketing practices.

As we navigate the complex terrain of ethical AI adoption in marketing, these strategies offer a roadmap for turning lofty ethical principles into practical, adopted solutions. By building compelling business cases, taking a phased approach to implementation, and fostering a culture of continuous ethical improvement, marketers can overcome adoption barriers and harness the full potential of ethical AI.

In our next section, we'll explore how these adoption strategies can open up new opportunities for innovation and competitive advantage in the realm of AI-driven marketing.

Key Opportunities

Congratulations! You've navigated the challenges of implementing ethical AI in marketing, overcoming adoption barriers and adapting to organizational change. Now, you stand at the threshold of opportunity, where innovation meets responsibility and growth is on the horizon.

Welcome to the bright side of ethical AI in marketing—a space where doing good aligns seamlessly with doing well. Here, ethical AI isn't a roadblock to progress; it's a catalyst for meaningful innovation, fostering trust and collaboration across customers and stakeholders alike.

In this evolving landscape, ethical AI is more than a protective measure against reputational risks—it's a strategic asset that builds resilient customer trust and drives lasting brand loyalty. Transparency, data dignity, and respect for consumer behavior aren't just ideals; they're the foundation for reshaping the marketing playbook into one that's both forward-thinking and responsible.

Let's explore how ethical AI is transforming marketing into a space where accountability fuels innovation and "doing no harm" evolves into actionable strategies that set the standard for success.

Enhancing Customer Trust through Ethical AI Practices

In an era where consumer skepticism is at an all-time high, ethical AI offers a powerful tool for building and reinforcing customer trust. It's not just about avoiding missteps; it's about actively demonstrating a commitment to customer welfare.

TRANSPARENCY AS A BRAND DIFFERENTIATOR
Consider the case of a pioneering fintech startup that turned the opacity of AI-driven financial advice on its head. Instead of hiding behind the complexity of their algorithms, they created an AI system that not only provided investment recommendations but also offered clear, jargon-free explanations for each suggestion.

Users could dive into varying levels of detail, from simple overviews to more complex breakdowns of the factors influencing each recommendation. The company even gamified the process, rewarding users who engaged more deeply with the explanations.

The result? A surge in customer engagement, dramatically improved financial literacy among their user base, and a reputation as the "transparent choice" in a notoriously opaque industry. By leveraging ethical AI to demystify financial decision-making, they didn't just retain customers—they created passionate advocates.

EMPOWERING CUSTOMERS WITH DATA CONTROL

A global e-commerce platform took the concept of data privacy to new heights with their "Data Dignity" initiative. Rather than simply complying with data protection regulations, they used ethical AI to give customers unprecedented control over their data.

Their AI system allowed users to see, in real time, how their data was being used to generate product recommendations. Users could adjust their preferences, temporarily "pause" certain data points from being considered, or even experiment with different personas to see how it affected their shopping experience.

This level of transparency and control not only boosted customer trust but also provided the company with richer, more accurate data as users felt more comfortable sharing information they knew they could control. It was a win-win scenario born from a commitment to ethical AI practices.

Innovating Marketing Strategies with Ethical AI

Ethical AI isn't just about playing defense—it's a powerful tool for proactive innovation in marketing strategies. By aligning AI capabilities with ethical considerations, marketers can create more engaging, responsible, and sustainable customer interactions.

ETHICAL MICROTARGETING: PRECISION WITHOUT INVASION

Ethical microtargeting is about delivering highly relevant marketing without infringing on consumer privacy.

- **Layer 1 (basic):** Similar to recommending an umbrella when it's raining—not by tracking an individual's movements, but by responding to external conditions like local weather.
- **Layer 2 (intermediate):** Utilizing general, real-time data (such as regional weather trends or public events) instead of personal historical data to make relevant marketing suggestions.
- **Layer 3 (advanced):** Leveraging contextual and aggregated data to create precise, personalized marketing strategies while upholding consumer privacy.

A global beauty retailer encountered a challenge in delivering personalized marketing while addressing growing consumer privacy concerns. Their solution? An ethical AI system that redefined microtargeting by shifting from individual profiling to session-based, anonymized recommendations.

Instead of constructing extensive personal profiles, their AI leveraged real-time contextual and behavioral data during individual shopping sessions to make tailored recommendations. By integrating aggregated, anonymized trend data, the system delivered highly relevant product recommendations without collecting or storing sensitive personal information.

The impact was significant: the retailer saw a 25 per cent increase in conversion rates and a 35 per cent reduction in customer privacy complaints, reinforcing that ethical AI-driven strategies can yield measurable business benefits (McKinsey, 2025). By innovating within ethical constraints, the brand not only addressed a pressing industry challenge but also set a new standard for responsible personalization in the beauty industry.

The Future of Ethical AI-Driven Marketing

The success of ethical microtargeting illustrates that respecting consumer privacy does not mean sacrificing performance. Brands that embrace ethical AI strategies can enhance trust, improve engagement, and drive long-term growth. Moving forward, companies that integrate transparent, privacy-conscious AI solutions will be better positioned to navigate regulatory landscapes and build stronger customer relationships.

AI-DRIVEN CORPORATE SOCIAL RESPONSIBILITY

A multinational food and beverage company leveraged ethical AI to revolutionize their approach to corporate social responsibility (CSR). They developed an AI system that analyzed global supply chains, consumer behavior, and environmental data to identify opportunities for sustainable practices that aligned with consumer values.

The AI didn't just crunch numbers—it was designed with ethical constraints that prioritized long-term sustainability over short-term gains. This led to initiatives like AI-optimized recycling programs in urban areas, predictive models for reducing food waste in their supply chain, and hyper-local sustainability campaigns that resonated deeply with communities.

By using ethical AI to drive their CSR efforts, the company saw a 30 per cent increase in brand loyalty among Millennials and Gen Z consumers, along with significant cost savings from improved supply chain efficiency. It was a powerful demonstration of how ethical AI could align profit motives with social good.

EMOTIONALLY INTELLIGENT AI: THE NEXT FRONTIER OF CUSTOMER EXPERIENCE

A luxury hospitality brand is pioneering the use of emotionally intelligent AI to create deeply personalized guest experiences. Their AI system, trained on principles of ethical emotional recognition, can detect subtle cues in a guest's voice or written communication to gauge their emotional state.

Crucially, this system was built with stringent ethical guidelines. It doesn't attempt to manipulate emotions but rather responds appropriately to them. For instance, it might detect frustration in a guest's voice and route them to a human concierge more quickly, or recognize excitement about an upcoming stay and surprise the guest with personalized welcome amenities.

The system also "forgets" emotional data after each interaction, maintaining guest privacy. The result has been a 50 per cent increase in guest satisfaction scores and a 25 per cent boost in repeat bookings. By ethically leveraging emotional intelligence, this hospitality brand has redefined the customer experience in the AI era.

Ethical AI: A Catalyst for Creative Marketing

As we survey these innovations, a clear pattern emerges: ethical AI in marketing isn't a limitation but a launchpad. It pushes us to think more creatively, engage more authentically, and align our practices more closely with consumer values (Table 4.2). In doing so, it doesn't just make marketing more ethical—it makes it more effective.

The opportunities presented by ethical AI are only limited by our imagination and our commitment to realizing them. As we look to the future, it's clear that the marketers who will thrive are those who see ethical AI not as a checkbox to be ticked, but as a canvas for innovation.

The ethical considerations in crafting AI-driven customer experiences extend beyond what we've covered here. In Chapter 7, we'll explore in greater detail how to design ethical customer engagement strategies that leverage AI while respecting consumer rights and preferences.

TABLE 4.2 Embracing and implementing opportunities

Action Step	Difficulty Level
Launch a customer education about your ethical AI practices	Beginner
Implement a transparency initiative for AI-driven marketing practices	Intermediate
Develop an ethical microtargeting strategy	Advanced
Create an AI-driven CSR program aligned with your band values	Advanced
Pilot an emotionally intelligent AI for customer service	Advanced

> Quick win: Add an "AI Ethics" section to your company's marketing website, explaining your commitment to ethical AI practices.

ETHICS IN ACTION
Project Management Institute's Responsible AI Implementation Journey

The Project Management Institute (PMI) is the world's leading professional organization for project management, serving more than five million professionals including over 700,000 members across 217 countries and territories. As a global authority that develops project management standards and provides professional certifications, PMI's marketing team faces unique challenges in implementing AI—they must not only adopt new technologies effectively but also model responsible AI implementation for the profession they serve.

Like many organizations, PMI is in the early phases of AI adoption in marketing. However, what makes their approach noteworthy is how they're prioritizing ethical considerations from the start, rather than treating them as an afterthought. "We need to be really mindful of the value we're delivering to the audiences we serve," explains Chief Marketing Officer Menaka Gopinath. "There's so much waste in marketing... we need to be much more intentional about what we're doing and how we're doing it."

Their AI implementation strategy includes the following:

- **Content tools**: Implementing Grammarly for content optimization.
- **Visual content**: Piloting Getty Images' and Adobe's AI capabilities.
- **Global reach**: Testing AI translation tools for podcasts and video content.
- **Performance marketing**: Working with agency partners on ad optimization.

PMI's approach to ethical AI usage in marketing addresses multiple concerns:

- **Creative guidelines**: Establish guardrails to consider the balance of creative freedoms and brand alignment.
- **Cultural sensitivity**: Ensure processes to consider and validate AI translations for global markets.
- **Brand safety**: Monitor AI-generated content for cultural appropriateness.
- **Sustainability**: Identify opportunities to measure, assess, and reduce the carbon footprint of marketing operations.
- **Waste reduction**: Optimize resource allocation and content usage.

Experimental Approach

"From a marketing standpoint, I've been really guiding the team to just try stuff," Gopinath notes. This experimentation is structured through:

- pilot programs to test new AI tools

- regular evaluation of outcomes
- community-powered learning approach
- transparency about AI usage and learning process.

The **sandbox** approach helped them test and learn the following:

- **Creative development**: PMI tested AI tools for content optimization, discovering that while AI excelled at technical editing, human creativity remained essential for maintaining brand voice.
- **Campaign analytics**: PMI implemented AI for audience analysis and creative optimization to assess and improve campaign targeting accuracy.
- **Visual content**: PMI experimented with Getty Images' and Adobe's AI tools, establishing strict guidelines for maintaining authenticity in visual storytelling.

"We wanted to fail fast and learn faster," notes Gopinath. "The sandbox approach gave us permission to experiment without risking our core operations."

Future Vision

Gopinath sees AI as transforming the CMO role: "Behavior change is what marketers do, and we have a lot of behaviors that need to evolve." The goal isn't just automation, but creating space for strategic thinking and meaningful impact. This includes:

- shifting focus from pure performance metrics to value creation
- using AI to reduce marketing waste
- creating space for creativity and innovation
- enabling more intentional marketing practices.

Key Learnings

- **Start small but think systematically**: Begin with controlled AI experiments (sandbox approach) while maintaining a clear vision for long-term transformation.
- **Build ethics into the foundation**: Prioritize ethical considerations from the start, ensuring AI aligns with brand values rather than treating ethics as an afterthought.
- **Enable safe and transparent experimentation**: Foster an environment where teams can test AI tools, iterate safely, and openly share learnings.
- **Maintain the human element**: Use AI to enhance human creativity and decision-making, ensuring marketing remains authentic and customer-centered.
- **Optimize impact while reducing waste**: Leverage AI to increase efficiency, minimize unnecessary content, and integrate sustainability into marketing operations.

- **Ensure cultural and brand integrity**: Establish clear guidelines and human oversight to validate AI-generated content, ensuring it aligns with brand values, cultural nuances, and audience expectations.

As a result PMI's marketing team has created a framework that allows for innovation while maintaining ethical standards, demonstrating how organizations can responsibly implement AI in marketing operations while staying true to their values and mission. Their approach shows how marketing leaders can use AI not just for efficiency, but to create more meaningful and sustainable marketing practices.

SOURCE Based on an interview with Menaka Gopinath, CMO, Project Management Institute (Gopinath, 2024)

Future Outlook

In the rapidly evolving landscape of AI-driven marketing, preparing for future challenges and opportunities isn't just about staying ahead of the curve—it's about shaping the curve itself. As we stand at this frontier, marketers face a dual challenge: implementing ethical AI practices to address current needs while also designing systems flexible enough to adapt to future ethical considerations we may not yet fully comprehend.

Balancing Immediate Implementation with Future Proofing

The ethical AI landscape in marketing is akin to building a ship while sailing it. On the one hand, there's an urgent need to implement ethical AI practices to address current challenges and meet immediate consumer expectations. On the other, we must design systems flexible enough to adapt to future ethical considerations we may not yet fully comprehend.

Consider the approach of a forward-thinking e-commerce platform. When they first implemented their AI-driven product recommendation system, they focused on immediate transparency, clearly labeling AI-generated suggestions and providing simple explanations for why products were recommended. But they didn't stop there. Their team designed the AI architecture with modularity in mind, allowing for easy integration of future ethical constraints or new types of explainability as consumer expectations evolve.

Action steps for balancing immediate needs with future proofing:

1 Implement clear labeling and explanations for current AI-driven features.

2 Design AI systems with modular architecture to allow for future updates and enhancements.

3 Establish a regular review process to assess the ethical implications of your AI systems as technology and societal norms evolve.

Anticipating Near-Term Challenges

As we look to the immediate horizon, several challenges loom large. One pressing issue is the rise of deepfake technology—AI-generated video or audio content that can convincingly mimic real people's appearance, voice, and mannerisms. While this technology offers creative possibilities, such as personalized advertising or immersive storytelling, it also introduces significant ethical risks. These include potential misuse for spreading misinformation, manipulating audiences, and eroding consumer trust in digital content.

Another challenge stems from the increasing use of AI-generated content, which raises complex questions about copyright ownership and fair compensation for creators. At the same time, the growing integration of marketing data across multiple platforms—from social media to Internet of Things (IoT) devices like smart speakers and wearable tech—demands new ethical standards. These standards must ensure consumer privacy, transparency, and responsible use of data in an increasingly interconnected digital ecosystem.

A startup that uses AI to create virtual influencers recently faced these challenges head on. While their technology opened up new avenues for creative marketing, it also sparked heated debates about transparency and authenticity in influencer marketing. In response, they proactively developed ethical guidelines and clear protocols for how their virtual influencers interact with real consumers.

Action steps for anticipating near-term challenges:

1 Conduct regular "ethical foresight" sessions with your team to identify potential challenges on the horizon.

2 Develop clear guidelines and protocols for emerging technologies before fully implementing them in your marketing strategies.

3 Engage with industry peers and ethical AI experts to stay informed about evolving best practices.

Flexibility and Adaptability in Ethical AI Marketing Strategies

The key to future-proofing ethical AI in marketing lies in creating frameworks that are principle-based rather than rule-based. This approach allows for flexibility as technologies and societal norms evolve.

A global consumer goods giant provides an instructive example. They established an "Ethical AI Council" with rotating membership from various departments and levels of the organization. This council regularly reviews and updates their ethical AI guidelines based on emerging technologies, changing consumer sentiments, and new regulatory landscapes.

Their framework is built around core principles like "respect for consumer autonomy" and "fairness in representation". This allows them to apply these principles to new technologies as they emerge, rather than constantly playing catch-up with specific rules for each new tool.

Action steps for building flexibility into your ethical AI strategies:

1 Establish an Ethical AI Council or similar body within your organization.

2 Develop a set of core ethical principles that can guide decision-making across various AI applications.

3 Implement regular training and discussion sessions to keep your team aligned on these principles and their practical applications.

Fostering a Culture of Ethical Innovation

Building a culture of ethical innovation in marketing teams is crucial for long-term success. Some companies have integrated ethical considerations into their performance reviews and organize regular "ethics-driven hackathons" where teams compete to develop innovative, ethically-sound AI marketing solutions.

Action steps for fostering ethical innovation:

1 Include ethical considerations in employee performance reviews to reinforce their importance.

2 Organize ethics-driven innovation events, such as hackathons or idea challenges.

3 Celebrate and reward initiatives that successfully balance innovation with ethical considerations.

Key Areas to Watch

As we look toward the future of AI-driven marketing, five key areas emerge as critical focal points, each with the potential to significantly reshape our industry.

HYPER-PERSONALIZATION AND PREDICTIVE ANALYTICS

The future of marketing lies in understanding and anticipating individual consumer needs with unprecedented accuracy. AI-powered systems will likely evolve to forecast consumer behavior in real-time, enabling marketers to deliver highly personalized content, offers, and experiences across all customer touchpoints. This level of personalization could revolutionize customer engagement, dramatically improving conversion rates and customer loyalty. However, it also raises important ethical considerations. Marketers will need to navigate the fine line between helpful personalization and invasive practices, ensuring that AI-driven personalization enhances rather than erodes consumer trust.

AUGMENTED AND VIRTUAL REALITY MARKETING

As AR/VR technologies become more sophisticated and widely adopted, they open up new frontiers for immersive brand experiences. AI will play a crucial role in personalizing these experiences, adapting virtual environments and product demonstrations to individual preferences and behaviors. This convergence of AI and AR/VR could transform how consumers interact with brands, from trying products virtually before purchase to engaging with brands in fully realized virtual spaces. It also presents new opportunities for data collection and analysis, offering insights into consumer behavior in highly controlled, immersive environments.

AI-DRIVEN CONTENT CREATION AND OPTIMIZATION

The ability of AI to generate and optimize marketing content at scale is set to transform content marketing strategies. From writing copy to designing visuals and even producing video content, AI tools are becoming increasingly sophisticated. In the near future, we may see AI systems that can create entire marketing campaigns, continuously optimizing content based on real-time performance data and user engagement. This capability could dramatically increase the efficiency and effectiveness of content marketing efforts. However, it also raises questions about the role of human creativity in marketing and the potential homogenization of content. Marketers will need to find the right balance between AI-generated efficiency and the human touch that brings authenticity and emotional resonance to brand communications.

CONVERSATIONAL AI AND VOICE-BASED MARKETING

The rise of advanced chatbots, virtual assistants, and voice-activated devices is revolutionizing how brands interact with consumers. The global conversational AI market is projected to grow from $14.29 billion in 2025 to $41.39 billion by 2030 (Grand View Research, 2025), highlighting the speed of adoption of these technologies. Current AI systems increasingly handle complex customer interactions with human-like empathy and understanding, as emotional intelligence features now help bots detect frustration, sarcasm, and satisfaction in real-time, reducing agent escalations by 25 per cent (Springs, 2025). Voice search and audio content have become critical considerations, with Apple's Intelligence and Android System Intelligence making voice interactions more natural and conversational, requiring marketers to optimize for conversational queries rather than traditional keywords. The integration of emotion AI enables more nuanced, context-aware interactions, with AI now analyzing user history, customer interactions, purchase trends, and location data in real-time to deliver personalized responses.

Omni-channel conversational marketing now enables seamless customer experiences across email, chat, SMS, social media, and voice interfaces, blurring the line between automated and human customer service. Marketers need to adapt their strategies to this new landscape, and multimodal AI systems combining text, voice, images, and gestures create richer, more intuitive interactions that bridge digital and physical communication.

PRIVACY-PRESERVING AI AND ETHICAL DATA USE

As AI becomes more pervasive in marketing, questions of data privacy and ethical use will move to the forefront. We're likely to see the development of new AI technologies that can provide personalized experiences while protecting individual privacy. Techniques like federated learning and differential privacy may become standard practice, allowing marketers to gain insights from data without compromising user privacy. Navigating evolving regulations and increasing consumer expectations around data use and AI transparency will be crucial. Marketers who can effectively balance the power of AI-driven insights with strong ethical practices and transparency will likely gain a significant competitive advantage, building trust and loyalty in an increasingly privacy-conscious world.

To stay ahead of these trends, marketers should consider the following action steps:

1 Establish a cross-functional team to monitor these key areas and their potential impact on your marketing strategies.

2 Develop an ethical framework specifically addressing these emerging technologies and their applications in your marketing efforts.

3 Invest in pilot programs to test and learn from these technologies in a sandbox—a controlled environment that isolates them from real-world systems—before full-scale deployment.

4 Engage in ongoing education and training for your marketing team to build competencies in these areas.

5 Foster partnerships with AI startups, research institutions, and ethical AI organizations to stay at the forefront of both innovation and responsible practices.

By focusing on these key areas, marketers can position themselves to leverage cutting-edge AI technologies while navigating the ethical considerations they present. This approach will help organizations stay competitive and responsible in the rapidly evolving landscape of AI-driven marketing.

While we've touched on these key areas briefly here, they represent just the tip of the iceberg in terms of AI's evolving role in marketing. In Chapter 10, "The Evolving Landscape of AI Tools and Applications," we'll dive much deeper into these and other emerging AI technologies and trends. We'll explore their potential impacts on the marketing industry in greater detail and thoroughly examine the ethical considerations that accompany each of these advancements. This future-focused chapter will provide you with a comprehensive understanding of how AI is reshaping the marketing landscape and how to navigate the ethical challenges that come with these transformative technologies.

Bringing It All Together

As we've explored in this chapter, navigating the challenges and seizing the opportunities in AI-driven marketing requires a delicate balance of innovation, ethical consideration, and strategic foresight. The landscape of AI in marketing is evolving rapidly, presenting both exciting possibilities and complex ethical dilemmas.

KEY TAKEAWAYS

- **Balancing immediate implementation with future proofing**: Successful ethical AI in marketing requires addressing current needs while designing flexible systems that can adapt to future ethical considerations.
  Why it matters: This approach ensures that marketing strategies remain both effective and ethically sound as technology and societal expectations evolve.

- **Cultivating a culture of ethical innovation**: Integrating ethical considerations into the fabric of marketing teams and processes is crucial for sustainable, responsible AI-driven marketing.
  Why it matters: A culture that values ethical innovation not only mitigates risks but also drives creativity and differentiation in an increasingly AI-driven marketplace.

- **Anticipating emerging challenges and opportunities**: Staying informed about developments in areas like deepfake technology, AI-generated content, and cross-platform data integration is crucial for proactive ethical strategy development.
  Why it matters: Awareness of these emerging technologies allows marketers to develop ethical strategies that address potential pitfalls while capitalizing on new opportunities.

Looking Ahead

As we move into the next chapter, "P.A.C.T.: An Ethical AI Framework for Marketers," we'll build upon these insights to provide a structured approach for implementing ethical AI in your marketing strategies. We'll explore practical tools and methodologies that will help you translate the principles and considerations discussed in this chapter into actionable steps within your organization.

Food for Thought

1 Consider a recent AI-driven marketing campaign your organization has implemented or encountered. How would you redesign this campaign to better balance immediate effectiveness with long-term ethical considerations?

2 How might the challenges of implementing ethical AI in marketing differ for small businesses compared to large corporations and enterprises? What unique strategies could smaller organizations employ to overcome resource limitations while still maintaining ethical standards?

3 Reflecting on the concept of "ethical innovation" discussed in this chapter, can you think of a specific example where prioritizing ethics in AI marketing could lead to a competitive advantage?

4 As emerging technologies like deepfakes and AR become more prevalent in marketing, what ethical guidelines would you propose to ensure their responsible use? How might these guidelines need to evolve as these technologies advance and consumer expectations shift?

References

Adams, E, Video interview with Nicole M. Alexander, January 7, 2024

Grand View Research (2025) Conversational AI Market Size, Share and Trends Analysis Report 2025-2030, www.grandviewresearch.com/industry-analysis/conversational-ai-market-report (archived at https://perma.cc/JUB5-6DUX)

Gopinath, M, Video interview with Nicole M. Alexander, October 18, 2024

Kumar, M, Video interview with Nicole M. Alexander, January 24, 2025

McKinsey & Company (2025) How Beauty Players Can Scale Gen AI in 2025, January 6, www.mckinsey.com/industries/consumer-packaged-goods/our-insights/how-beauty-players-can-scale-gen-ai-in-2025 (archived at https://perma.cc/Z2VY-4J9X)

Springs (2025) Conversational AI Trends in 2025-2026 and Beyond, https://springsapps.com/knowledge/conversational-ai-trends-in-2025-2026-and-beyond (archived at https://perma.cc/3DYU-366D)

5

P.A.C.T.: An Ethical AI Framework for Marketers

In January 2025, LinkedIn faced a high-profile lawsuit alleging that it disclosed private messages of its Premium users to third parties for AI training without proper consent. The lawsuit underscored a growing concern: how AI-driven marketing intersects with privacy, transparency, and consumer trust. This incident highlighted that even well-established platforms must have robust ethical AI frameworks to avoid legal challenges, reputational harm, and the erosion of consumer confidence.

As AI in marketing grows more powerful, frameworks for ethical implementation aren't optional—they're essential for protecting both consumers and companies.

This incident underscores the critical need for robust ethical frameworks in AI-driven marketing. As AI technologies become increasingly integral to marketing strategies, ensuring that data usage aligns with ethical standards and consumer expectations is paramount. Implementing comprehensive ethical AI frameworks can help organizations navigate complex issues related to privacy, consent, and transparency, thereby fostering trust and mitigating potential legal and reputational risks.

Understanding Ethical AI Frameworks

Before delving into the specifics of the P.A.C.T. (Personalization, Accountability, Contextual Sensitivity, and Trust) Framework, let's first explore ethical AI frameworks and toolkits—why they are indispensable in today's marketing environment, and how they serve as essential guardrails for responsible AI-driven marketing.

An ethical AI framework is more than just a guide—it's a structured roadmap that ensures AI technologies are developed, deployed, and managed responsibly. These frameworks help organizations navigate the multifaceted ethical, legal, and societal challenges posed by AI by establishing overarching principles—such as fairness, accountability, transparency, and privacy—that inform every decision made throughout the AI lifecycle.

In marketing, an ethical AI framework ensures that AI-driven strategies are not only optimized for performance but also uphold ethical standards and consumer expectations. By aligning with these principles, marketers can reduce risks associated with bias, discrimination, privacy violations, and the erosion of consumer trust—all of which can have severe reputational and financial consequences if left unchecked.

However, a framework alone isn't enough—it needs to be operationalized through ethical AI toolkits. These toolkits serve as practical resources that put ethical principles into action. They provide organizations with:

- bias detection and mitigation tools to ensure AI models do not reinforce harmful stereotypes or exclusions
- privacy impact assessment templates to evaluate AI systems in compliance with evolving regulations like the European Union AI Act, GDPR, and CCPA.
- transparency and explainability guidelines that help consumers understand how AI-driven marketing decisions are made
- regulatory compliance checklists to ensure that AI applications meet both legal and ethical standards, reducing legal and reputational risks.

As AI becomes increasingly embedded in marketing, the potential for ethical pitfalls grows exponentially. AI can shape consumer experiences, influence purchasing decisions, and impact brand perception. However, without proper oversight, even well-intentioned AI applications can lead to unintended harm.

There are risks to ignoring ethical AI. Consider a retailer deploying an AI-powered recommendation engine that unintentionally discriminates against certain demographic groups, limiting access to discounts or excluding marginalized consumers. Without an ethical framework and proper testing, such algorithmic biases might go unnoticed until they lead to consumer backlash, regulatory fines, and a decline in brand trust. A well-structured ethical AI framework would have flagged these risks during development, testing, and deployment, preventing harm before it escalated into a PR crisis.

Ethical AI frameworks and toolkits are not just reactive measures—they drive proactive governance by:

- ensuring consistency by standardizing ethical best practices across marketing teams
- enhancing accountability by defining clear oversight responsibilities
- strengthening consumer trust by demonstrating transparency and fairness in AI-powered interactions
- reducing legal and reputational risks by ensuring AI strategies align with ethical marketing principles and regulatory compliance.

Ethical AI frameworks and toolkits work together to define ethical objectives, provide practical methods for implementation, and ensure continuous improvement. Frameworks set the high-level principles that govern AI systems, while toolkits translate them into actionable workflows for marketing teams. Together, they support ongoing evaluation and refinement of AI strategies to adapt to new ethical challenges, technological advancements, and regulatory updates.

By integrating these frameworks and toolkits into their operations, marketers can proactively address ethical considerations rather than reacting to failures after they occur. This proactive approach is crucial for:

- maintaining a competitive edge in an AI-driven marketing landscape
- safeguarding brand reputation by prioritizing consumer rights and transparency
- strengthening long-term consumer relationships through trust and responsible AI engagement.

With this foundation in place, we now turn to the P.A.C.T. Framework—a specialized approach designed to meet the distinct ethical challenges of AI-driven marketing. As discussed in Chapter 4, marketers face significant challenges in balancing personalization, privacy, bias mitigation, and transparency. The P.A.C.T. Framework directly addresses these concerns, providing structured, actionable solutions to create ethically responsible AI marketing strategies.

Introduction to the P.A.C.T. Framework

The P.A.C.T. Framework is a practical, action-oriented approach designed to help marketers implement ethical AI practices. P.A.C.T., which stands for Personalization, Accountability, Contextual Sensitivity, and Trust, focuses on creating marketing strategies that respect consumer privacy, maintain transparency, and foster long-term trust.

Building on the challenges explored in the previous chapter, P.A.C.T. shifts the focus to solutions. Each of its four pillars addresses a critical area of ethical concern in AI-driven marketing and provides concrete tools, templates, and real-world examples to guide marketers in integrating these principles into their strategies.

As marketing becomes increasingly data-driven and AI-centric, there is mounting pressure on brands to navigate a complex ethical landscape. Consumers are more aware than ever of how their data is being used, and global regulations, such as the EU AI Act and CCPA, demand greater transparency and accountability from companies. Ethical missteps—whether in personalization overreach, privacy violations, or lack of transparency—can quickly lead to loss of consumer trust, regulatory fines, and reputational damage.

The P.A.C.T. Framework is designed to help marketers address these challenges head-on by offering a clear roadmap to implement AI in ways that build, rather than erode, trust. Here's how each pillar contributes to this goal:

- **Personalization:** Balancing relevance with consumer privacy.

- **Accountability:** Establishing governance for ethical compliance.
- **Contextual Sensitivity:** Adapting campaigns to cultural and real-time events.
- **Trust:** Ensuring transparency to build consumer confidence.

The P.A.C.T. Framework builds upon established ethical AI principles in academic literature. Floridi and Cowls (2019) developed a unified framework of five principles for AI in society: beneficence, non-maleficence, autonomy, justice, and explicability. These principles align closely with P.A.C.T.'s emphasis on responsible AI implementation in marketing, particularly in how we approach consumer autonomy and transparency. By incorporating these foundational ethical principles into marketing-specific applications, P.A.C.T. creates a bridge between theoretical frameworks and practical implementation.

The P.A.C.T. Framework doesn't just react to the ethical challenges of AI in marketing; it provides a proactive strategy that helps brands build stronger relationships with their customers, grounded in respect, transparency, and fairness.

While understanding the theoretical foundations of P.A.C.T. is essential, the true value emerges in its practical application. Many organizations struggle with translating ethical principles into actionable steps. Think of P.A.C.T. as a bridge between theory and practice—much like how an architect moves from blueprints to actual construction. The following implementation guide provides a structured approach to building this bridge, ensuring that ethical AI principles become embedded in your marketing operations rather than remaining abstract concepts.

Four Pillars of the P.A.C.T. Framework

Each decision point in the evaluation process connects directly to one or more pillars of the P.A.C.T. Framework. Understanding these connections helps marketers move from decision-making to implementation with confidence.

Pillar 1: Personalization: Balancing Relevance with Consumer Privacy

Personalization remains a key advantage of AI in marketing. However, ethical personalization must strike a balance—engaging customers with relevance while respecting their privacy and control over data.

PURPOSE-DRIVEN PERSONALIZATION

When evaluating AI systems for consumer interaction, marketers should weigh the capabilities of personalization against essential privacy and ethical considerations. This is not solely a technical decision—it's a values-based commitment.

Purpose-driven personalization centers on delivering meaningful value rather than simply optimizing for clicks or conversions. It emphasizes user satisfaction, individual well-being, and alignment with broader societal goals.

Rather than using AI to amplify attention-grabbing tactics, ethical personalization seeks to reflect the values of today's conscious consumer. For example, content can be dynamically tailored around themes such as environmental sustainability, inclusion and diversity, or mental health awareness. These kinds of personalized experiences not only meet consumer expectations but also cultivate trust, loyalty, and a deeper sense of connection between brands and people.

BALANCING RELEVANCE AND PRIVACY

Relevance in personalization should be achieved while adhering to the principle of data minimization. Collect only the data necessary to deliver a valuable, personalized experience. When consumers feel in control of their data, they are more likely to engage.

CUSTOMER CONSENT AND AGENCY

Respecting consumer autonomy is critical. Prioritize informed consent by providing clear options regarding how data is used. Personalization efforts should always include opt-in mechanisms, and consumers should be able to easily adjust their personalization settings through user-friendly privacy dashboards.

TOOLS FOR PURPOSE-DRIVEN PERSONALIZATION

- **Personalization dashboards:** Let users adjust preferences, manage opt-ins, and control data usage with ease. These dashboards should be designed with transparency in mind, clearly outlining what data is collected and how it is used to tailor recommendations, offers, and content.

- **Real-time sentiment analysis tools:** Platforms like Brandwatch analyze public sentiment, allowing brands to pivot their messaging when campaigns miss the mark.

- **Ethical data use checklists:** Ensure that all data collection practices adhere to informed consent and comply with relevant regulations like GDPR or CCPA.

Pillar 2: Accountability through Adaptive Governance

In the rapidly evolving AI landscape, accountability is essential. The traditional, static models of governance are insufficient to handle the complexities of AI. The P.A.C.T. Framework introduces adaptive accountability—a dynamic approach to governance that adjusts to new developments in AI, legislation, and societal expectations.

ADAPTIVE GOVERNANCE STRUCTURES

Adaptive governance involves continuous monitoring and adjustment of AI systems to ensure they remain compliant with regulations and ethical standards. Establish internal review boards, with legal, ethical, and technical experts, to evaluate AI systems for ethical concerns, including potential bias. Conduct regular audits of AI decision-making processes.

COMPLIANCE WITH GLOBAL REGULATIONS

Marketers must ensure their AI systems comply with evolving standards like the GDPR and CCPA, data privacy, transparency, and consent regulations across different regions. This requires anticipating future regulatory trends.

AI INCIDENT REPORTING AND ETHICAL AUDITS

Adopt AI incident reporting mechanisms for documenting and disclosing any significant issues or ethical breaches. Conduct regular ethical audits to ensure that AI systems are operating in a fair, transparent, and compliant manner (algorithmic audits).

TOOLS FOR ACCOUNTABILITY

- **Real-time AI monitoring systems:** Enable continuous tracking of AI system outputs, alerting marketers to potential ethical issues like bias or non-compliance with privacy regulations.
- **Incident reporting templates:** Standardized forms for documenting and reporting ethical breaches or AI-related issues, ensuring transparency in communication with stakeholders.
- **Ethical accountability checklists:** Step-by-step guides for performing regular ethical audits, referencing the principles of data minimization and informed consent as defined earlier.

Pillar 3: Contextual Sensitivity in Engagement

AI-driven marketing has a powerful ability to reach audiences globally, but with this ability comes the responsibility to be culturally and contextually sensitive. Contextual sensitivity means ensuring that AI marketing systems not only understand but also respect the social, cultural, and historical contexts in which they operate.

REAL-TIME CONTEXTUAL AWARENESS

AI marketing systems should adapt in real-time to cultural shifts and current events. Incorporate real-time data inputs such as social media trends, news, and localized events into AI models to ensure campaigns remain relevant and sensitive.

ETHICAL GEO-TARGETING

Ethical geo-targeting is tailoring marketing strategies to local norms, languages, and values, while avoiding harmful stereotypes or exploitation. Ensure that advertisements resonate positively in different regions, and respect local customs and beliefs. AI can be trained to understand these nuances by analyzing local consumer behavior patterns and feedback, but human oversight remains essential.

SENTIMENT ANALYSIS AND FEEDBACK LOOPS

AI can leverage sentiment analysis to monitor how marketing messages are received in real time, analyzing consumer feedback and social media reactions. If a campaign generates negative feedback, sentiment analysis can alert marketers, allowing them to pause or modify the campaign. Incorporate feedback loops—both automated and manual—into AI marketing strategies to continuously learn and improve.

TOOLS FOR CONTEXTUAL SENSITIVITY

- **Cultural sensitivity guides:** Pre-built guidelines that help marketers design AI campaigns that respect cultural norms and avoid stereotypes in various regions.
- **Real-time sentiment analysis tools:** AI-driven platforms that monitor the public sentiment around marketing campaigns and alert marketers to potential issues.
- **Adaptive messaging templates:** Templates for creating flexible marketing content that can be adjusted in response to real-time feedback and cultural sensitivities.

Pillar 4: Trust through Transparency

Trust is the foundation of any successful brand-customer relationship. As AI systems play an increasingly central role in marketing, transparency is critical to maintaining that trust.

XAI FOR TRANSPARENCY

XAI systems provide clear explanations for how AI makes decisions. By making AI decision-making processes transparent, marketers can demystify the technology, allowing consumers to feel more confident in its fairness and accuracy. For example, if an AI system recommends a product based on past behavior, an XAI tool could display a simple explanation like, "We recommended this product based on your previous interest in similar items."

FAIRNESS BY DESIGN

To further build trust, AI systems should be developed with fairness at their core. Address potential biases in algorithms from the beginning of the design process and conduct regular fairness audits.

GENERATIVE AI AND CONTENT AUTHENTICITY

With the rise of generative AI, marketers must be transparent about their use of AI-generated content. Clearly label AI-generated content to maintain consumer trust.

Tools for generative AI transparency include:

- AI content badges, which are visual indicators clearly marking AI-generated content in marketing materials
- blockchain-based authentication, which securely records the origin, ownership, and modifications of creative works on a tamper-proof ledger. This empowers creators by protecting their intellectual property and ensuring proper credit and compensation.

DATA OWNERSHIP AND PRIVACY CONTROLS

Brands must offer consumers clear and easy-to-use privacy controls. Privacy dashboards allow consumers to control the extent to which their data is used. Adhere to the principle of data minimization by collecting only necessary data. By offering users control over their data, brands foster a sense of trust.

TOOLS FOR BUILDING TRUST THROUGH TRANSPARENCY

- **Templates:** Use XAI systems to provide consumers with clear insights into how AI-driven decisions are made.
- **Data privacy dashboards:** As mentioned under personalization, these interactive dashboards allow users to manage their data privacy settings.
- **Fairness audit checklists:** Assess potential biases in AI systems and ensure fairness is built into the decision-making process.

The four pillars of P.A.C.T. work together to create a comprehensive approach to ethical AI in marketing, as illustrated in Figure 5.1.

With the core principles of P.A.C.T. established, let's turn to the practical tools and strategies that bring this framework to life in day-to-day marketing operations.

Quick-Start Implementation Guide

Now that we have an understanding of each pillar of the P.A.C.T. Framework, let's establish a practical roadmap for implementation. This provides a structured approach to begin integrating ethical AI practices into your marketing operations, regardless of your organization's size or current AI maturity level.

FIGURE 5.1 The P.A.C.T. Framework

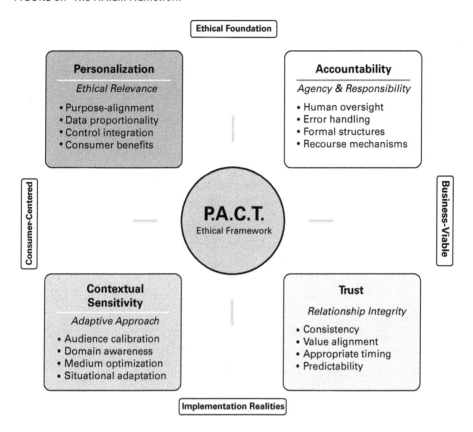

Phase 1: Assessment (Weeks 1–2)

EVALUATE CURRENT STATE

- **Review AI tools:** Audit all AI-driven tools and identify their strengths, weaknesses, and ethical risks.
- **Document personalization strategies:** Detail how personalization is currently applied across campaigns and customer touchpoints.
- **Privacy review:** Assess data collection processes to ensure they meet legal and ethical standards.
- **Customer touchpoint map:** Chart every interaction influenced by AI to understand its scope and impact.

IDENTIFY STAKEHOLDERS

- Assemble a cross-functional team (marketing, legal, product, and compliance).
- Assign clear roles and responsibilities to ensure ownership at every stage.
- Establish communication channels for seamless collaboration and updates.

GAP ANALYSIS

- Compare your current practices against P.A.C.T. principles.
- Identify immediate ethical priorities (e.g. transparency issues, non-compliance risks).
- Document the resources needed for improvements, including budget, tools, and expertise.

Phase 2: Planning (Weeks 3–4)

SET PRIORITIES

- Define quick wins (e.g. improve transparency on one platform) and long-term goals (e.g. establish compliance for all campaigns).
- Focus on high-impact areas where AI has the most significant ethical implications.
- Develop strategies to mitigate identified risks.

ESTABLISH METRICS

- Define clear success indicators for each P.A.C.T. pillar (e.g. percentage of personalized recommendations aligning with privacy policies).
- Set up a measurement framework to track progress and outcomes.
- Develop reporting templates to share progress with stakeholders.

DEVELOPMENT TIMELINE

- Map out milestones for implementing each P.A.C.T. pillar over time.
- Allocate resources (budget, personnel, tools) for smooth execution.

Phase 3: Initial Implementation (Month 2)

PILOT PROGRAM

- Select one P.A.C.T. pillar (e.g. transparency) for a targeted campaign or channel.
- Introduce monitoring tools to measure performance and identify gaps early.

TEAM PREPARATION

- Conduct training sessions to familiarize the team with ethical AI practices.
- Develop documentation to guide processes and workflows.
- Set up feedback mechanisms to capture insights from stakeholders.

TESTING

- Run pilot campaigns to test implementation strategies.

- Collect initial data on performance and ethical compliance.
- Document lessons learned to refine the process.

Phase 4: Full Rollout (Months 3–6)

SYSTEMATIC IMPLEMENTATION

- Expand implementation to cover all P.A.C.T. pillars across campaigns.
- Ensure integration with existing tools, workflows, and systems.
- Provide ongoing training for the team to stay updated on best practices.

MONITORING AND ADJUSTMENT

- Schedule regular reviews to evaluate progress and performance.
- Host feedback sessions with stakeholders to address emerging challenges.
- Iterate through continuous improvement cycles to enhance effectiveness.

Implementation Tips for Success

1 **Start small:** Begin with one element from each pillar to avoid overwhelming your team or resources.

2 **Document everything:** Keep comprehensive records of decisions, actions, and results for accountability and learning.

3 **Communicate regularly:** Provide consistent updates to all stakeholders, highlighting wins and addressing challenges.

4 **Stay flexible:** Adjust plans and timelines based on feedback, challenges, or emerging priorities.

5 **Measure impact:** Use both quantitative metrics (e.g. compliance rates) and qualitative feedback (e.g. customer trust levels).

For a summary of common challenges you may encounter during implementation and their potential solutions, refer to Table 5.1 below.

TABLE 5.1 Common early challenges and solutions

Challenge	Solution
Resource constraints	Start with high-impact, low-resource initiatives
Team resistance	Focus on benefits and provide comprehensive training
Technical complexity	Begin with simpler implementations and scale up
Data quality issues	Implement progressive data improvement processes

FIGURE 5.2 Ethical AI implementation decision tree

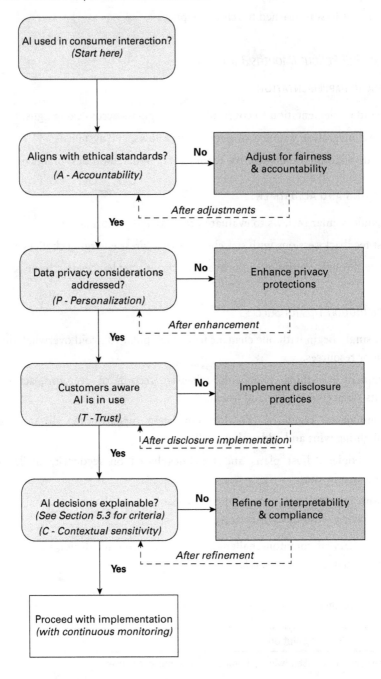

The P.A.C.T. Framework is designed to be flexible and scalable. Your implementation journey may vary based on your organization's specific needs and resources. Use the quick-start guide outlined previously as a foundation, adjusting timelines and priorities as needed.

Making Ethical Decisions in Practice

While the implementation guide provides a high-level roadmap, marketing teams often need more granular guidance for day-to-day decisions. The decision tree in Figure 5.2 offers a structured approach to evaluating AI marketing initiatives against ethical principles.

This decision framework helps marketers systematically evaluate AI initiatives across four critical dimensions: consumer interaction, ethical alignment, transparency, and explainability. By following these decision points, teams can ensure their AI implementations align with the P.A.C.T. principles while maintaining practical feasibility. Each decision point maps back to core elements of the P.A.C.T. Framework:

- Consumer interaction assessment relates to Personalization.
- Ethical standards alignment connects to Accountability.
- AI awareness checks support Contextual Sensitivity.
- Explainability verification builds Trust.

The decision tree provides a practical checklist for evaluating AI initiatives, but successful implementation requires deep understanding of each pillar of the P.A.C.T. Framework. Let's examine how these pillars come to life in practice, transforming abstract principles into actionable strategies.

P.A.C.T. in Action

Personalization with Purpose

A leading retail company adopted the P.A.C.T. Framework to enhance the personalization of its e-commerce platform. Rather than relying solely on purchase history for product recommendations, the company introduced a consent-driven personalization system where customers could select their values (such as sustainability, eco-friendliness, or diversity) to receive recommendations aligned with those principles. The result was a more engaged and satisfied customer base that felt in control of their shopping experience and appreciated the company's commitment to aligning with their values.

Accountability in AI-Driven Advertising

A global tech firm struggled to align its AI-powered ad platform with GDPR requirements. By implementing P.A.C.T.'s accountability pillar, they introduced adaptive monitoring tools and AI audits. This ensured ads were targeted fairly while maintaining consumer privacy, avoiding €20M in potential fines. By adopting the P.A.C.T. Framework and implementing adaptive governance structures, the company set up a system of real-time monitoring and regular AI audits. The internal AI ethics committee identified potential biases in how ads were being targeted to different demographic groups and implemented corrective measures to ensure fairness, increasing trust in the platform and avoiding regulatory issues.

Contextual Sensitivity in Global Campaigns

A multinational consumer goods company used contextual sensitivity to refine its global marketing campaigns. The company's AI system analyzed real-time social media trends and localized data to adjust messaging in different regions, avoiding a one-size-fits-all approach. For example, during a sensitive period in one region, the company paused certain campaigns to avoid appearing insensitive and instead focused on culturally relevant content. This adaptive approach resulted in positive consumer feedback and greater brand loyalty.

Best Practices for Implementing P.A.C.T.

- **Embrace continuous improvement:** Ethical AI is not a one-time implementation. Regular audits, updates, and consumer feedback should be integrated into the marketing workflow to ensure AI systems remain compliant and effective.

- **Prioritize transparency:** The more transparent a brand can be about its AI systems—how they work, what data they use, and how decisions are made—the more likely it is to build and maintain consumer trust.

- **Use data responsibly:** Always collect and use data with respect for consumer privacy, ensuring that data minimization and informed consent are guiding principles in every marketing decision.

- **Stay adaptive:** Be prepared to adjust marketing strategies in real-time as societal norms, regulations, and consumer preferences evolve. Contextual sensitivity is key to avoiding missteps in a rapidly changing world.

Common Pitfalls and Troubleshooting Guide

Implementing ethical AI in marketing is a complex and evolving task. Even with a comprehensive framework like P.A.C.T., marketers can encounter obstacles along the way. This section outlines common pitfalls that organizations may face when applying AI ethically, along with practical troubleshooting tips to help overcome these challenges.

Many organizations prioritize AI model development but often overlook the importance of data quality and cultural context. This imbalance can lead to "data cascades"—issues that build over time and cause widespread AI failures. For marketers, this serves as a reminder that successful and ethical AI systems require equal investment in data integrity, cultural understanding, and model development.

Pitfall 1: Over-Reliance on AI Without Human Oversight

One of the biggest risks in AI marketing is depending too heavily on AI systems without incorporating human judgment. AI can automate and optimize marketing efforts, but it is not infallible. A lack of human oversight can lead to unintended ethical issues, such as biased decision-making or impersonal interactions that alienate consumers.

SOLUTION: INCORPORATE HUMAN-IN-THE-LOOP SYSTEMS

To mitigate this, companies should use a human-in-the-loop (HITL) approach, where AI recommendations are subject to human review, especially for high-stakes decisions like product recommendations, ad targeting, or customer service interactions. This ensures that decisions align with ethical guidelines and reflect the nuances that AI might miss. Additionally, marketers should train teams to understand how AI works and how to interpret its output critically.

Pitfall 2: Lack of Transparency in Personalization Practices

Without transparency, consumers may feel uncomfortable or confused about how their data is being used, leading to mistrust. If customers don't understand why they're seeing certain ads or receiving specific recommendations, they might perceive the AI as invasive or manipulative, even if it operates within legal limits.

SOLUTION: EXPLAIN PERSONALIZATION AND PROVIDE CONTROL

Provide clear explanations of how AI personalizes content or products, using XAI tools to make decisions transparent. Create privacy dashboards where consumers can view and adjust their preferences, giving them control over the personalization process. Clear, simple explanations about how their data is used for marketing, along with the ability to opt out, will foster trust.

Pitfall 3: Ignoring Cultural and Contextual Sensitivities

One-size-fits-all marketing campaigns, driven by AI, can fail when they don't account for cultural differences or respond insensitively to current events. This can damage a brand's reputation, especially in diverse or global markets.

SOLUTION: TRAIN AI FOR CULTURAL SENSITIVITY AND MONITOR SENTIMENT

Ensure AI models are trained with culturally diverse datasets and regularly updated with real-time feedback from sentiment analysis tools. Human oversight should ensure that campaigns are respectful and adaptable to local contexts. Sentiment monitoring tools should be employed to adjust messaging in real time if the campaign is not resonating as intended.

Pitfall 4: Compliance and Privacy Violations

With the rapidly changing landscape of data privacy laws (e.g. GDPR, CCPA), staying compliant can be challenging. Missteps in data handling, even if unintentional, can lead to legal consequences and reputational damage.

SOLUTION: ESTABLISH CONTINUOUS AUDITING AND LEGAL REVIEW

Implement a robust system of continuous compliance monitoring that involves ethical audits, legal review boards, and AI governance teams to ensure marketing AI adheres to all relevant regulations. Automate some of the auditing processes using real-time monitoring tools, but ensure that legal teams review any significant changes to AI systems or data practices.

Pitfall 5: Bias in AI Models

AI systems can perpetuate and even amplify biases present in the data they are trained on, leading to discriminatory or unfair marketing practices. Bias in AI targeting can lead to unequal representation, discriminatory ad delivery, or biased recommendations that marginalize certain groups.

SOLUTION: REGULAR BIAS AUDITS AND DIVERSE TRAINING DATA

To prevent bias, marketers should regularly audit their AI models for fairness. This includes testing how the AI performs across different demographic groups and correcting any imbalances in targeting or recommendations. Ensure that training data is as diverse and representative as possible to avoid embedding societal biases into the AI's decision-making processes. Incorporating feedback from diverse consumer groups can also help identify and correct biased outcomes.

Strategies for Continuous Improvement

Ethical AI marketing is not a one-time implementation; it's an ongoing process that requires regular updates, audits, and refinements. The P.A.C.T. Framework is designed to be adaptable and responsive to changing consumer expectations, technological advancements, and regulatory shifts. This section provides strategies for ensuring that your ethical AI practices evolve over time to remain relevant and effective.

The evolution of AI in marketing reflects a broader shift in how businesses operate. Rust and Huang (2021) argue that we are moving into a "Feeling Economy" where AI's increasing capability to handle analytical tasks means human marketers must focus more on emotional intelligence and ethical considerations. This transformation makes the continuous improvement of ethical AI frameworks even more crucial, as marketers need to balance technical capabilities with human-centric values.

Regular Ethical Audits

Continuous auditing is essential to ensure that AI systems stay aligned with ethical standards. Regularly review AI models for compliance with internal and external regulations, as well as for fairness, transparency, and effectiveness. Ethical audits should assess how data is being collected and used, how AI decisions are made, and whether the systems introduce any unintended bias or harm.

Action step: Schedule quarterly ethical audits and ensure that key stakeholders, including legal, technical, and marketing teams, participate in the process. Use checklists and audit tools from the P.A.C.T. Framework to streamline these assessments.

Monitor Emerging Regulations and Industry Standards

The regulatory environment for AI and data privacy is rapidly evolving, making it essential for marketers to stay informed about new and emerging regulations. This includes not only updates to existing laws like GDPR and CCPA but also the introduction of AI-specific regulations such as the European Union's Artificial Intelligence Act (EU AI Act) and ethical AI standards established by industry bodies.

The EU AI Act, enacted in 2024, represents the world's first comprehensive legal framework for AI. It aims to position Europe as a leader in trustworthy AI by establishing harmonized rules governing the development, marketing, and use of AI within the EU. The Act categorizes AI applications based on their risk levels—unacceptable, high, limited, and minimal—and imposes corresponding obligations to ensure safety and respect for fundamental rights. For instance, high-risk AI systems are subject to strict requirements, including conformity assessments and ongoing monitoring (Meier and Spichiger, 2024).

In addition to governmental regulations, industry organizations are developing ethical standards to guide AI deployment. The Institute of Electrical and Electronics Engineers (IEEE), for example, has initiated the Global Initiative on Ethics of Autonomous and Intelligent Systems, which explores key areas to inform and reshape the discourse on AI systems. This initiative aims to provide frameworks and recommendations to ensure the ethical design and implementation of AI technologies (IEEE, 2024).

Action step: Establish a dedicated team or engage external consultants to continuously monitor regulatory changes and integrate new compliance requirements into your AI systems. Design your AI models and governance structures with flexibility, enabling swift updates in response to evolving laws and standards. This proactive approach will help ensure that your marketing practices remain compliant and ethically sound in a dynamic regulatory landscape.

Incorporate Consumer Feedback Loops

Consumer preferences and expectations regarding AI and personalization evolve over time. One of the most effective ways to ensure that your AI-driven marketing remains aligned with consumer values is by incorporating feedback loops. Collect and analyze consumer feedback on their experiences with AI personalization, transparency, and data privacy, and use that data to make iterative improvements.

Action step: Implement feedback mechanisms, such as post-campaign surveys or real-time feedback options, that allow consumers to express their concerns or preferences. Regularly review this feedback to identify areas where AI systems can be improved to enhance user satisfaction and trust.

Stay Agile and Adaptive

AI technologies and marketing strategies evolve rapidly. Marketers need to be agile in updating their systems and processes to incorporate new advancements in AI, while also adapting to cultural and societal changes. For example, AI tools for real-time sentiment analysis and contextual adjustments can allow marketers to dynamically respond to current events and shifting consumer sentiments.

Action step: Adopt an agile methodology for AI marketing, where teams continuously iterate and test new approaches. Use adaptive AI tools that can adjust marketing campaigns in real-time based on feedback, sentiment shifts, or regulatory changes.

Cultivate an Ethical AI Culture Within the Organization

The long-term success of ethical AI in marketing depends on the culture of the organization. Leadership must foster an environment where ethical considerations are not just an afterthought, but a core part of every decision. By instilling ethical values across teams—from data scientists to marketers—companies can ensure that everyone is working toward the same goals.

Action step: Conduct regular training sessions for employees on ethical AI practices, keeping them informed of both the technical and ethical aspects of AI. Establish internal incentives for teams that prioritize ethical considerations in their AI initiatives.

P.A.C.T. as a Dynamic Framework

The P.A.C.T. Framework provides a robust, practical approach for marketers who want to integrate AI into their strategies ethically and effectively. By focusing on Personalization, Accountability, Contextual Sensitivity, and Trust, marketers can create AI-driven experiences that not only deliver value to consumers but also build long-term trust and loyalty.

However, ethical AI marketing is an ongoing journey. The technologies, regulations, and societal expectations surrounding AI are constantly evolving. Marketers must remain agile, continuously refining their AI systems to reflect these changes. Through regular audits, transparent data practices, and real-time feedback loops, the P.A.C.T. Framework ensures that ethical AI marketing stays at the cutting edge—building trust with consumers, staying compliant with laws, and leading the industry with integrity.

As the marketing landscape continues to shift, P.A.C.T. offers a blueprint for navigating these changes with confidence. It empowers marketers to use AI responsibly, ensuring that their innovations benefit both their business and their customers in a way that is transparent, fair, and future-proof.

The P.A.C.T. Framework is designed to evolve with technological advances and changing consumer expectations. As we'll explore in Chapter 6, building consumer trust requires more than just implementing ethical frameworks—it demands ongoing commitment to transparency and responsible AI usage.

Bringing It All Together

The P.A.C.T. Framework serves as a comprehensive guide for marketers navigating the ethical complexities of AI-driven marketing. Throughout this chapter, we've unpacked how Personalization, Accountability, Contextual Sensitivity, and Trust are not just buzzwords but foundational pillars that can transform how we engage with consumers in the age of AI.

KEY TAKEAWAYS

- **Purpose-driven personalization**: This goes beyond merely tailoring content—it involves aligning marketing efforts with consumer values and respecting their privacy and autonomy. By focusing on delivering genuine value and obtaining informed consent, we build deeper connections and foster long-term loyalty.

Why it matters: Purpose-driven personalization not only strengthens relationships but also mitigates privacy concerns, ensuring consumers feel valued and respected.

- **Accountability through adaptive governance**: In a landscape where regulations and technologies evolve rapidly, traditional governance models fall short. Adaptive governance requires continuous monitoring, ethical audits, and cross-functional collaboration to ensure compliance with global regulations and ethical standards.
  Why it matters: Proactive governance minimizes ethical risks, ensures compliance, and enhances the reliability and credibility of AI systems.

- **Contextual sensitivity in engagement**: Recognizing and respecting cultural nuances is crucial in a global market. By employing real-time contextual awareness, ethical geo-targeting, and sentiment analysis, organizations can create campaigns that resonate authentically with diverse audiences.
  Why it matters: Culturally sensitive engagement prevents missteps that could harm brand reputation and ensures marketing resonates across diverse markets.

- **Trust through transparency**: Transparency is essential for building and maintaining consumer trust. Implementing XAI, ensuring fairness-by-design, and providing robust data ownership controls empower consumers and demystify AI processes.
  Why it matters: Transparency strengthens consumer confidence, demystifies AI, and positions brands as ethical leaders in a competitive marketplace.

Looking Ahead

In Chapter 6, we'll explore the pivotal role of trust in AI-driven marketing—how consumers perceive and interact with AI, and why trust is the foundation of lasting customer relationships. We'll examine common concerns about AI, demystify its use, and provide practical strategies for building transparency into AI interactions.

From communicating ethical AI practices effectively to embedding fairness and transparency into marketing strategies, Chapter 6 will guide you in addressing consumer fears and creating trust-based relationships. By aligning ethical integrity with business goals, you'll be equipped to navigate consumer perceptions of AI, driving both trust and innovation in this evolving landscape.

Food for Thought

1 How can your organization implement purpose-driven personalization that aligns with your customers' values? Consider ways to obtain informed consent and provide value without infringing on privacy.

2 Think about how cross-functional teams can collaborate to monitor and audit AI systems effectively.

3 Reflect on a recent marketing campaign. Were cultural nuances and real-time events adequately considered? How could real-time sentiment analysis have improved its reception?

4 In what ways can you enhance transparency around your AI systems? Consider how XAI and data privacy dashboards could empower your consumers.

References

Floridi, L and Cowls, J (2019) A Unified Framework of Five Principles for AI in Society, *Harvard Data Science Review*, 1 (1), doi.org/10.1162/99608f92.8cd550d1 (archived at https://perma.cc/EKV4-YSBC).

IEEE (2024) The IEEE Global Initiative 2.0 on Ethics of Autonomous and Intelligent Systems, standards.ieee.org/industry-connections/activities/ieee-global-initiative/ (archived at https://perma.cc/E5WH-MLLV)

Meier, K and Spichiger, R (2024) The EU AI Act: What It Means for Your Business, EY, March 15, www.ey.com/en_ch/insights/forensic-integrity-services/the-eu-ai-act-what-it-means-for-your-business (archived at https://perma.cc/T6RQ-J7F5)

Rust, R T and Huang, M -H (2021) *The Feeling Economy: How Artificial Intelligence Is Creating the Era of Empathy*, Springer International Publishing, Cham

PART THREE

Building Consumer Trust through Ethical AI Marketing

6

Consumer Trust and Perception of AI in Marketing

While previous chapters laid the groundwork for ethical AI implementation (Chapter 2), human-centered design (Chapter 3), and practical frameworks (Chapter 5), this chapter focuses on the psychology behind consumer trust in AI marketing systems. After all, even the most ethically designed AI will fall flat if consumers don't trust it.

Recent research highlights intriguing paradoxes in consumer attitudes toward AI-driven marketing. Consumers encounter AI-powered marketing interactions frequently, often without realizing it. According to a 2022 Pew Research Center survey, 27 per cent of Americans reported interacting with AI at least several times a day, while another 28 per cent said they interact with AI about once a day or several times a week (Pew Research Center, 2023). As AI adoption continues to expand across industries, marketing applications—from personalized recommendations to chatbots—are increasingly shaping consumer experiences. According to McKinsey & Company (2023), AI-powered personalization can deliver five to eight times the ROI on marketing spend and significantly boost customer engagement.

In this rapidly evolving landscape, trust in AI has become a crucial factor for successful adoption and long-term engagement. The World Economic Forum underscores that "trust is the foundation for AI's widespread acceptance," and emphasizes the necessity for companies to adopt self-governance frameworks that prioritize transparency, accountability, and fairness (World Economic Forum, 2025).

This chapter expands on the P.A.C.T. Framework—Personalization, Accountability, Contextual Sensitivity, and Trust—introduced in Chapter 5. While P.A.C.T. offers a structured approach to ethical AI marketing, this chapter explores its application in real-world trust dynamics—examining how each component influences consumer perception across different industries and cultural contexts. We also introduce the Trust Measurement Framework (TMF) to provide marketers with a structured approach to evaluating consumer trust in AI.

Beyond theoretical models, this chapter analyzes real-world examples of companies successfully fostering consumer trust in AI. By examining a diverse range of industries, we will distill the core principles that distinguish successful trust-building endeavors from those that falter, offering valuable insights applicable across sectors.

By the end of this chapter, you'll not only understand why consumers trust or distrust AI marketing but also gain actionable strategies to measure and cultivate trust in ways that align with both business goals and consumer psychology.

The Psychology of AI Trust

Consumer trust in AI marketing systems operates fundamentally differently from traditional marketing trust mechanisms. Where traditional marketing trust builds through brand familiarity and consistent experiences, AI trust involves additional psychological dimensions related to automation, decision-making autonomy, and perceived control. Understanding these differences is crucial for organizations seeking to build and maintain consumer trust in their AI marketing initiatives.

Cognitive Dimensions

Neurological studies offer intriguing insights into how our brains react to AI. Research from Stanford University reveals that we process information differently when interacting with AI-powered systems. For example, when evaluating AI-generated product recommendations, our brains activate distinct neural pathways compared to those triggered by recommendations from a human salesperson. This crucial difference highlights the need for marketers to understand how consumers cognitively process AI-driven interactions. There are three key cognitive factors that have emerged as critical influences on AI trust, including perceived control, understanding of mechanisms, and value recognition.

Emotional Dimensions

Consumer trust in AI marketing is deeply influenced by emotional factors, which often override logical evaluations. These emotional responses shape trust in several key ways:

- **Anxiety and privacy concerns:** Despite AI's convenience, 67 per cent of consumers express anxiety about how their data is used, reflecting persistent privacy concerns (Pew Research Center, 2023). This tension creates a paradoxical relationship where consumers benefit from AI-driven marketing while simultaneously fearing its potential misuse.
- **Trust through repeated interactions:** Emotional trust in AI systems develops iteratively through repeated, successful interactions, particularly when systems demonstrate high accuracy, consistent performance, and empathetic behavior. Experimental studies

show that emotional and behavioral trust accumulate over time, with early experiences strongly shaping later perceptions. In repeated legal decision-making tasks, users exhibited growing trust toward high-performing AI, with initial interactions significantly influencing long-term reliance (Kahr et al., 2023). Emotional trust can follow nonlinear pathways—dipping after failures but recovering through empathetic interventions or improved system performance (Tsumura and Yamada, 2023).

- **Honesty and transparency in AI content:** Consumers increasingly value transparency regarding AI-generated content. Companies that openly disclose when AI has been used—for instance, in creating product descriptions—can empower customers by helping them feel more informed and in control of their choices. Such openness often strengthens customer trust and fosters positive perceptions of brands actively embracing transparency in their marketing practices.

Cultural Variations in AI Trust

The global nature of modern marketing requires a nuanced understanding of cultural differences in AI trust. These variations arise from deeply ingrained societal values, historical relationships with technology, and norms around privacy, automation, and decision-making. For marketers leveraging AI in customer engagement, recognizing these cultural distinctions is crucial for developing trustworthy AI-driven campaigns, personalized experiences, and region-specific data strategies.

Diverging Cultural Trust in AI

Recent research reveals significant disparities in AI trust across global markets. A KPMG (2023) global survey found that 72 per cent of Chinese consumers express trust in AI-driven services, while in the U.S., trust levels plummet to just 32 per cent. This stark difference reflects broader societal attitudes toward government-led AI innovation, data privacy concerns, and varying historical experiences with technology.

Another study found that AI-related job displacement fears vary greatly by region. In countries like the U.S., India, and Saudi Arabia, consumers express significant concerns about AI replacing human roles in professional sectors such as medicine, finance, and law. In contrast, consumers in Japan, China, and Turkey exhibit lower levels of concern, signaling a higher acceptance of AI in professional settings (Quantum Zeitgeist, 2025). The Quantum Zeitgeist study shows that regions like Japan, China, and Turkey exhibit lower levels of concern about AI replacing human jobs compared to regions like the U.S., India, and Saudi Arabia, where such fears are more pronounced.

This insight is invaluable for marketers crafting AI-driven customer service, financial tools, and healthcare applications, as perceptions of AI reliability and utility vary significantly by region. As trust in AI diverges globally, understanding the role of cultural privacy norms becomes essential for marketers aiming to build trust through AI-driven services.

Cultural Privacy Targeting in AI Marketing

As AI-driven marketing becomes more integrated globally, the concept of cultural privacy targeting—the practice of aligning data collection, privacy messaging, and AI transparency with cultural values—has gained increasing importance. Consumer attitudes toward AI adoption and data privacy are highly regional, requiring market-ers to adapt their strategies accordingly.

In more collectivist societies like Japan, AI applications that prioritize societal or community well-being are generally more accepted than those centered on individual convenience. This is evident in Japan's Society 5.0 initiative—a national vision intro-duced in 2016 that seeks to build a "super-smart" society by integrating AI, IoT, robotics, and big data to solve social challenges such as an aging population and strains on healthcare systems. Businesses are central to this transformation, with government and industry collaboration encouraging companies to adopt digital technologies not just for efficiency, but to contribute to public welfare. Across sectors—from manufac-turing and healthcare to urban planning—firms are reimagining business models to align with societal needs, creating innovations that are both economically viable and socially beneficial. In this context, AI is viewed more favorably when positioned as a tool to enhance collective well-being and address structural challenges. For instance, AI-powered health monitoring technologies in Japan have seen increased adoption when positioned as tools that contribute to broader public health outcomes.

Conversely, Germany, as an individualistic society with strong privacy norms and high uncertainty avoidance, places significant emphasis on consumer control over personal data. The EUs GDPR and Germany's support for the proposed Artificial Intelligence Act reinforce expectations for robust transparency, fairness, and user autonomy in AI systems. According to the OECD (2024), campaigns in Germany that clearly communicate data usage, safeguard individual rights, and provide opt-in consent mechanisms experience higher levels of public trust and adoption.

These contrasting cultural orientations illustrate the strategic need for contextual-ized AI marketing—ensuring that data transparency and privacy are not treated as one-size-fits-all, but rather as culture-aware dimensions that shape trust and acceptance.

Hofstede's (2011) cultural dimensions theory offers further insights into AI trust variations:

- High individualism + high uncertainty avoidance (e.g. Germany, U.S.) → Consum-ers demand transparency, data protection, and human oversight in AI marketing.
- Collectivist cultures with lower uncertainty avoidance (e.g. Japan, China, South Korea) → AI is seen as a tool that enhances societal progress, and data-sharing concerns are often lower when the societal benefits are clear (Gupta et al., 2021).

For marketers deploying AI in different regions, these insights help determine which features to emphasize:

- Control and explainability in Western markets (focused on privacy and autonomy)
- Seamless automation and societal progress in East Asian markets (focused on communal benefits and technological enhancement)

Understanding the cultural dimensions of AI trust is key for marketers crafting successful AI-powered campaigns. By aligning AI personalization efforts with local cultural expectations and privacy norms, marketers can improve consumer trust and adoption in both individualistic and collectivist societies. This culturally informed approach helps brands tailor privacy messaging and AI transparency to the unique preferences of consumers in various regions, building stronger relationships and enhancing overall engagement.

Religious and Ethical Influences on AI Trust

Religious and ethical frameworks also shape AI marketing trustworthiness:

- Islamic-majority nations evaluate AI through *maṣlaḥah* (public interest) and *maqāṣid al-sharī'a* (objectives of Islamic law), which prioritize both societal welfare and ethical alignment with divine principles. As Elmahjub (2023) explains, *maṣlaḥah* offers a flexible framework that accommodates both duty-based and utility-based reasoning, allowing AI to be evaluated in terms of both benefit and moral integrity. Marketers and developers who design AI systems in accordance with these values are more likely to build trust in Muslim-majority societies, where ethical legitimacy is closely tied to religious norms.
- In Hindu-majority regions, AI's integration into spiritual and ethical decision-making (e.g. AI-powered astrology or matchmaking) must be seen as augmenting, not replacing, human wisdom to be accepted (ISACA, 2024).

For AI marketers, culturally sensitive AI applications require localized adaptation, ensuring that automated decision-making aligns with ethical, religious, and moral expectations.

Avoiding Overgeneralization in AI Trust Strategies

While cultural differences are clear, overgeneralizing consumer attitudes can lead to marketing missteps. A 2024 ISACA report warns against rigid AI segmentation, emphasizing that trust attitudes evolve with:

- media influence (e.g. growing fears of AI misinformation)

- regulatory changes (e.g. the EU AI Act's impact on European consumer confidence)
- generational shifts (younger, digitally native consumers are often more AI-trusting, regardless of cultural background).

For AI marketing, this highlights the need for flexible, real-time AI trust monitoring rather than static cultural assumptions.

Marketers should adapt AI trust-building strategies based on region-specific consumer expectations:

- **North America and Europe:** AI explainability, data transparency, and ethical AI labels increase trust.
- **East Asia:** AI-driven personalization and seamless automation work best when framed as benefiting society.
- **Islamic-majority nations and ethical consumer segments:** AI must be clearly aligned with fairness and ethical governance.
- **Global emerging markets:** AI trust is rapidly increasing, making these markets prime opportunities for AI-driven financial inclusion and digital transformation.

These regional nuances in AI trust are illustrated in Table 6.1, which presents a comparative snapshot of consumer trust in AI across several global markets. The data, drawn from the 2023 KPMG International survey, underscores how cultural values such as collectivism, uncertainty avoidance, and openness to innovation, shape public attitudes toward AI. For example, trust levels in Germany and Japan remain low, reflecting high uncertainty avoidance and strong privacy expectations, while countries like India and Brazil exhibit notably higher trust, driven by optimism around AI's role in societal and economic progress.

TABLE 6.1 AI trust across different cultures

Country	% Trusting AI	Cultural factors
Finland	<25%	High certainty avoidance; emphasis on privacy
Japan	<25%	High certainty avoidance; historical experiences with technological disruption
Brazil	>50%	Openness to innovation; collectivist values
India	>50%	Rapid technological advancement; emphasis on economic growth
China	>50%	Collectivist values; government support for AI development
South Africa	>50%	Technological leapfrog; focus on social development

SOURCE KPMG International and The University of Queensland, 2023

Industry-Specific Trust Variations

Trust in AI systems varies significantly across industries, shaped by factors such as the nature of consumer interactions, the stakes involved, and the sensitivity of data. Each sector presents unique challenges and opportunities for building trust in AI applications.

Financial Services

The financial sector handles highly sensitive personal data and high-stakes decisions, necessitating exceptional levels of trust. Consumers are particularly cautious about AI-driven financial systems, demonstrating significantly higher demands for reliability and transparency compared to other industries.

Transparency in explaining AI-based decisions, such as credit scoring, loan approvals, and investment recommendations, is critical for fostering trust. Research from PwC (2024) highlights that 85 per cent of consumers are more likely to trust AI-driven financial services when they clearly explain decision-making processes.

When financial institutions prioritize explainability, customer trust and adoption often improve. For example, Morgan Stanley introduced the GPT-4-powered AI @ Morgan Stanley Assistant in 2023 to support financial advisors with explainable access to the firm's research and insights. By Q3 2024, 98 per cent of financial advisor teams were actively using the platform, underscoring the value of transparent, AI-enhanced tools in building internal trust and boosting adoption (OpenAI, 2024). Similarly, industry studies by Accenture indicate that financial firms emphasizing transparent AI experience around a 20 per cent boost in customer satisfaction and loyalty (Venturini et al., 2023).

Healthcare

In healthcare, where AI can directly influence patient outcomes, trust plays a critical role. Research shows that the more complex and high-stakes an AI-driven decision is, the less trust people tend to have in it. A nationally representative survey published in JAMA Network Open found that while many U.S. adults are open to AI in healthcare, their trust drops significantly when it's used for key decisions like diagnosis or treatment recommendations—especially compared to more routine administrative tasks (Kullar et al., 2022).

Hybrid approaches combining AI analysis with human oversight significantly enhance patient trust. The *Journal of Medical Internet Research* highlights that integrating AI into clinical workflows, alongside clear communication and physician involvement, improves user acceptance and addresses patient concerns effectively (Woodcock et al., 2022).

Retail and E-Commerce

The relationship between consumers and AI in retail is increasingly complex, with trust levels varying based on factors such as purchase complexity and transparency of AI use. A 2025 Capgemini report revealed that 71 per cent of consumers want generative AI integrated into their shopping experiences, with 58 per cent already using AI tools for produce or service recommendations—more than double the rate reported in 2023. This shift signals a growing, albeit cautious, reliance on AI in retail decision-making.

As consumers become more aware of AI's capabilities, trust hinges on clear communication and responsible deployment. Notably, 66 per cent of consumers want to be informed when companies use AI to enable interactions, highlighting the importance of transparency in AI-driven engagement (Capgemini Research Institute, 2023).

Retailers leveraging AI to personalize experiences are seeing measurable benefits. According to Capgemini, 67 per cent of organizations believe generative AI helps build brand identity, while over 65 per cent cite improvements in trend analysis, cost efficiency, and content generation (Capgemini Research Institute, 2025). These findings suggest that when used ethically and transparently, AI not only improves marketing performance but also strengthens consumer relationships.

Travel and Tourism

In the travel industry, AI is revolutionizing how consumers plan their journeys by personalizing recommendations, streamlining itinerary planning, and offering immersive destination previews. For example, *The New York Times* uses AI to analyze historical data and refine its "Places to Go" lists, illustrating AI's growing influence in shaping consumer travel decisions (Virshup, 2025). Similarly, Google's AI-powered travel features offer itinerary suggestions, immersive 3D previews, and destination insights.

Recent research highlights a significant rise in the adoption of AI for travel planning. A Deloitte (2025) survey found that between October 2023 and October 2024, the proportion of travelers using generative AI for trip planning doubled from 8 per cent to 16 per cent, with Millennials leading the trend at a 25 per cent adoption rate. Despite this growing usage, many travelers still expect human interaction during their trips, signaling the importance of integrating AI with personalized service.

CHALLENGES AND ETHICAL CONSIDERATIONS IN AI TRAVEL MARKETING

AI-powered travel marketing faces several ethical challenges:

- **Transparency:** Many consumers are unaware of how AI influences their travel choices. Marketers should disclose AI's role in shaping recommendations to build trust.

- **Bias:** AI algorithms may prioritize destinations based on marketing budgets rather than cultural significance or unique experiences, leading to biased recommendations.

- **Trust:** While AI enhances efficiency, many consumers still trust human-curated travel recommendations over automated suggestions. A balanced approach combining AI efficiency with human expertise is essential for building trust.

ETHICAL AI TRAVEL MARKETING STRATEGIES

To address these concerns, ethical AI travel marketing should prioritize the following:

- **Disclosure:** Clearly disclose AI's involvement in recommendations to enhance transparency and consumer trust (Virshup, 2025).

- **Fairness:** Ensure AI systems spotlight diverse and underrepresented destinations, not just popular or well-funded locations (Virshup, 2025).

- **Human-AI collaboration:** Combining AI-generated insights with human expertise fosters credibility and enhances consumer trust.

Telecommunications

Telecom providers face the challenge of balancing personalization with privacy concerns. AI-powered customer support tools, such as chatbots, can increase efficiency, but consumers often prefer systems that escalate complex issues to human agents. Transparency, privacy compliance, and adaptability to customer needs are critical to building trust in AI systems.

Education

AI is increasingly used in personalized learning, student assessments, and administrative tasks like scheduling and resource allocation. Trust in AI within education is crucial, as it directly impacts student outcomes. Transparency in how AI systems make recommendations or assess students is essential. Concerns around bias in AI algorithms, especially in grading systems, need to be addressed to ensure fairness.

- Trust factors: Data privacy (student data), explainability of AI-driven assessment tools, fairness in AI grading systems.

Automotive and Transportation

AI is transforming the automotive industry, from autonomous vehicles to AI-driven traffic management systems. Trust in AI is vital, especially in autonomous driving and predictive maintenance, where safety is at stake. Consumers need assurance that AI systems are safe, reliable, and efficient.

- Trust factors: Safety, transparency of decision-making in autonomous systems, regulatory standards.

Pharmaceuticals and Biotechnology

AI plays an increasing role in drug discovery, clinical trials, and personalized medicine. Given the sensitive nature of healthcare and high risks involved, trust in AI systems is critical. Bias in clinical trials or healthcare applications can have severe consequences, so ensuring fairness and accuracy is paramount.

- Trust factors: Safety, regulatory compliance, fairness in clinical trial design, transparency in treatment recommendations.

Measuring Trust in AI Marketing Systems

As AI becomes central to how brands engage customers—from personalization engines to chatbots—measuring consumer trust in these systems is no longer optional. It's essential. And yet, many marketing teams still rely on outdated metrics like Net Promoter Score (NPS) or basic satisfaction surveys to evaluate the impact of AI. These tools are helpful for broad feedback but miss the nuance and dynamics of trust in AI-powered experiences

Recent research, including work from MIT Media Lab (n.d.) and leading behavioral scientists, makes one thing clear: Trust in AI is multi-dimensional, and it's shaped by how people feel, think, and behave in real-time when interacting with automated systems. Traditional metrics like NPS and CSAT (Customer Satisfaction Score) tell you if a customer is satisfied—but not why they trust (or don't trust) your AI systems. They don't account for how transparent your algorithm is, how well it explains itself, or how emotionally resonant the interaction feels. In AI-driven environments, you need a smarter way to understand trust.

A Modern Framework for Trust: What CMOs Should Know

MIT Media Lab's work on trust in human-AI interaction offers a powerful lens for marketers. It breaks trust into three key dimensions:

Behavioral Trust

This is about what customers do, not what they say. When customers engage frequently, opt in to data sharing, or return to your AI tools repeatedly, that's a sign of behavioral trust. How to track it:

- Repeat engagement with AI-driven tools (e.g. product recommenders, chatbots)

- Opt-in rates for personalization features
- Drop-off points in AI-led journeys

Emotional Trust

Trust is not just rational, it's emotional. The tone of a voice assistant, the empathy in a chatbot's reply, or how "human" a recommendation feels all play into emotional trust. How to track it:

- Sentiment analysis from chat transcripts and reviews
- Customer frustration or delight signals from support tickets
- Tone and emotional language in user feedback

Cognitive Trust

This is where understanding meets confidence. When your AI explains itself clearly—or when customers understand what it can and can't do—they're more likely to trust the output. How to track it:

- Feedback on explainability ("I understood why I got this recommendation")
- Click-through or acceptance rates of AI-generated content or decisions
- Post-interaction surveys that assess clarity

Today's marketers are moving toward real-time trust dashboards—tools that monitor how users interact with AI systems across channels. These dashboards track behavior, sentiment, and comprehension all at once.

According to MIT Media Lab researchers, combining these signals provides a richer picture of trust than any single survey can. It also gives teams the agility to address trust breakdowns as they happen—like confusion over AI-generated content or friction in AI-powered customer journeys.

Customers don't expect AI to be perfect. But they do expect it to be honest and understandable. That's why brands should:

- label AI-generated content clearly
- explain how decisions like pricing, recommendations, or targeting are made
- give customers control over data and personalization.

Building trust is less about tech perfection and more about perceived fairness, clarity, and respect. Measuring that trust means going deeper than satisfaction. Use behavioral, emotional, and cognitive signals to track trust in real-time—and design AI systems that earn it.

FIGURE 6.1 The consumer trust pyramid: AI marketing strategies

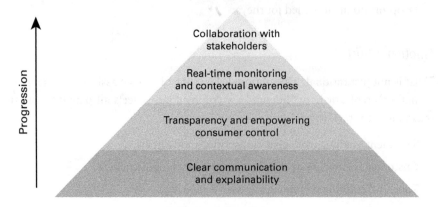

Strategies for Building Sustainable Consumer Trust

Building on the foundations laid in previous chapters, marketers can employ a range of strategies to cultivate lasting consumer trust in their AI-driven marketing initiatives. These strategies not only address the challenges outlined in this chapter but also align with the overarching principles of ethical AI implementation.

Establishing sustainable consumer trust in AI marketing requires a layered approach, starting with foundational practices and advancing to more complex, collaborative strategies. In Figure 6.1, each layer represents progressive steps in establishing trust, from foundational practices to the advanced strategy of collaborative stakeholder involvement.

Core Strategies (Base Layer)

At the foundation of the pyramid are core strategies, which include clear communication and explainability. These strategies represent the essential elements that establish initial trust in AI-driven marketing.

- **Clear communication:** Consumers need to understand when and how AI is being used in their interactions with a brand. Communicating clearly about the role of AI builds transparency and minimizes confusion or misconceptions. Simple, jargon-free language is key here.
- **Explainability:** Offer understandable AI insights, even in complex scenarios. Explainability involves providing easy-to-understand explanations of AI processes—without overwhelming technical details—so consumers can grasp how their data is used and how decisions are made.

These core strategies form the strong foundation necessary for all other trust-building efforts. These strategies represent essential practices every brand should implement to establish a baseline of trust and transparency.

Foundational Strategies (Lower Middle Layer)

Building on core strategies, foundational strategies introduce more direct consumer empowerment. Key elements in this layer are transparency and empowering consumer control.

- **Transparency:** While the core strategies involve communicating AI's presence and purpose, foundational transparency goes a step further by sharing additional details on how AI impacts the consumer experience. For example, this might include clarifying how consumer data is used to make personalized recommendations or showing users how specific AI-driven decisions were reached.

- **Empowering consumer control:** Trust is strengthened when consumers feel in control of their data and can make choices about their AI-driven experiences. By providing intuitive privacy settings, opt-in or opt-out options, and other customizations, brands give consumers a sense of agency. Empowering consumers in this way helps to address potential concerns about data privacy and control, leading to greater overall trust.

The foundational strategies layer in the pyramid visually builds on core strategies by adding a level of engagement and autonomy, deepening the trust established at the base.

Intermediate Strategies (Upper Middle Layer)

The intermediate strategies layer involves more dynamic and responsive practices, such as real-time monitoring and contextual awareness. These strategies help brands stay attuned to consumer expectations and shifts in trust on an ongoing basis.

- **Real-time monitoring:** Monitoring consumer trust in real-time enables brands to track consumer sentiment and respond promptly to issues as they arise. By leveraging tools that track behavioral and emotional indicators of trust, brands can adapt their AI-driven interactions to maintain positive consumer relationships. Real-time monitoring ensures that brands can take corrective actions if trust begins to waver.

- **Contextual awareness:** This strategy acknowledges that consumer expectations vary depending on context, including cultural norms, industry standards, and personal data sensitivity. Contextual awareness involves tailoring AI-driven marketing approaches to reflect these differences, such as adjusting privacy controls based on regional preferences or providing more in-depth explanations for sensitive transactions like financial or health-related decisions.

As shown in the pyramid's upper middle layer, intermediate strategies build on the foundations of transparency and control by adding real-time responsiveness and adaptability, which are key for fostering deeper trust in a dynamic, AI-driven landscape.

Advanced Strategy (Top Layer)

At the top of the pyramid lies the advanced strategy of stakeholder collaboration. This approach represents the most mature level of trust-building and involves creating partnerships with consumers, industry bodies, and regulatory authorities to promote ethical and transparent AI practices.

- **Stakeholder collaboration:** Long-term trust is established not only through transparency but also by actively involving stakeholders in shaping AI practices. This might include working directly with consumer advocacy groups, collaborating with regulatory agencies to comply with evolving privacy laws, or creating forums where consumers can provide feedback on AI interactions. Engaging stakeholders in this way shows a brand's commitment to ethical AI use and helps maintain trust even as AI technology evolves. By involving stakeholders actively and incorporating feedback into AI practices, brands showcase a commitment to ethical growth, aligning AI with evolving consumer and societal standards.

The consumer trust-building strategies pyramid highlights a progression of strategies that work together to establish and maintain consumer trust in AI marketing. Each layer builds on the one below, starting with the fundamental practices of clear communication and explainability and culminating in collaborative efforts with consumers and industry stakeholders. By following this layered approach, marketers can develop a robust, sustainable framework for trust-building that adapts to both consumer expectations and technological advancements.

Enhance Transparency and Explainability

As the "transparency paradox" suggests, simply providing more information is not enough to build trust. Marketers should focus on delivering clear, jargon-free explanations of how AI systems operate, drawing on the XAI techniques discussed in Chapter 5. By demystifying the inner workings of AI and offering consumers visibility into decision-making processes, brands can foster a sense of understanding and control that is crucial for trust development.

Empower Consumers with Control and Consent

Reinforcing the "personalization with purpose" and "respect for autonomy" principles from Chapters 3 and 5, marketers should prioritize giving consumers granular control over their data and how it is used. Intuitive privacy dashboards, robust opt-in/opt-out mechanisms, and clear data usage policies empower consumers to make informed choices, reducing the risk of perceived privacy violations and enhancing trust.

Cultivate a Culture of Ethical AI

As outlined in Chapter 4, the successful implementation of ethical AI in marketing requires a holistic, organization-wide commitment. By fostering a culture of ethical AI, as we'll explore in Chapter 9, marketers can demonstrate their brand's steadfast dedication to responsible innovation. This includes establishing cross-functional governance structures, providing comprehensive employee training, and visibly celebrating teams that prioritize ethical considerations in their AI initiatives.

Leverage Contextual Awareness and Adaptability

The Contextual Sensitivity pillar of the P.A.C.T. Framework (Chapter 5) becomes increasingly important as brands navigate the evolving landscape of consumer trust. By maintaining real-time awareness of cultural shifts, current events, and industry-specific norms, marketers can adapt their AI-driven strategies to avoid tone-deaf messaging and remain authentically relevant to their target audiences. This agility not only builds trust but also positions the brand as a responsive, trustworthy partner.

Implement Robust Trust Measurement and Monitoring

By adopting the comprehensive TMF described in this chapter, marketers can gain a deeper, more nuanced understanding of how consumers perceive and engage with their AI systems. By continuously tracking behavioral, emotional, and cognitive trust indicators, brands can identify emerging issues, refine their strategies, and demonstrate a commitment to trust-building that resonates with consumers.

Collaborate with Consumers and Stakeholders

Meaningful trust is built through open, ongoing dialogue. By establishing feedback loops that allow consumers to share their concerns and preferences, as well as collaborating with industry bodies and regulatory authorities, marketers can demonstrate a genuine commitment to trust-building. This collaborative approach, as explored in Chapters 4 and 9, fosters transparency, accountability, and a shared sense of purpose that underpins sustainable consumer trust.

The Future of Consumer Trust in AI Marketing

As the integration of AI into marketing continues to accelerate, the ability to maintain and cultivate consumer trust will be a defining factor in long-term success. Marketers must embrace the ethical principles and practical frameworks outlined in this and previous chapters to navigate the complex, ever-evolving landscape of AI trust.

By prioritizing transparency, empowering consumer autonomy, and demonstrating a steadfast commitment to responsible innovation, brands can transform the perception of AI from a potentially invasive or manipulative force to a trusted partner in the customer journey. This trust-centric approach not only mitigates risks but also opens the door to new opportunities for genuine, value-driven engagement that benefits both the business and the consumer.

Looking ahead, the future of AI marketing will be shaped by the industry's ability to keep pace with changing consumer attitudes, technological advancements, and regulatory frameworks. Marketers who can demonstrate agility, foresight, and an unwavering dedication to ethical practices will be well-positioned to thrive in an AI-driven world where trust is the new currency of success.

Bringing It All Together

We've discussed the complex dynamics of consumer trust in AI marketing, including the importance of a strategic approach to transparency and consumer control. By addressing key transparency challenges—such as balancing information overload and respecting contextual privacy—brands can foster sustainable trust.

KEY TAKEAWAYS

- **The psychology of AI trust**: This involves both cognitive dimensions (perceived control, understanding of mechanisms, value recognition) and emotional factors (fear, comfort, authenticity) that significantly influence consumer perceptions and behaviors. *Why it matters*: Understanding the psychological underpinnings of AI trust enables marketers to design AI systems and interactions that resonate with consumers on both rational and emotional levels, fostering deeper connections and trust.

- **Cultural variations**: AI trust across regions and industries require marketers to develop nuanced, context-specific strategies for building consumer confidence in AI-driven initiatives. *Why it matters*: Recognizing and adapting to cultural differences in AI trust is crucial for brands operating in diverse markets, as a one-size-fits-all approach may fail to address the unique concerns and expectations of different consumer segments.

- **Trust Measurement Framework**: This provides a comprehensive approach to assessing consumer trust in AI marketing systems, integrating behavioral, emotional, and cognitive indicators for a holistic understanding of trust dynamics.
  Why it matters: By adopting a multidimensional TMF, marketers can gain actionable insights into the factors driving consumer trust, enabling data-driven strategies for building and maintaining confidence in AI-powered marketing initiatives.

- **Emerging trust challenges**: Such as the authenticity crisis surrounding AI-generated content and the transparency paradox, demand proactive strategies for maintaining consumer trust in an evolving AI landscape.
  Why it matters: Staying ahead of emerging trust challenges is essential for brands seeking to establish long-term, sustainable relationships with consumers in an AI-driven world. Failure to address these issues proactively can erode trust and damage brand reputation.

Looking Ahead

In Chapter 7, we'll explore ethics in customer engagement, offering strategies to integrate transparency, empathy, and autonomy into AI interactions. From practical guidelines on transparency in content creation to frameworks for ethical AI practices, readers will gain tools for making their AI strategies both effective and ethically grounded. Building on the trust foundations we've established, we'll explore how brands can leverage HCAI to create meaningful, trust-building interactions with consumers across various touchpoints and industry verticals.

We'll examine practical ways to infuse transparency, empathy, and respect for consumer autonomy into AI-driven engagement strategies. We'll also provide guidance on integrating ethical AI practices into your marketing workflows, ensuring that your brand's values are consistently reflected in every customer interaction.

By combining the trust-building strategies from this chapter with the ethical engagement principles we'll explore next, you'll be well-equipped to navigate the complexities of consumer trust in the age of AI, fostering lasting relationships that drive both business success and positive societal impact.

Food for Thought

1 Reflect on your transparency approach. Are you prioritizing disclosures on high-impact areas like data usage and personalization while avoiding information overload? How might contextual privacy settings help you build a balanced trust strategy?

2 Reflect on the industry-specific trust variations discussed in this chapter. How might you adapt your AI marketing strategies to better suit the unique needs and expectations of your target consumers?

3 As new AI-powered technologies like generative content continue to evolve, what ethical guidelines would you propose to ensure their responsible use in marketing?

4 Consider the Trust Measurement Framework introduced in this chapter. How might you integrate behavioral, emotional, and cognitive trust indicators into your organization's marketing analytics practices?

References

Capgemini Research Institute (2023) Almost 60% of Organizations Are Implementing or Exploring Generative AI in Marketing, December 11, www.capgemini.com/news/press-releases/almost-60-of-organizations-are-implementing-or-exploring-generative-ai-in-marketing/ (archived at https://perma.cc/8B8Y-5VPE)

Capgemini Research Institute (2025) 71% of Consumers Want Generative AI Integrated into their Shopping Experiences, January 9, www.capgemini.com/news/press-releases/71-of-consumers-want-generative-ai-integrated-into-their-shopping-experiences/ (archived at https://perma.cc/5TE4-JXPW)

Deloitte (2025) Are Consumers Ready to Embrace Generative AI for Travel Planning, CMO Today, *The Wall Street Journal*, April 1, deloitte.wsj.com/cmo/are-consumers-ready-to-embrace-generative-ai-for-travel-planning-a1660d7e (archived at https://perma.cc/8AGL-zzzz)

Elmahjub, E (2023) Artificial Intelligence (AI) in Islamic Ethics: Towards Pluralist Ethical Benchmarking for AI, *Philosophy & Technology*, 36, 73. https://doi.org/10.1007/s13347-023-00668-x (archived at https://perma.cc/YAN4-WQPP)

Google Public Policy (2022) An AI Opportunity Agenda for Japan, https://publicpolicy.google/resources/japan_ai_opportunity_agenda_en.pdf (archived at https://perma.cc/VC36-M6YQ)

Hofstede, G (2011) Dimensionalizing Cultures: The Hofstede Model in Context, *Online Readings in Psychology and Culture*, 2 (1), scholarworks.gvsu.edu/cgi/viewcontent.cgi?article=1014&context=orpc (archived at https://perma.cc/B7EP-94CQ)

ISACA (2024) AI Ethics: Navigating Different Cultural Contexts, December 6, www.isaca.org/resources/news-and-trends/isaca-now-blog/2024/ai-ethics-navigating-different-cultural-contexts (archived at https://perma.cc/3XLA-MRDE)

Kahr, P K, Meijer, S A, Willemsen, M C, and Snijders, C C P (2023) It Seems Smart, But It Acts Stupid: Development of Trust in AI Advice in a Repeated Legal Decision-Making Task, *Proceedings of the 28th International Conference on Intelligent User Interfaces*, doi.org/10.1145/3581641.3584058 (archived at https://perma.cc/SZF8-TSK2)

KPMG International and The University of Queensland (2023) *Trust in Artificial Intelligence: A Global Study*, assets.kpmg.com/content/dam/kpmg/au/pdf/2023/trust-in-ai-global-insights-2023.pdf (archived at https://perma.cc/MPZ2-UWJY)

Khullar, D, Casalino, L P, Qian, Y, Lu, Y, Krumholz, H M, and Aneja, S (2022) Perspectives of patients about artificial intelligence in health care, JAMA Network Open, 5(5), e2210309, https://jamanetwork.com/journals/jamanetworkopen/fullarticle/2791851 (archived at https://perma.cc/RYN4-72VY)

McKinsey & Company (2023) The State of AI in 2023: Generative AI's Breakout Year, www.mckinsey.com/capabilities/quantumblack/our-insights/the-state-of-ai-in-2023-generative-ais-breakout-year (archived at https://perma.cc/V29V-QU6R)

MIT Media Lab (n.d.) Research Projects, accessed April 8, 2025

OECD (2024) OECD Artificial Intelligence Review of Germany, www.oecd.org/en/publications/2024/06/oecd-artificial-intelligence-review-of-germany_c1c35ccf.html (archived at https://perma.cc/5DBS-LVLV)

OpenAI (2024) Customer stories: Morgan Stanley, https://openai.com/index/morgan-stanley (archived at https://perma.cc/37A4-6XS7)

Pew Research Center (2023) Public Awareness of Artificial Intelligence in Everyday Activities, February, www.pewresearch.org/wp-content/uploads/sites/20/2023/02/PS_2023.02.15_AI-awareness_REPORT.pdf (archived at https://perma.cc/V3SE-L2BM)

PwC (2024) Voice of the Consumer Survey, May 15, www.pwc.com/gx/en/issues/c-suite-insights/voice-of-the-consumer-survey.html (archived at https://perma.cc/HNV9-2RLW)

Quantum Zeitgeist (2025) How Cultural Differences Shape Fear of AI in the Workplace, Quantum News, February 22, quantumzeitgeist.com/how-cultural-differences-shape-fear-of-ai-in-the-workplace-a-global-study-across-20-countries/ (archived at https://perma.cc/3EFL-LTKM)

Tsumura, T and Yamada, S (2023) Making an Agent's Trust Stable in a Series of Success and Failure Tasks Through Empathy, arXiv. arxiv.org/abs/2306.09447 (archived at https://perma.cc/L7HN-B3ZC)

Venturini, F, Bhardwaj, A, Vyas, S, Imbroda, A, Orlando, A, and Parvathy, U (2023) Embracing the Loyalty Equation, Accenture, www.accenture.com/content/dam/accenture/final/accenture-com/document-3/Embracing-The-Loyalty-Equation.pdf (archived at https://perma.cc/DW2D-9AHF)

Virshup, A (2025) How AI Tools Helped the Travel Team Study its "Places to Go" lists, The New York Times, January 19, www.nytimes.com/2025/01/19/travel/how-ai-tools-helped-the-travel-team-study-its-places-to-go-lists.html (archived at https://perma.cc/5BQ3-8BQ5)

Woodcock, C, Mittelstadt, B, Busbridge, D, and Blank, G (2022) The Impact of Explanations on a Layperson Trust in Artificial Intelligence-driven Symptom Checker Apps: Experimental Study, Journal of Medical Internet Research, 23 (11): e29386, doi.org/10.2196/29386 (archived at https://perma.cc/KQJ4-WQD5)

World Economic Forum (2025) How AI Can Move from Hype to Global Solutions, www.weforum.org/stories/2025/01/ai-transformation-industries-responsible-innovation/ (archived at https://perma.cc/5ALX-MDXB)

7

Ethical Consumer Engagement in AI Marketing

The rise of AI in marketing has created an unprecedented capability to engage with customers at scale. Yet as we explored in Chapter 6, capability without trust is at best ineffective and at worst destructive to customer relationships. The challenge we now face is how to transform the theoretical frameworks and trust principles we've discussed into practical engagement strategies that respect our customers while driving business results.

A 2024 interview with Chris Duffey, Adobe's AI Strategy and Innovation Lead, explored the escalating challenges and opportunities in ethical AI engagement. As AI systems become increasingly sophisticated, the boundary between ethical and unethical practices is growing ever more nuanced. Duffey provided firsthand insights into how Adobe has operationalized ethical AI at scale, balancing groundbreaking innovation with deep-seated concerns over creator rights and consumer trust. His perspective on generative AI—as both a revolutionary creative tool and a potential source of ethical dilemmas—offers critical lessons for any organization looking to foster trust while pushing the envelope in technological advancement.

In this chapter, we'll build on the P.A.C.T. Framework introduced in Chapter 5 to create actionable strategies for ethical AI engagement. By examining Adobe's approach to generative AI, we'll uncover how organizations can balance innovation with accountability to foster trust. This sets the stage for Chapter 8, where we'll formalize these strategies into governance structures.

From P.A.C.T. to Practice: Operationalizing Ethical Engagement

The P.A.C.T. Framework provides the ethical foundation for AI marketing. This section translates its principles into practical strategies, using Adobe's generative AI as a model for operationalizing personalization, accountability, cultural intelligence, and trust.

Personalization → Value-Driven Interactions

The first element of P.A.C.T., Personalization, must evolve beyond technical capability into value-driven interaction. Every decision about personalization must consider not just what's possible, but what builds trust and creates long-term value for all stakeholders. Ethical AI personalization requires empathetic engagement—understanding the impact of AI-driven recommendations and interactions across diverse user groups.

Adobe's Firefly generative AI platform demonstrates this evolution. As Duffey emphasizes, "We're not just building AI; we're building a sustainable creative ecosystem." This is reflected in their commitment to detailed attribution for AI-generated works, ensuring that original creators receive proper recognition and credit. Adobe's approach to personalization goes beyond generic AI recommendations—it is context-sensitive, culturally aware, and designed to respect individual agency.

One of the most effective strategies Adobe employs is "progressive customization"—a phased approach where personalization starts with low-risk, universally beneficial AI suggestions before deepening engagement based on earned trust. This model allows AI-driven marketing to scale without overwhelming users or crossing ethical boundaries. The key takeaway for marketers: True personalization isn't about what AI can do—it's about what makes consumers feel valued, informed, and respected.

Accountability → Responsible Engagement

The second element of P.A.C.T. shifts AI accountability from mere compliance to proactive responsibility. Adobe exemplifies this shift through clear ownership policies, ethical data usage, and transparent content authentication, setting new industry standards for responsible AI engagement.

Rejecting common industry practices like web scraping and unauthorized data usage, Adobe ensures that its AI models train only on licensed or user-approved content. This commitment is reinforced by its intellectual property indemnification policy, a safeguard that legally protects enterprise customers from intellectual property risks associated with AI-generated content.

A cornerstone of Adobe's approach is the Content Authenticity Initiative (CAI), which Chris Duffey describes as "creating digital nutrition labels for content in the age of AI." This system of provenance tracking and verification underscores how a company's dedication to responsible engagement can inspire industry-wide transformation. As Duffey explains, "Transparency isn't just about disclosure. It's about enabling informed trust in digital content." By embedding trust mechanisms directly into its AI architecture, Adobe ensures that provenance tracking is not an afterthought but a fundamental pillar of ethical AI engagement.

As AI-generated media floods digital channels, consumers increasingly question the authenticity and origin of content. CAI directly addresses this challenge by providing a provenance-tracking framework, allowing businesses to embed transparent, verifiable credentials into their digital assets.

Though Adobe played a foundational role in launching CAI, the initiative has evolved into an open-source, industry-wide standard that enables organizations to verify content origins at scale. Through the C2PA technical standard, companies can embed tamper-evident credentials, documenting critical details such as AI tool usage, human oversight, and modification history. This framework is already integrated into Adobe Firefly, Microsoft's AI-powered image tools, and major news media workflows, reinforcing ethical AI engagement across industries.

For brands, CAI is more than a technical safeguard—it's a trust-building mechanism. Organizations such as *The New York Times*, Nikon, and Publicis Groupe have adopted CAI's standards to protect their audiences from deceptive AI-generated content while reinforcing credibility. As AI-generated misinformation becomes a growing concern, content transparency is no longer optional—it's a competitive advantage.

Adobe's responsible AI engagement strategy, including CAI, demonstrates how ethical AI practices drive both consumer trust and business value. Beyond efficiency metrics, the company actively monitors trust indicators, community sentiment, and real-world AI adoption feedback, reinforcing the idea that sustained transparency fosters stronger consumer relationships and long-term industry leadership.

Contextual Sensitivity → Cultural Intelligence

The third element of P.A.C.T. is Contextual Sensitivity, which becomes especially critical as AI-driven marketing engages global audiences. Adobe's approach to Firefly demonstrates how AI systems must evolve beyond localization into true cultural intelligence.

Instead of one-size-fits-all AI experiences, Adobe develops adaptive frameworks that respect cultural variations in creativity, ownership, and ethical standards. Some societies prioritize individual artistic ownership, while others value communal artistic heritage. Firefly is designed to adjust its recommendations, content structures, and even engagement strategies based on these cultural factors.

This level of cultural intelligence extends beyond language. It includes regional sensitivities, ethical AI perceptions, and content authenticity expectations. For instance, "transparency" isn't a universally understood or accepted concept—its interpretation varies by country, industry, and user demographic. Adobe's implementation of CAI reflects this nuance by adopting flexible frameworks that uphold ethical standards while respecting local regulations and expectations.

In the age of generative AI, where the distinction between human and machine creativity is increasingly blurred, cultural intelligence ensures that AI-driven marketing remains both ethical and effective. Companies that integrate culturally adaptive

AI strategies will be better positioned to engage diverse global audiences while minimizing ethical risks.

Trust → Authentic Connections

The final element of P.A.C.T. is Trust, the foundation of all ethical AI engagement strategies. Trust isn't a feature—it's a relationship that companies must actively cultivate.

Adobe's approach to Firefly offers valuable insights into how trust can be prioritized over short-term AI capabilities. One of their most groundbreaking decisions was to compensate Adobe Stock contributors whose work was used to train Firefly's AI models. This wasn't just an industry first—it was a statement: Human creativity must be recognized and rewarded in the age of AI.

Additionally, Adobe has established clear, accessible terms of service that explicitly protect creator rights. Unlike many AI companies that bury critical policies in legal jargon, Adobe's policies directly address creators' concerns, stating: "You own your content. Adobe makes no claims, and never has, to owning your content, regardless of how it was created."

This commitment to authentic connections extends beyond Adobe's own ecosystem. The company actively supports the Federal Anti-Impersonation Right (FAIR) Act, a proposed U.S. law designed to protect artists and individuals from AI-driven impersonation—such as deepfakes that mimic an artist's style, voice, or likeness without consent.

By advocating for policy reforms that safeguard creators, Adobe demonstrates that trust isn't just about ethical business practices—it requires industry-wide leadership. This is the ultimate lesson for AI marketers: Building trust means going beyond compliance to actively defend stakeholder interests.

The Implementation Framework: Making Ethics Actionable

Ethical AI engagement requires more than understanding principles—it demands scalable implementation. As Chris Duffey puts it, "The journey to ethical AI engagement isn't just a technical challenge—it's a trust-building exercise at every step." Adobe's phased approach offers a practical blueprint for organizations to follow.

Phase One: Foundation Building

The journey begins with "ethical infrastructure"—the basic systems and processes that enable responsible AI engagement. For Adobe, this meant developing clear policies about training data sources before they even began building Firefly. They established bright lines: no web scraping, no unauthorized data use, no ambiguous ownership claims.

Phase Two: Engagement Design

With the foundation in place, the next phase focused on designing engagement patterns that would build trust while delivering value. Adobe's approach here was particularly sophisticated, creating "trust-aware interfaces"—interaction patterns that adapt based on the user's trust level and engagement history.

For example, when a user first encounters Firefly, the system begins with basic, clearly bounded interactions, offering a limited set of features and functionalities. This initial phase focuses on familiarizing the user with the core mechanics and establishing a foundation of understanding. As users become more comfortable and see consistent value delivery, more sophisticated features become available, expanding the scope of possible interactions and creative outputs. This progressive engagement model ensures that trust and capability grow in tandem, allowing users to gradually explore the full potential of Firefly while minimizing potential overwhelm or misuse.

Phase Three: Scale and Integration

Scaling ethical AI engagement requires more than just expanding technical capacity. Adobe's experience demonstrates how organizations can grow AI capabilities while strengthening their ethical commitments. When Adobe began integrating Firefly across their Creative Cloud, Document Cloud, and Experience Cloud platforms, they faced a crucial challenge: maintaining consistent ethical standards across diverse use cases and user populations.

To address this, Adobe developed "ethical scaling principles"—guidelines that adapt to different contexts without compromising core values. For example:

- **Creative Cloud:** Individual creators using Firefly in applications like Photoshop and Illustrator benefit from built-in safeguards, including clear ownership policies and tools that help maintain transparency in content creation. Content Credentials ensure that artists retain ownership and attribution, fostering trust and protection for creative work.

- **Document Cloud:** In applications like Adobe Acrobat, Firefly powers AI-driven features such as document summarization and PDF editing. Here, ethical scaling focuses on protecting sensitive information and ensuring data privacy, especially in enterprise settings. By embedding safeguards for confidentiality and security, Adobe supports ethical AI use for professional and legal documents.

- **Experience Cloud:** In marketing and customer experience contexts, Adobe's AI capabilities enable personalized, data-driven campaigns. Ethical scaling principles prioritize commercial safety, ensuring responsible use of customer data and offering intellectual property indemnification to enterprise clients. This reinforces trust in AI-powered experiences while addressing the complexities of enterprise-scale marketing.

ETHICAL INTEROPERABILITY IN PRACTICE

Integration across platforms revealed the need for "ethical interoperability"—the ability to preserve ethical properties like ownership, usage rights, and provenance as content moves between systems. For instance, content generated with Firefly in Creative Cloud retains its Content Credentials when used in Experience Cloud for marketing campaigns or in Document Cloud for contracts. This ensures ethical continuity, maintaining transparency and trust as content flows through Adobe's ecosystem.

By embedding ethical practices directly into its AI architecture and scaling principles, Adobe demonstrates that expanding AI capabilities need not dilute ethical commitments. Instead, ethical engagement can serve as a foundation for innovation, ensuring trust remains intact as AI grows across diverse applications and industries.

Phase Four: Measurement and Refinement

Perhaps the most challenging aspect of ethical AI engagement is measuring its effectiveness. Adobe's approach here offers valuable insights into how organizations can evaluate both the technical and ethical performance of their AI systems. They developed a "dual metrics framework" that tracks both traditional performance indicators and ethical impact measures.

Traditional metrics showed impressive results: Enterprise customers reported up to 60 per cent time savings in content creation, with one Fortune 500 company projecting $5.5 million in potential savings. But Adobe went further, tracking what they call "trust metrics": creator participation rates, opt-in levels for advanced features, and community feedback on AI-generated content.

Crucially, they found that ethical engagement and business performance weren't in tension—they reinforced each other. Higher trust metrics consistently correlated with stronger business outcomes, supporting the premise we explored in Chapter 6 that trust isn't just an ethical imperative, it's a business advantage.

Phase Five: Ecosystem Development

The final phase of implementation moves beyond the organization's boundaries to help shape the broader AI ecosystem. Adobe's leadership in founding the CAI demonstrates how individual corporate action can catalyze industry-wide change.

This ecosystem approach is particularly crucial as we look ahead to the governance challenges we'll explore in Chapter 8. By actively participating in policy development, companies can help ensure that future regulations align with practical business needs while protecting stakeholder interests.

The ecosystem phase also involves "ethical network effects." As more organizations adopt ethical AI practices, the benefits multiply. This creates a virtuous cycle where ethical behavior becomes increasingly advantageous from a business perspective.

IMPLEMENTATION CHALLENGES AND SOLUTIONS

No implementation journey is without its challenges. Adobe's experience highlights several common obstacles and effective approaches to addressing them.

First is the challenge of balancing innovation with ethical constraints. Adobe reframed ethical constraints as design parameters to drive innovation. Smaller organizations can take similar steps by starting with manageable, high-impact changes, such as piloting transparency initiatives or using open-source tools for provenance tracking.

These efforts, combined with creative solutions, build "ethical momentum." Ethical momentum refers to the compounding effect of consistent ethical actions, where small steps build upon each other to create significant positive change over time. For instance, instead of building proprietary systems like Adobe's Content Credentials, consider using open-source tools to implement provenance tracking. Similarly, pilot transparency initiatives—such as clearly labeling AI-generated content—with a single department before scaling across the organization. These focused efforts, combined with creative solutions to constraints, can generate a ripple effect of trust that benefits the entire AI ecosystem.

Second is the challenge of stakeholder alignment. Different groups—creators, enterprise customers, end users—often have competing needs and expectations. Adobe's approach was to find "ethical common ground"—areas where stakeholder interests naturally align. Their focus on commercial safety, for instance, benefits both creators (protecting their rights) and enterprise customers (reducing legal risk).

The Adobe Example

As we've seen throughout this chapter, Adobe's approach to generative AI offers a masterclass in ethical consumer engagement. Now let's examine their journey in detail, understanding how they transformed ethical principles into a practical reality in one of technology's most challenging domains.

ETHICS IN ACTION
Adobe's Bet on Ethical AI Innovation

When Adobe began developing Firefly, their generative AI platform, they faced a fundamental challenge that echoes throughout the AI industry: How do you harness the power of AI while respecting creator rights and maintaining trust? Most generative AI companies had trained their models on vast datasets scraped from the internet, raising serious ethical concerns about copyright, consent, and fair compensation.

The easy path was available—following industry norms and training on publicly available data would have been faster and cheaper. Instead, Adobe chose what they call a "trust-first" approach that would set new standards for ethical AI engagement.

Reimagining AI Development

Adobe's first crucial decision was to break with industry convention regarding training data. Rather than mining the web for content, they built their training dataset exclusively from Adobe Stock and openly-licensed content where copyright had expired. This wasn't just an ethical choice—it was a strategic one that would influence every aspect of their AI engagement strategy.

This decision came with significant challenges. The training dataset would be smaller than those of competitors who scraped the web indiscriminately. Development would be more expensive, requiring licensing fees and creator compensation. Questions were raised as to whether the resulting AI could match the capabilities of systems trained on larger datasets.

But Adobe understood something fundamental about trust that we explored in Chapter 6: Trust isn't just about what you can do; it's about what you choose *not* to do. By publicly committing to ethical training practices and backing that commitment with concrete policies and compensation structures, they began building trust before Firefly generated its first image.

Ethical Innovation in Practice

Adobe's approach reveals several key principles for ethical AI engagement that any organization can apply:

- **Ethical by design**: This means building AI systems with ethical principles baked in from the start—like adding trust as a key ingredient, not a topping added later. Firefly includes built-in safeguards against copyright infringement and mechanisms to ensure commercial safety. These aren't bolt-on features, they're fundamental to how the system operates.

- **Transparency through action**: Adobe didn't just promise to respect creator rights—they developed concrete mechanisms to demonstrate that respect, such as the CAI

- **Commercial safety by design**: Recognizing that businesses need assurance when using AI tools, Adobe has taken steps to protect users from intellectual property infringement claims. Essentially, they're offering an "insurance policy" for content created with Firefly. If a user faces legal action because their Firefly-generated work is alleged to infringe on someone else's copyright, Adobe will step in to defend them and cover any associated costs. This commitment to intellectual property indemnification requires robust technical measures, but more importantly, it stems from Adobe's dedication to ethical AI training practices. By training Firefly on a carefully curated dataset of properly licensed content, they minimize the risk of generating infringing output, making such guarantees possible.

Measurable Impact

The results of Adobe's ethical approach have been remarkable, challenging the assumption that ethical constraints limit business success. But perhaps more important are trust metrics. Adobe's transparent approach has earned unprecedented support from the creative community. The CAI has grown to over 3,000 members, including major platforms like Microsoft and ARM Holdings, a leading designer of the chip technology that powers billions of devices worldwide.

How Adobe Advances Ethical AI Engagement

While examining Adobe's approach to ethical AI engagement through Firefly, we see both validation of proven practices and significant advances in implementation. "We didn't want to just follow best practices—we wanted to set new standards," explains Duffey. Let's examine how Adobe's approach compares and extends traditional ethical AI frameworks.

Evolution of Ethical Checkpoints

Traditional approaches to ethical AI often implement basic compliance checkpoints. For instance, we've seen companies deploy simple filters for problematic content or basic opt-in mechanisms. Adobe's system, however, represents a significant evolution in ethical AI architecture.

TRADITIONAL APPROACH

- Basic content filtering
- Simple compliance checks
- Limited user control

Adobe's Enhanced Framework represents a significant evolution beyond traditional approaches. Their system implements multiple verification layers that assess not only technical accuracy but also cultural sensitivity and ethical alignment. The framework includes:

- proactive copyright protection through automated scanning and verification systems
- commercial safety verification ensuring content meets business and regulatory requirements
- creator compensation mechanisms that fairly reward contributors
- cross-platform provenance tracking maintaining content authenticity across applications.

Advancing the Progressive Trust Model

Previous implementations of progressive trust, like the ones we examined earlier, often focused primarily on data collection and access. Adobe's approach expands this concept significantly.

TRADITIONAL PROGRESSIVE TRUST

- Stage 1: Basic data collection
- Stage 2: Enhanced features
- Stage 3: Full system access

ADOBE'S ENHANCED MODEL

- Stage 1: Licensed content training
- Stage 2: Transparent creation
- Stage 3: Creator compensation
- Stage 4: Industry standard setting

"We don't just ask for trust—we earn it through consistent, transparent value delivery," notes Duffey. This expanded model has driven remarkable results for enterprise customers.

Cultural Intelligence: From Matrix to Dynamic System

Previous approaches to cultural intelligence often relied on mapping cultural preferences to AI behaviors. Adobe's implementation through Firefly and the CAI represents a more dynamic, adaptive approach.

TRADITIONAL CULTURAL MATRIX

- Fixed regional preferences
- Static behavior mapping
- Limited adaptation

ADOBE'S DYNAMIC SYSTEM

- Real-time cultural context adaptation
- Cross-border creative rights protection
- Multi-stakeholder value alignment
- Adaptive transparency standards

"Cultural intelligence isn't just about avoiding mistakes—it's about creating genuine value across different contexts," Duffey explains. This approach has enabled Adobe to scale their ethical AI practices globally while maintaining consistent principles. Cultural intelligence, as Duffey explains, is a multifaceted concept that extends far beyond simply preventing cultural missteps. It involves the ability to generate authentic and meaningful value across a wide array of cultural contexts. This approach has been instrumental in allowing Adobe to successfully implement and expand their ethical AI practices on a global scale, all while upholding a consistent set of core principles.

In essence, cultural intelligence enables organizations to navigate the complexities of diverse cultural landscapes, ensuring that their practices and principles are not only understood but also respected and valued across different cultures. This goes beyond mere translation or adaptation; it requires a deep understanding of cultural nuances and the ability to integrate them into the very fabric of the organization's operations.

Metrics and Measurement: Beyond Basic KPIs

While traditional ethical AI implementations track basic metrics like opt-in rates and user satisfaction, Adobe has developed a more comprehensive measurement framework.

TRADITIONAL METRICS

- User opt-in rates (+44 per cent industry average)
- Trust scores (+28 per cent typical improvement)
- Reduced complaint rates (–15 per cent standard)

ADOBE'S ENHANCED ANALYTICS

- Creator ecosystem health
- Cross-platform content authenticity

- Commercial safety metrics
- Industry standard adoption
- Global creative rights protection

Adobe measures success not just through user metrics, but through their impact on the broader creative ecosystem. This comprehensive view has helped them build "ethical momentum"—where each successful implementation builds a foundation for further ethical advances.

Value–Trust Exchange: Redefining the Relationship

Traditional value–trust exchanges often focus on immediate user benefits. Adobe's approach introduces a more comprehensive model.

TRADITIONAL EXCHANGE

- Feature access for data
- Personalization for information
- Services for permissions

ADOBE'S ECOSYSTEM APPROACH

- Creator compensation
- Commercial safety guarantees
- Industry standard development
- Long-term ecosystem sustainability

Trust doesn't just grow, it multiplies when organizations create transparent systems that benefit everyone involved. Adobe's approach shows how ethical AI can amplify trust, creating a ripple effect of goodwill and collaboration.

Lessons for Implementation

Adobe's advances in ethical AI engagement offer several key lessons for organizations.

- Systemic integration:
  - Embed ethical considerations at the architectural level.
  - Build systems that scale ethics alongside capabilities.
  - Create mechanisms for continuous ethical evolution.
- Ecosystem thinking:
  - Consider all stakeholders in ethical frameworks.

- o Build systems that create mutual value.
- o Develop industry-wide standards and practices.
- Measurement evolution:
  - o Move beyond traditional metrics.
  - o Track ecosystem health indicators.
  - o Measure long-term ethical impact.
- Cultural adaptation:
  - o Build dynamic cultural intelligence.
  - o Create flexible ethical frameworks.
  - o Enable cross-cultural value creation.

Adobe's advances in ethical AI engagement provide a blueprint for organizations seeking to implement their own ethical AI strategies. However, translating these insights into practical action requires careful consideration of organizational context and capabilities. Let's examine how organizations can build the necessary infrastructure to support ethical AI engagement at scale.

Implications for Organizations

As we look toward the future, it's clear that consumer expectations around AI transparency and ethics are rapidly evolving. What Adobe recognized early—and what other organizations must now understand—is that these expectations aren't just about privacy or data protection. They extend to baseline questions of fairness, attribution, and value exchange.

Consider how Adobe's Content Credentials system has begun reshaping consumer expectations around digital content authenticity. Adobe's "digital nutrition labels" are creating new standards for transparency in AI-generated content. Organizations that fail to meet these emerging standards risk losing consumer trust and market position.

Building Ethical AI Infrastructure

One of the most valuable insights from Adobe's journey is the importance of ethical AI infrastructure. This isn't just about technical systems—it's about creating the organizational capabilities and processes that enable ethical AI engagement at scale. As we'll explore further in Chapter 8, this infrastructure forms the foundation for effective AI governance.

Adobe's approach to infrastructure goes beyond systems and processes, focusing on building organizational muscle memory for ethical decision-making at every level. This perspective has shaped Adobe's approach to three critical infrastructure elements:

- **Clear ethical boundaries:** Adobe's commitment to using only licensed content and compensating creators set a new standard for responsible AI development. While not every organization needs to build its own training datasets, every organization needs clear principles governing how they acquire and use AI capabilities.

- **Value exchange mechanisms:** Adobe's approach to creator compensation and commercial safety demonstrates how organizations can build trust through clear, concrete benefits. "Trust isn't abstract," notes Duffey. "It's built through consistent, verifiable actions that deliver real value to stakeholders."

- **Adaptive oversight systems:** As AI capabilities evolve, so too must ethical frameworks and engagement strategies. Adobe's continued development of the CAI shows how ethical infrastructure must grow and adapt alongside technological capabilities.

The Role of Industry Leadership

Adobe's experience also highlights the crucial role of industry leadership in ethical AI adoption. By developing and openly sharing standards through initiatives like CAI, they've helped create "ethical network effects" —where the value of ethical practices increases as more organizations adopt them.

This kind of leadership is increasingly important as AI technology becomes more powerful and ubiquitous. "Leadership in ethical AI isn't just about your own practices," Duffey emphasizes. "It's about elevating the entire industry." Adobe's approach to industry leadership encompasses three key dimensions:

1 **Standard setting:** Through the CAI, Adobe has established transparency standards that now influence the entire creative industry. This initiative demonstrates how one company's commitment to ethics can catalyze industry-wide change.

2 **Policy advocacy:** Adobe's support for the Federal Anti-Impersonation Right Act demonstrates the importance of proactive engagement with regulatory frameworks.

3 **Ecosystem development:** By creating systems that benefit all stakeholders—from individual creators to enterprise customers—Adobe has shown how ethical AI can create sustainable value networks. The company's approach to creator compensation and commercial safety has established new benchmarks for ethical AI business models.

Preparing for the Future

Looking ahead, several key trends will shape the future of ethical AI engagement. Drawing from Adobe's experience, we can identify critical areas of focus for organizations.

AI Technology Evolution

As AI capabilities grow more sophisticated, ethical frameworks must evolve in parallel. Adobe's continuous development of the CAI exemplifies this evolutionary approach. Their experience shows that today's consumers increasingly demand not just AI capabilities, but ethical AI capabilities that prioritize transparency and user value. Organizations must ensure their ethical frameworks and engagement strategies keep pace with technological advancement. Adobe's continuous development of the CAI provides a model for this kind of evolutionary approach.

The growing focus on AI regulation requires proactive preparation. Adobe's experience shows the value of getting ahead of regulatory requirements rather than scrambling to comply. Their work on content authentication and creator rights has positioned them well for emerging regulatory frameworks.

As AI becomes more prevalent in daily life, consumers are becoming more sophisticated in their understanding and expectations. Organizations must be prepared for increasingly informed and discerning customers who demand both transparency and tangible value from AI interactions.

Bringing It All Together

Throughout this chapter, we've explored how to transform ethical AI principles into practical engagement strategies that build lasting customer relationships. Adobe's journey demonstrates that successful AI engagement requires more than just technical excellence—it demands ethical commitment, transparent practices, and consistent value delivery.

KEY TAKEAWAYS

- **Infrastructure drives ethics**: Building robust ethical AI infrastructure is foundational to success. Organizations need systems, processes, and cultural practices that make ethical decision-making intuitive and scalable.
  Why it matters: Without proper infrastructure, ethical initiatives remain superficial and fail to create lasting impact.

- **Progressive trust building**: Successful ethical AI implementation requires a phased approach that builds trust incrementally through consistent value delivery and transparent practices.
  Why it matters: Organizations that rush AI deployment without building trust first risk long-term damage to customer relationships and brand reputation.

- **Cross-platform integration**: Ethical principles must be consistently applied across all platforms and use cases while adapting to different contexts and user needs.
  Why it matters: As AI systems become more interconnected, maintaining ethical consistency across platforms becomes crucial for building sustained trust.

- **Measurement beyond metrics**: Success in ethical AI requires tracking both traditional performance indicators and broader impact measures like ecosystem health and stakeholder trust.
  Why it matters: Organizations need comprehensive measurement frameworks to demonstrate that ethical practices drive business value.

Looking Ahead

The strategies outlined in this chapter—rooted in personalization, accountability, cultural intelligence, and trust—lay the foundation for effective governance. Without robust governance structures, even the best engagement practices can falter under the pressures of scaling and evolving technologies. In Chapter 8, we'll explore how organizations can sustain ethical practices through governance mechanisms such as AI ethics committees and cross-platform accountability frameworks. Together, these approaches ensure trust and innovation remain at the core of AI marketing strategies.

Food for Thought

1 What are the critical first steps in building ethical AI infrastructure for your organization's specific context and scale?

2 How can you design a progressive trust-building approach that aligns with your organization's capabilities and customer expectations?

3 What mechanisms would help ensure ethical consistency as your AI implementations expand across different platforms and use cases?

4 Which metrics would best capture both the business impact and ethical effectiveness of your AI initiatives?

Reference

Duffey, C. Video interview with Nicole M. Alexander, November 11, 2024.

8

Governance and Oversight in Ethical AI Marketing

Effective governance and oversight frameworks for ethical AI in marketing are essential to transforming aspirational principles into sustained, actionable practices. Earlier chapters have stressed trust, transparency, and a human-centric philosophy as cornerstones of responsible AI-driven marketing. Yet, these ideals cannot thrive in a vacuum. Governance structures serve as the connective tissue binding these principles to the realities of corporate life, ensuring that innovative AI solutions—such as those described in Chapter 4's exploration of market opportunities and Chapter 5's P.A.C.T. (Personalization, Accountability, Contextual Sensitivity, Trust) Framework—are not only profitable but also fair, compliant, and ethically sound.

The rationale for robust oversight arises from the increasing complexity and scope of AI applications in marketing. Advanced algorithms drive hyper-personalization, continuously refine predictive consumer analytics, and adjust pricing strategies based on intricate behavioral models. While these capabilities unlock tremendous value, they also elevate the risks of bias, privacy infringements, and manipulative targeting (Floridi and Cowls, 2019). Without structured governance, organizations may fall into ethical pitfalls despite having good intentions. As discussed in Chapter 6 and Chapter 7, the erosion of consumer trust can be swift and severe if AI-driven marketing ventures beyond acceptable ethical boundaries.

Governance frameworks offer a safeguard, translating high-level ethical commitments into daily decision-making processes. Far from hindering innovation, strong oversight enhances business resilience. Firms that rigorously apply governance measures are better positioned to win consumer confidence, preempt legal liabilities, and cultivate long-term loyalty. They create a stable environment for sustainable growth, ensuring that the brand's ethical standing becomes an enduring asset. This chapter charts a path forward, detailing how organizations can create internal governance structures, navigate regulatory obligations, design effective oversight mechanisms, engage stakeholders, measure progress, and learn from industry exemplars.

Internal Governance Structures and Roles

As discussed in Chapter 3's call for HCAI and Chapter 5's introduction of the P.A.C.T. Framework, meaningful ethical action begins with internal alignment. Internal governance structures are the backbone of any oversight program, ensuring that ethical principles do not remain theoretical but shape the day-to-day execution of AI-driven marketing initiatives.

Identifying Governance Pitfalls and Solutions

While governance frameworks are vital, several common pitfalls must be addressed:

- **Inflexibility in governance:** Governance structures can sometimes be too rigid, stifling creativity and quick decision-making. Organizations may struggle to balance the need for ethical oversight with the desire for flexibility in marketing campaigns.
  Solution: Adopt "flexible" governance frameworks that allow for creativity but provide clear ethical guardrails. Allow for innovation within defined ethical boundaries, ensuring business objectives are not sacrificed for ethical compliance.
- **Resistance from marketing teams:** Marketing teams focused on growth may resist governance that hinders their work. There may be concerns that increased oversight could slow down campaigns.
  Solution: Engage marketing teams early in the development of governance structures to align ethical guidelines with marketing objectives. Integrate ethics into the creative process to prevent friction.
- **Lack of accountability:** Poorly defined roles and responsibilities in governance structures can make it difficult to hold teams accountable for ethical failures.
  Solution: Define clear roles for accountability, ensuring that every department has a responsible party for ethical oversight. Implement escalation paths for ethical red flags.

Defining Clear Roles and Responsibilities

Many companies now appoint a Chief AI Ethics Officer or establish dedicated AI Ethics Committees that bring together marketing strategists, data scientists, ethicists, privacy officers, and legal advisors. This cross-functional composition ensures that strategic marketing objectives (explored in Chapter 1 and Chapter 4) are balanced against ethical considerations, legal requirements, and technical feasibility.

Effective governance requires a clear distinction between different types of oversight. Dataiku, a leading AI and data science platform, helps organizations operationalize AI while ensuring governance and compliance. As Triveni Gandhi

(2024), Responsible AI Lead at Dataiku, explains, "We distinguish three things—AI governance, which is the rules and processes that align your risk appetite with your objectives; responsible AI, which covers the machine learning and data analytics pipeline work needed for alignment in practice; and MLOps, which helps operationalize these principles." This layered approach creates clear accountability at every level of the organization.

Gandhi emphasizes that this structure isn't about restricting innovation but ensuring responsible ownership: "Each team involved in the development cycle should be documenting the checks done on models before moving them forward so there is a clear line of accountability in the AI pipeline." This clear line of responsibility encourages teams to take ownership of ethical considerations rather than treating them as someone else's problem.

Marketers play a critical role in these governance bodies. As the leaders driving AI applications with direct customer impact, marketers provide an essential perspective on balancing ethical priorities with engagement and revenue goals. Their involvement from the outset ensures governance policies reflect real-world implementation challenges.

Accountability and Escalation Channels

An essential component of oversight involves clearly defined escalation protocols. If a marketing analyst suspects algorithmic bias—such as consistently lower ad exposure to certain demographic groups—they should know immediately whom to contact. Documented escalation paths ensure that ethical red flags are promptly raised to the AI Ethics Committee or Chief AI Ethics Officer, rather than being ignored or suppressed. Regular internal audits and "ethics checkpoints" before major campaign launches embed these reporting protocols into the operational workflow.

A leading e-commerce platform successfully implemented an escalation protocol where suspected algorithmic issues were flagged by marketing teams and reviewed weekly by an AI ethics board. This approach uncovered a subtle bias in search result rankings, leading to corrective updates that improved fairness across demographics and boosted consumer trust.

Roles Beyond the C-Suite

While leadership roles like Chief AI Ethics Officer are critical, governance should extend to the grassroots level. Ethics ambassadors within teams can act as liaisons between oversight committees and operational staff, fostering a culture of accountability across the organization. Their proximity to day-to-day activities ensures that ethical considerations remain embedded in routine decision-making.

Cultural Integration of Governance

Ethical AI governance takes root when it becomes part of the organizational DNA. Incentive structures should reward employees who champion integrity and ethical alignment, even if short-term profits might be compromised. Regular ethics training, scenario-based workshops, and performance metrics tied to responsible AI use reinforce that everyone—marketer, developer, or executive—plays a role in sustaining the brand's moral compass. Over time, such cultural embedding ensures that oversight is not perceived as bureaucratic overhead but as a defining feature of corporate identity.

While cultural integration represents the ideal state of ethical AI governance, the path to achieving it reveals a fundamental tension between organizational controls and human behavior. Even the most thoughtfully designed frameworks can falter when they clash with practical business needs—a reality that becomes strikingly clear when we examine one of the most pressing challenges organizations face today: the emergence of shadow AI.

THE SHADOW AI CHALLENGE: WHEN GOVERNANCE MEETS HUMAN NATURE

Picture a marketing team racing to meet a campaign deadline. The company-approved AI tool is secure but limited. A creative director, frustrated by these constraints, opens ChatGPT on her personal phone to generate content variations—a scenario playing out in organizations worldwide.

This phenomenon, which Dr. Henry Shevlin of the Leverhulme Centre for the Future of Intelligence at Cambridge calls "shadow AI usage," represents a pressing governance challenge organizations face today (Shevlin, 2024). "A lot of employees do shadow AI usage... where the model that they get to access through work can't do all the fancy stuff that an LLM like ChatGPT can do. So when they want to do something like that they'll do it on their phone."

The implications run deeper than simple rule-breaking. When employees bypass official systems, they create invisible data flows that security teams can't monitor. Marketing departments are particularly vulnerable, given their constant need for creative content and rapid campaign iterations. A copywriter might paste confidential brand guidelines into an unauthorized AI tool, or a designer might upload proprietary visual assets to generate variations—all without malicious intent, but with potentially serious consequences.

The instinctive response might be to implement stricter controls. However, as we've seen throughout this book, effective governance isn't about building higher walls, it's about creating better pathways. Organizations need frameworks that acknowledge human nature and business realities while maintaining security. This might mean:

- implementing more capable approved tools that match external AI capabilities
- creating clear guidelines for what data can and cannot be used with AI tools

- developing rapid approval processes for new AI use cases
- building transparency through open dialogue about AI needs and limitations.

The challenge of *practical ethics* sets the stage for understanding how leading organizations balance control with enablement in the age of AI. Salesforce offers a compelling example of how ethical governance can align with human nature rather than restrict it.

In 2018, Salesforce established the Office of Ethical and Humane Use of Technology, a cross-functional initiative designed to embed ethical considerations across every stage of product development and deployment (Salesforce, 2020b). This team brings together professionals from engineering, product, legal, and policy backgrounds to ensure that emerging technologies reflect the company's values: trust, customer success, innovation, and equality.

At the heart of this initiative is Salesforce's Trusted AI Principles, which guide the company's AI development. These five core principles—responsibility, accountability, transparency, empowerment, and inclusiveness—provide a framework for evaluating AI systems and aligning them with ethical norms (Salesforce, 2023b).

Salesforce operationalizes these values through cross-functional collaboration, product reviews, and internal education. For example, the development of Einstein, Salesforce's AI platform, involved ethical reviews from early stages. These reviews included bias testing, privacy safeguards, and explainability checks to ensure that the AI's decisions could be clearly communicated to users (Salesforce, 2020a).

To deepen ethical awareness, Salesforce created an "Ethics by Design" learning module for employees. This program, available through Salesforce Trailhead, equips teams with tools to identify bias, design for transparency, and understand the social impact of their technologies (Salesforce Trailhead, n.d.).

In addition to internal structures, Salesforce established an AI Ethics Advisory Council, composed of external experts in academia, civil society, and industry. This body provides strategic guidance and helps anticipate emerging ethical risks tied to AI deployment (Salesforce, 2020b).

Salesforce also extends its ethical commitments into emerging areas like generative AI. In 2023, the company introduced a set of generative AI guidelines focused on safety, accuracy, transparency, empowerment, and sustainability to ensure innovation remains grounded in trust and responsibility (Salesforce, 2023a).

Salesforce's approach illustrates that building responsible innovation at scale is not only possible—it is imperative. By combining leadership, principles-based governance, training, and external oversight, Salesforce has created a robust model for embedding ethics into technology.

For marketing leaders looking to emulate Salesforce's approach, some key takeaways include:

- establish a dedicated ethics office or committee with cross-functional expertise

- develop actionable, principles-based AI governance frameworks
- integrate ethics reviews into product development from the outset
- mandate internal training programs focused on bias, fairness, and transparency
- engage independent experts to challenge assumptions and guide responsible growth
- continuously audit AI systems to align with evolving ethical and legal standards.

By making AI ethics a foundational part of governance and operations, marketing organizations can build trust with customers and stakeholders while harnessing the power of AI responsibly.

Addressing Internal Resistance and Facilitating Change

Even with a robust governance framework in place, organizations may encounter internal resistance when implementing ethical AI oversight. Such resistance can arise for various reasons: employees may fear increased scrutiny or penalties for mistakes; teams accustomed to growth-at-all-costs strategies might view ethical constraints as hindrances; or technical staff may be skeptical of non-technical oversight committees influencing algorithmic decisions. Addressing this resistance is critical to ensuring that governance practices not only take root but also thrive.

In cases of active resistance, leaders must be clear that core ethical standards and oversight protocols are non-negotiable. The organization's commitment to responsible AI is a strategic imperative, not an optional initiative. While open dialogue to surface valid concerns is always welcome, non-compliance with established governance policies is a serious matter that will be addressed accordingly. The focus should be on collaborative problem-solving to uphold ethical principles in ways that are as efficient and enabling as possible.

COMMUNICATING THE RATIONALE

Effective change management begins with clear, transparent communication about why ethical AI oversight matters. Instead of framing oversight as a top-down directive, leadership should explain how robust governance upholds the organization's values, protects consumer trust, and safeguards long-term brand health. Sharing real-world examples—from the e-commerce platform that neutralized bias in search rankings to the multinational retailer that improved demographic parity—illustrates that ethical governance can yield tangible business benefits and competitive advantages.

LEADERSHIP ENDORSEMENT AND ROLE MODELING

Leaders play a pivotal role in overcoming internal resistance. When executives and department heads publicly support ethical AI initiatives, they signal that these efforts are integral to the company's future. By visibly participating in ethics training sessions, incorporating governance goals into performance evaluations, and acknowledging employees who champion ethical considerations, leaders demonstrate that ethics is not an optional add-on but a core strategic priority.

INCLUSIVE POLICY DESIGN AND ITERATIVE FEEDBACK

Involving employees in the policy-making process helps quell skepticism. For instance, before finalizing escalation protocols or fairness metrics, organizations can host internal forums, soliciting feedback from data scientists, marketers, and front-line staff. By incorporating suggestions from these groups, the final policies are more likely to feel co-created rather than imposed. Encouraging employees to identify practical challenges and propose solutions also fosters a sense of ownership, reducing pushback by giving staff a voice in shaping the oversight framework.

TARGETED TRAINING AND PEER MENTORSHIP

Resistance often arises when employees feel unprepared to meet new ethical standards. Providing targeted training that clarifies expectations—such as how to recognize and report potential biases or how to use explainability tools—reduces uncertainty. Pairing employees who are new to ethical AI procedures with "ethics ambassadors" or peer mentors can also ease the transition. Mentors can share strategies for integrating ethical checkpoints into existing workflows, thereby demonstrating that ethical governance need not disrupt daily operations.

ALIGNING INCENTIVES AND RECOGNITION

Altering incentive structures can help overcome internal inertia. Recognizing teams that proactively identify and resolve ethical concerns—through commendations, awards, or internal communications—reinforces that ethical stewardship is valued. When employees see that raising potential issues or suggesting improvements is encouraged, not penalized, they are more likely to embrace governance efforts. Over time, these incentives shift the organizational culture so that employees view ethical oversight as a contributor to, rather than a constraint on, innovation.

CONTINUOUS LEARNING AND ADAPTATION

Change management is not a one-time event. Just as governance frameworks evolve in response to new regulations or emerging technologies, internal adoption strategies must also adapt. Regular surveys, feedback sessions, and reflection workshops help organizations gauge how well employees understand and support governance measures. If resistance persists, leaders can revisit messaging strategies, refine training materials, or introduce new peer-support initiatives. Demonstrating a willingness to iterate in response to employee feedback underscores that governance is a shared journey rather than a static mandate.

While theoretical frameworks provide a foundation for ethical AI governance, examining how leading organizations implement these principles in practice offers valuable insights. Drawing from my interview with Stephanie Bannos-Ryback, Head of Business Transformation at Ipsos North America (Bannos-Ryback, 2024), we explore how one of the world's largest market research firms built and scaled ethical AI governance across a global organization.

ETHICS IN ACTION
Ipsos' Governance Model

Operating across multiple jurisdictions and handling sensitive consumer data, Ipsos faced a complex challenge: ensuring their AI solutions complied with various data privacy regulations while maintaining consistent ethical standards globally. Their response offers valuable lessons for organizations seeking to implement robust AI governance at scale.

At the heart of Ipsos's approach lies a carefully structured governance system that balances central oversight with local autonomy. The foundation rests on a central strategic steering committee that provides unified vision and direction for the organization's AI initiatives. This committee works in concert with three specialized subcommittees, each focusing on critical aspects of AI implementation: infrastructure development, commercial solutions, and change management. Supporting these committees is a dedicated engineering team responsible for AI development and implementation, ensuring technical excellence aligns with strategic objectives and commitments to privacy, security, and quality.

Key governance components:

- Central strategic steering committee providing unified vision and direction.
- One central committee and three subcommittees (infrastructure, commercial solutions, change management).
- Dedicated AI engineering team ensuring technical excellence.
- Local execution teams with market-specific expertise.

Understanding that global standards must adapt to local realities, Ipsos established robust local execution teams. Market-specific liaisons serve as bridges between global directives and regional requirements, ensuring that AI implementations respect local regulations, client needs and talent skill sets. These liaisons work closely with champion networks embedded across various business units, creating a web of expertise that spans the organization. Local legal teams with region-specific AI knowledge provide additional support, offering crucial guidance on regional compliance requirements.

The compliance mechanisms supporting this structure are equally sophisticated. Rather than attempting a one-size-fits-all approach, Ipsos developed region-specific platforms that address local requirements while maintaining global standards. Strict data retention policies, carefully aligned with jurisdictional standards, ensure consistent data governance across regions. Regular security assessments and testing protocols provide ongoing validation of these systems, creating a dynamic security framework that evolves with emerging threats and requirements.

Critical success factors include:

- balancing global consistency with local market flexibility
- establishing clear lines of communication between global and local teams
- creating robust feedback mechanisms for continuous improvement
- maintaining rigorous security and compliance standards.

Perhaps most crucially, Ipsos developed robust knowledge integration systems that enable continuous learning and improvement. Their talent strategy includes a mandatory generative AI certification program, with leadership actively demonstrating its importance through early completion. Rather than relying solely on global e-learning, Ipsos emphasizes hands-on, use-case based training delivered by local champions who understand their teams' specific needs. These champions form a network that connects local teams to the central committee, ensuring bi-directional knowledge flow and rapid dissemination of best practices.

This approach allows Ipsos to focus on developing talent with deep domain expertise, creating a workforce that combines AI literacy with strong research discipline expertise— essential for maintaining their position as a trusted advisor to clients.

Key takeaways for organizations:

- Start with a strong central governance framework.
- Build in flexibility for local market adaptation.
- Invest in knowledge-sharing infrastructure.
- Maintain continuous feedback loops.
- Prioritize security and compliance from the outset.

While Ipsos's internal governance model demonstrates how organizations can effectively manage AI ethics within their operations, external oversight and regulatory compliance add another crucial dimension to ethical AI governance. As we'll explore next, navigating the complex landscape of global regulations requires careful attention to both internal controls and external requirements.

External Oversight and Regulatory Compliance

The external environment further shapes governance imperatives. Laws, regulations, and guidelines continually evolve to address the complexities of AI's role in society.

Marketers operating at scale cannot rely solely on internal principles; they must adapt to shifting legal landscapes and societal expectations, as covered in earlier chapters' discussions about trust and fairness from a consumer vantage point (Chapter 6) and ethical consumer engagement (Chapter 7).

Navigating Regulatory Complexity

Frameworks like the EU's GDPR and the CCPA impose stringent mandates on data usage, consent, and consumer rights to explanation and redress. Forthcoming regulations—such as the proposed EU AI Act—will likely classify AI systems by risk level, demanding heightened oversight for high-risk marketing applications that influence financial decisions or target vulnerable populations.

Organizations often struggle to maintain compliance across regions with disparate and sometimes conflicting regulations. For instance, while GDPR emphasizes user consent and the right to explanation, certain markets in Asia-Pacific prioritize data sharing for economic growth. Navigating these nuances requires a sophisticated and agile governance strategy.

Global and Cross-Cultural Adaptation

Firms with a global footprint must harmonize governance frameworks across multiple jurisdictions while accounting for cultural sensitivities and local norms. This requires balancing universal ethical standards with region-specific expectations for privacy, fairness, and transparency. Some strategies for global governance:

- **Tiered compliance architecture:** Develop a modular governance framework where core ethical principles (e.g. fairness, transparency) remain consistent globally, but regional adaptations address specific legal or cultural requirements. For example, ensure GDPR-compliant consent mechanisms in Europe while offering culturally resonant transparency reports in Asia.

- **Regional governance boards:** Establish regional ethics committees or advisory boards to provide localized insights. These boards can evaluate how marketing algorithms align with local norms and flag potential issues that might not be apparent from a global perspective.

- **Localized consumer engagement:** Tailor ethical AI practices to regional consumer expectations. For instance, a survey-driven approach in Europe might emphasize data protection, whereas an interactive workshop format in Asia could focus on building trust through community engagement.

A global beauty brand leveraged a modular governance framework to address privacy laws in the EU (GDPR) while respecting consumer norms in Asia-Pacific, where attitudes toward data sharing were more flexible. The approach included localized consent mechanisms and region-specific transparency reports, maintaining consumer trust across diverse markets. As a result, the company improved compliance metrics and earned recognition as an industry leader in responsible AI practices (Capgemini Research Institute, 2022).

Proactive Regulatory Engagement

While regulatory compliance is essential, organizations that engage proactively with policymakers can help shape the future of ethical AI standards. This forward-looking approach not only prepares businesses for emerging legal landscapes but also positions them as thought leaders in responsible AI innovation. By actively contributing to the regulatory process, companies can influence policy development, align their practices with future requirements, and demonstrate their commitment to ethical leadership.

Proactive regulatory engagement begins with advocacy. Organizations can participate in public consultations, offering feedback on draft legislation or sharing real-world use cases to highlight the practical implications of proposed rules. For instance, a financial services firm contributed to the European Union's draft AI Act by detailing the technical challenges of implementing explainability in high-stakes decision-making tools (European Commission, 2021). Such contributions allow policymakers to craft regulations that balance rigorous accountability with operational feasibility.

Engagement with industry associations further amplifies an organization's voice. Groups like the Partnership on AI provide platforms for collaborative dialogue, where companies can exchange insights and advocate for industry-wide standards. Members have influenced global conversations on AI transparency, fairness, and accountability. Similarly, the IEEE Standards Association develops internationally recognized ethical guidelines, offering businesses an opportunity to shape and adopt cutting-edge practices.

More broadly, this insight supports the merit and necessity of global collaborative approaches to AI governance and international standard setting, such as by the JTC1, IEEE, the OECD (2020) and the Global Partnership on AI, to help mitigate AI risks and support responsible use. It also underscores the importance of striving for consistency in AI regulatory and legislative frameworks across countries and markets. By actively participating in these global initiatives and advocating for harmonized standards, marketing leaders can not only ensure compliance but also contribute to shaping a more coherent and ethical AI landscape worldwide.

Consider the case of a healthcare company that collaborated with IEEE to co-develop standards for explainability in clinical decision-making tools. Through this partnership, the company not only ensured its systems met emerging regulatory expectations but also gained a competitive edge by enhancing trust among patients and stakeholders (IEEE Standards Association, 2021).

Global engagement is equally important. In regions with nascent AI regulations, such as Africa and South America, organizations have an opportunity to play a foundational role. In Africa, for example, businesses have supported policy creation by launching pilot programs and engaging in public–private partnerships that introduce best practices in data governance and AI ethics (UNESCO, 2021). In South America, where countries like Brazil are advancing data privacy laws inspired by GDPR, global companies have contributed to regional policy discussions by sharing insights from their experiences in more regulated markets.

Consider the approach taken by Microsoft in Africa. Recognizing the need for responsible AI development on the continent, Microsoft has actively partnered with various African governments to help shape AI policy frameworks. This engagement involves a multidisciplinary team from Microsoft, including researchers, engineers, and policy experts, collaborating with policymakers to identify and tailor policy interventions for cloud and AI technologies. Their goal is to ensure that AI is developed and used in ways that align with the specific needs and policy landscapes of African countries, fostering responsible innovation and societal benefit. This collaboration not only contributes to the development of emerging regulations but also demonstrates Microsoft's commitment to ethical AI practices in the regions where they operate (Microsoft On the Issues, 2024).

Proactive engagement enables organizations to shape the regulatory environment to align with ethical and practical considerations. By influencing standards and preparing for their implementation, businesses can build trust with regulators, stay ahead of compliance challenges, and lead in fostering responsible AI practices.

Regulatory Diversity: Navigating Regional Standards

AI governance and compliance are significantly shaped by the regulatory landscape in which an organization operates. As nations and regions develop their own frameworks for data privacy, AI accountability, and consumer rights, organizations must navigate these diverse requirements to ensure both compliance and alignment with ethical principles. This complexity necessitates a flexible and strategic approach.

The regulatory landscape surrounding AI in marketing continues to evolve rapidly, requiring organizations to develop adaptive compliance capabilities. This evolution is reflected in significant regional variations in the adoption of AI governance measures.

Figure 8.1 reveals striking regional differences in AI governance adoption. Latin America leads with an average of 2.51 measures per organization, followed by Asia (2.31) and Europe (2.26). These variations reflect not only different regulatory frameworks—such as GDPR in Europe and LGPD in Brazil—but also distinct approaches to balancing innovation with oversight.

North America's more moderate adoption rate (2.16 measures) suggests a different regulatory philosophy, while the significantly lower adoption rate in other regions

FIGURE 8.1 Regional adoption of AI governance measures

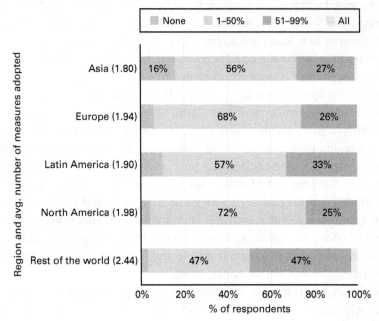

Adoption of AI-related fairness measures by region
Source: Global State of Responsible AI report, 2024 | Chart: 2024 AI Index report

(1.90) highlights the global disparities in AI governance maturity. These regional differences create unique challenges for global organizations implementing ethical AI marketing practices.

Regional Frameworks and Key Considerations

EUROPE: GDPR AND THE AI ACT

- **Key requirements:** The European regulatory framework for AI in marketing rests on two foundational pillars:

  o GDPR established core principles for data protection and privacy that remain crucial for AI marketing operations. It mandates explicit consent for data collection and processing, grants consumers rights to access their data and understand automated decisions and requires organizations to implement robust data protection measures.

  o The AI Act, introduced in 2021 and adopted in 2024, takes a risk-based approach to AI regulation. For marketing applications, it introduces several critical requirements:

    – Risk classification: Marketing AI systems must be evaluated to determine their risk level. Systems that could significantly influence consumer behavior or target vulnerable populations may be classified as high-risk, requiring additional oversight.

– Transparency requirements: Organizations must clearly disclose when AI systems are being used in marketing campaigns, particularly for AI-generated content and chatbots.

– Documentation: Technical documentation must detail how AI systems comply with requirements, including impact assessments and risk mitigation strategies.

– Human oversight: Organizations must maintain meaningful human oversight of AI marketing systems, especially for high-risk applications.

• **Challenges:** Organizations face several key challenges in complying with this dual framework:

o Integration of requirements: Marketing teams must ensure their AI systems simultaneously meet GDPR's data protection standards and the AI Act's risk management requirements.

o Explainability: The combined regulations create a higher standard for explaining how AI marketing systems work, requiring both data processing transparency (GDPR) and algorithmic impact disclosure (AI Act).

o Cross-border operations: Companies must navigate how these regulations affect marketing campaigns that extend beyond the EU while maintaining consistent ethical standards.

• **Opportunities:** Despite these challenges, the regulatory framework offers several advantages:

o Trust building: Compliance with these comprehensive regulations can serve as a strong trust signal to consumers.

o Competitive advantage: Organizations that embrace these requirements can differentiate themselves through demonstrated commitment to responsible AI use.

o Future proofing: The framework provides a clear roadmap for developing sustainable, ethical AI marketing practices that are likely to align with future global standards.

A major European retailer exemplifies successful navigation of these requirements. They implemented a unified compliance framework that:

• integrates GDPR data protection principles into their AI development lifecycle

• includes regular risk assessments aligned with AI Act requirements

• maintains detailed documentation of their AI systems' design and impact

• provides clear disclosures to consumers about AI use in personalized marketing.

This approach not only ensured compliance but led to a 20 per cent increase in consumer trust metrics and reduced regulatory compliance costs by streamlining their governance processes.

UNITED STATES: CCPA AND STATE PRIVACY LAWS

- **Key requirements:** The U.S. regulatory landscape for AI in marketing is evolving through state-level initiatives:
  - CCPA and its amendment, the California Privacy Rights Act, establish core requirements for data privacy and automated decision-making. These laws mandate clear disclosures about data collection and use, grant consumers rights to access and delete their data, and require businesses to honor opt-out requests for data sales and automated processing.
  - Other state laws, such as Virginia's Consumer Data Protection Act and Colorado's Privacy Act, create additional compliance requirements with varying standards for AI system transparency and consumer rights.
- **Challenges:** Organizations face several key challenges in this fragmented regulatory environment:
  - Multi-state compliance: Companies must navigate varying requirements across different states, often requiring sophisticated compliance frameworks that can adapt to local regulations.
  - Regulatory evolution: The rapid development of state-level privacy laws requires organizations to continuously update their governance strategies.
  - Implementation complexity: Without federal standards, organizations must determine how to apply consistent AI governance practices while meeting diverse state requirements.
- **Opportunities:** Strategic compliance with U.S. privacy laws offers several advantages:
  - Consumer empowerment: By providing clear data rights and control mechanisms, organizations can build trust through demonstrated respect for consumer autonomy.
  - Market leadership: Companies that exceed basic requirements often gain reputation benefits as privacy leaders in the U.S. market.
  - Cross-state preparedness: Organizations that build strong trust frameworks based on current state laws are better positioned to adapt as other states introduce similar legislation.

A leading U.S. technology company demonstrates effective navigation of this landscape. They implemented a comprehensive compliance program that:

- applies the strictest state-level requirements across all operations

- provides consumers with granular control over their data and AI-driven interactions
- maintains detailed documentation of AI systems and their impact.

This approach resulted in a 15 per cent increase in consumer trust metrics and established the company as a privacy leader in the market.

CHINA: PERSONAL INFORMATION PROTECTION LAW AND AI REGULATIONS

- **Key requirements:** Personal Information Protection Law (PIPL) establishes fundamental requirements for data handling and AI systems. These include stringent data localization rules requiring companies to store personal data within China's borders unless specifically approved for cross-border transfer. The law mandates explicit consent requirements and creates strict accountability mechanisms for data processing.
- China's AI regulations, including the Internet Information Service Algorithmic Recommendation Management Provisions, add specific requirements for AI systems:
  - Algorithm registration: Companies must register their algorithmic recommendation systems with authorities and provide detailed technical documentation.
  - Transparency mandates: Organizations must clearly inform users when AI systems are making recommendations or decisions.
  - User control: Consumers must have options to opt out of personalized recommendations and algorithmic decision-making.
  - Special protection: Enhanced safeguards are required for minors and other vulnerable populations.
- **Challenges:** Organizations face several significant challenges in this comprehensive regulatory environment:
  - Data localization complexity: Multinational organizations must establish separate data infrastructure within China while maintaining global operations.
  - Regulatory interpretation: Companies must navigate evolving interpretations of requirements as authorities provide ongoing guidance.
  - Technical integration: Organizations need sophisticated systems to ensure compliance with both data protection and AI-specific requirements.
- **Opportunities:** Compliance with Chinese regulations offers strategic advantages:
  - Local trust building: Strong compliance with PIPL and AI regulations helps build trust with Chinese consumers who highly value data protection and sovereignty.
  - Government relations: Demonstrating robust compliance can improve relationships with regulatory authorities, building trust at both consumer and institutional levels.

o Market access: Organizations that excel in compliance often find it easier to maintain and expand their presence in China's sophisticated digital market.

A major e-commerce platform demonstrates successful compliance navigation in China. Their approach includes:

- establishing dedicated data centers within China
- implementing comprehensive algorithm registration and documentation systems
- creating transparent user controls for AI-driven recommendations.

This strategy led to a 25 per cent increase in user engagement and strengthened their market position through demonstrated regulatory commitment.

INDIA: DIGITAL PERSONAL DATA PROTECTION ACT AND EMERGING AI FRAMEWORK

- **Key requirements:** India's evolving digital regulatory landscape combines established data protection with emerging AI governance.
- The Digital Personal Data Protection Act (DPDPA) creates a framework that balances innovation with consumer protection:
  o Data processing rules: Organizations must follow specific guidelines for collecting and processing personal data.
  o Consent requirements: Clear consent mechanisms are mandatory for data collection and AI-driven decision-making.
  o Cross-border data flows: The law establishes procedures for international data transfers while protecting national interests.
- India's emerging AI framework, including the National Strategy on Artificial Intelligence, adds considerations for AI deployment:
  o Ethical AI guidelines: Organizations must ensure AI systems align with principles of fairness and transparency.
  o Sector-specific rules: Different industries face varying requirements for AI deployment and oversight.
  o Innovation support: The framework encourages responsible AI development while protecting consumer interests.
- **Challenges:** Organizations must navigate several key issues:
  o Regulatory evolution: The rapid development of India's digital regulations requires flexible compliance strategies.
  o Implementation timeline: Companies must balance quick adoption with thorough implementation.
  o Market diversity: Organizations need to account for India's diverse consumer base and varying digital literacy levels.

- **Opportunities:** Early adoption of strong compliance frameworks offers significant advantages:

  o Market leadership: Organizations that proactively embrace data protection and AI governance principles can establish themselves as trusted pioneers in India's growing digital economy.

  o Consumer education: Companies can build trust by helping consumers understand their data rights and AI interaction options.

  o Future-ready operations: Demonstrating commitment to responsible AI use helps build long-term trust as India's regulatory landscape matures.

A leading Indian financial services company exemplifies effective compliance preparation. It has:

- implemented comprehensive data protection measures ahead of regulatory deadlines
- developed transparent AI disclosure systems for automated services
- created consumer education programs about AI-driven financial services.

Their proactive approach resulted in a 30 per cent increase in digital service adoption and established them as a trusted market leader.

Managing regulatory diversity is more than a compliance exercise—it's an opportunity to demonstrate a global commitment to ethical AI practices. Organizations that navigate this complexity effectively earn consumer trust, minimize legal risks, and position themselves as leaders in responsible innovation across diverse markets. By embracing flexibility and cultural intelligence, firms can turn regulatory challenges into a competitive advantage.

Effective Oversight Mechanisms

Turning lofty principles into tangible safeguards requires practical oversight mechanisms. Drawing on tools and strategies hinted at in Chapter 5's P.A.C.T. Framework, effective oversight mechanisms offer concrete processes for detecting, correcting, and preventing ethical failings.

Audits, Impact Assessments, and Certifications

Regular third-party audits, fairness assessments, and algorithmic impact assessments (AIAs) shine a light on biases or non-compliant practices that may lurk beneath complex AI models (Raji et al., 2020). These evaluations examine input data sources, training methodologies, modeling choices, and output distributions. Certifications from recognized bodies or adherence to standardized reporting guidelines (e.g. model cards) can further enhance credibility, signaling to consumers and regulators that the firm's oversight is robust and transparent (Mitchell et al., 2019).

Continuous Monitoring and Feedback Loops

Oversight is never a one-and-done exercise. Dynamic feedback loops alert decision-makers to emerging issues in near real-time. Post-deployment monitoring, combined with retrospective reviews and lessons-learned sessions, fosters a culture of continuous improvement. For instance, if an audit reveals bias in a recommendation engine, subsequent model updates incorporate improved training sets, stronger fairness constraints, and refined oversight mechanisms to ensure the problem does not recur.

For example an entertainment streaming platform implemented continuous monitoring for its recommendation algorithms. Feedback loops, informed by consumer surveys and sentiment analysis, identified that certain genres were under-represented in personalized suggestions. Updates to the algorithm resulted in a 25 per cent increase in user engagement and satisfaction.

Engaging Key Stakeholders in Governance

Governance gains strength and legitimacy when it embraces a broad array of perspectives. As Chapters 6 and 7 emphasized, ethics cannot be detached from the people it ultimately affects—customers, communities, and society at large.

Ethics-by-Design Workshops

Interactive ethics-by-design workshops can serve as participatory platforms where consumers collaborate directly with AI and marketing teams to define priorities. For example, when developing a personalization algorithm, workshops may highlight concerns about privacy or perceived manipulation, allowing teams to incorporate these insights early in development. This approach ensures governance reflects the lived experiences and expectations of end-users.

Consumer Trust Metrics

Establishing metrics that gauge public trust is essential to tracking governance success. Surveys, focus groups, and sentiment analysis on social media can measure consumers' perceptions of ethical practices. For instance, a retailer might survey customer attitudes before and after implementing explainable AI tools, using the feedback to refine its oversight framework.

A major telecommunications company conducted quarterly consumer trust surveys focused on its AI-driven customer service tools. Insights from the surveys revealed a need for greater transparency in how customer data was used. By implementing AI explainability dashboards, the company improved trust scores by 18 per cent within a year.

Empowering Consumers through Governance

Beyond safeguarding consumers, effective AI governance can actively empower them. When oversight frameworks prioritize transparency and fairness, they transform consumers from passive recipients of marketing content into informed participants who understand how and why certain messages reach them. For example, explainability dashboards and accessible privacy controls not only reassure consumers about data usage but also give them the means to influence their own marketing experiences. When a user can review the reasoning behind personalized recommendations or opt out of certain targeting methods, they gain agency, cultivating a sense of trust and respect.

This empowerment also aligns with emerging consumer expectations. As individuals become more aware of AI-driven personalization, they appreciate brands that explain their data practices, involve them in product design decisions, and invite feedback on ethical considerations. Over time, these participatory approaches strengthen the consumer-brand relationship, signaling that ethical oversight is not just a compliance measure but a value-added service. By inviting consumer voices into the governance dialogue, organizations foster an environment where informed choice, mutual respect, and meaningful collaboration become hallmarks of their ethical AI marketing efforts.

Indicators of Effective AI Governance

Metrics are a cornerstone of effective governance, providing organizations with the tools to track progress, identify areas for improvement, and demonstrate accountability. While ethical AI principles lay the foundation, quantifiable KPIs ensure these principles are translated into measurable outcomes. For AI-driven marketing, meaningful metrics must address fairness, transparency, compliance, and organizational responsiveness while being tailored to the unique needs of each organization.

To effectively measure fairness, organizations can track demographic parity in marketing outcomes. For example, a company might evaluate whether personalized recommendations are equitably distributed across demographic groups without disproportionate exclusions. Another metric could be the conversion rates for targeted campaigns across various demographics, assessed before and after a fairness audit to ensure inclusive practices (Raji et al., 2020).

Transparency is another critical area where metrics provide clarity. One such metric is explainability coverage, which measures the percentage of deployed AI models accompanied by documentation accessible to non-technical stakeholders (Mitchell et al., 2019). Additionally, organizations can develop a consumer trust index to monitor sentiment and trust levels, gathered through surveys, focus groups, or sentiment analysis of consumer feedback (Floridi and Cowls, 2019). These insights reveal how effectively transparency efforts resonate with audiences.

Privacy and compliance metrics are equally vital. Time-to-compliance for consumer data deletion requests can track how efficiently an organization adheres to privacy regulations, while incidence rates of data misuse provide a clear picture of internal safeguards' effectiveness. These metrics help organizations maintain trust while mitigating legal risks.

Organizational responsiveness completes the picture. Metrics like issue escalation response time measure how quickly ethical concerns are identified and resolved. A shorter resolution window demonstrates that governance frameworks are not just present but actively functioning.

Setting benchmarks is essential to interpreting these metrics effectively. For instance, a global retailer aiming for 90 per cent compliance with explainability standards within 18 months establishes both a clear target and a timeline for achieving it. Success metrics can be adjusted iteratively as governance maturity evolves, allowing for continuous improvement in response to new challenges.

A multinational retailer provides an illustrative case of metrics driving governance improvements. The company discovered through a bias audit that 40 per cent of its ad campaigns disproportionately targeted higher-income demographics, neglecting middle-income and rural consumers. In response, it introduced fairness constraints in its targeting algorithms and set KPIs to measure demographic parity. Within a year, these changes reduced disparities by 85 per cent, increased engagement by 15 per cent, and resulted in fewer consumer complaints about perceived exclusion (Raji et al., 2020). By aligning metrics with strategic goals, the company transformed its governance framework into a tool for equity and inclusion.

Metrics not only measure the effectiveness of governance efforts but also reinforce their value across the organization. By turning ethical commitments into actionable KPIs, businesses can ensure their governance frameworks are responsive, impactful, and continuously improving.

Benchmarking and Collaboration

Governance frameworks thrive on shared learning and industry-wide collaboration.

Standardization Efforts

Adopting standardized frameworks, such as ISO AI Standards or IEEE guidelines, ensures consistency across governance practices. These frameworks provide benchmarks for fairness, transparency, and accountability, offering a unified approach to addressing ethical challenges.

An automotive company adopted ISO AI Standards to ensure fairness in AI-driven advertising campaigns. The standardization streamlined compliance efforts across multiple regions, reducing operational complexity and earning recognition from consumer advocacy groups.

Shared Learnings

Collaborative initiatives such as the Partnership on AI and the World Economic Forum's AI governance projects encourage open dialogue. By sharing lessons learned, organizations can accelerate the maturity of their governance efforts while reducing the trial-and-error phase for others.

A consortium of retail brands collaborated through the Partnership on AI to establish best practices for mitigating algorithmic bias. The shared learnings enabled smaller firms to implement advanced bias-detection tools without incurring significant development costs.

Sustaining Effective Oversight

Establishing governance and oversight frameworks for ethical AI in marketing is not a one-time exercise but an ongoing journey. As technologies evolve, consumer preferences shift, and regulations adapt, so too must oversight structures. Regular policy reviews, continuing professional development, and ongoing dialogue with stakeholders are essential to keeping governance efforts relevant and impactful.

Ultimately, governance sustains the ethical principles introduced at the start of this book. By operationalizing trust, transparency, and human-centered values, organizations can confidently harness AI's potential. Governance becomes more than a safeguard—it becomes a catalyst for ethical excellence, facilitating innovation that respects the dignity of consumers, the mandates of regulators, and the aspirations of marketers.

Bringing It All Together

Throughout this chapter, we've examined how governance and oversight frameworks can transform ethical AI principles into sustained, actionable practices. Real-world examples and strategic insights reveal that effective governance is not just a safeguard but a driver of innovation, resilience, and consumer trust in AI-driven marketing.

KEY TAKEAWAYS

- **Principles to integration**: Effective governance structures ensure that high-level ethical principles become integral to daily decision-making. From internal alignment to accountability and escalation protocols, robust governance frameworks operationalize ethics across all levels of an organization.
  Why it matters: Practical governance mechanisms prevent ethical failures, promote fair outcomes, and build resilience against reputational and financial risks.

- **Collaboration**: Engaging diverse stakeholders—internal and external—enhances the legitimacy and effectiveness of governance frameworks. Interdisciplinary collaboration, consumer participation, and shared learning across industries ensure governance remains inclusive and impactful.
  Why it matters: Collaboration fosters trust, ensures policies address real-world needs, and accelerates the adoption of best practices, benefiting entire industries.

- **Measurability**: Quantifiable metrics and KPIs help organizations track and improve their governance efforts. Metrics for fairness, transparency, and compliance provide actionable insights and align ethical goals with business objectives.
  Why it matters: Measuring progress turns ethical commitments into tangible outcomes, ensuring accountability and continuous improvement.

- **Long-term success**: Strong oversight frameworks safeguard organizations from regulatory and reputational risks while enabling sustainable growth. Companies that embrace governance as a core business strategy gain competitive advantages, from consumer loyalty to market differentiation.
  Why it matters: Governance is not a constraint—it's a catalyst for trust, innovation, and enduring success in an increasingly AI-driven world.

Looking Ahead

With governance frameworks and oversight mechanisms now in place, the next step is ensuring they become an integral part of your organization's identity. In Chapter 9, we move beyond structural and regulatory measures to explore how companies can nurture an environment where ethical principles guide every decision. By focusing on leadership influence, talent development, and sustained commitment, we will examine how to weave these values into the very fabric of daily operations. As the market evolves and consumer expectations shift, Chapter 9 will provide insights for fostering a culture that not only supports but thrives on ethical AI practices.

Food for Thought

1 How can you translate broad ethical principles into specific, day-to-day practices within your AI marketing workflows to prevent bias and promote fairness?

2 Which metrics and KPIs would best capture the success of your AI governance efforts, and how can you set realistic targets to foster continual improvement?

3 How can your organization navigate global compliance demands while respecting regional cultural norms, without diluting core ethical commitments?

4 In what ways can interdisciplinary collaboration, including engagement with policy experts and consumer advocates, proactively shape emerging AI regulations and industry standards?

References

Bannos-Ryback, S, Video interview with Nicole M. Alexander, October 18, 2024

Capgemini Research Institute (2022) The AI-Powered Enterprise: Unlocking the Potential of AI at Scale, Capgemini, www.capgemini.com/insights/research-library/the-ai-powered-enterprise/ (archived at https://perma.cc/JC58-YHZQ)

European Commission (2021) Proposal for a Regulation Laying Down Harmonised Rules on Artificial Intelligence (Artificial Intelligence Act), European Commission, digital-strategy.ec.europa.eu/en/library/proposal-regulation-laying-down-harmonised-rules-artificial-intelligence-artificial-intelligence (archived at https://perma.cc/HA8F-VVWH).

Floridi, L and Cowls, J (2019) A Unified Framework of Five Principles for AI in Society, *Harvard Data Science Review*, 1 (1), doi.org/10.1162/99608f92.8cd550d1 (archived at https://perma.cc/44Z9-TF3V)

Gandhi, T, Video interview with Nicole M. Alexander, December 13, 2024

IEEE Standards Association (2021) *IEEE 7010-2020 – IEEE Recommended Practice for Assessing the Impact of Autonomous and Intelligent Systems on Human Well-Being*, IEEE Standards Association, standards.ieee.org/ieee/7010/7718/ (archived at https://perma.cc/E77Z-E4HP)

Microsoft On the Issues (2024) Governing AI in Africa: Policy frameworks for a new frontier, January 28, blogs.microsoft.com/on-the-issues/2024/01/28/governing-ai-in-africa-policy-framework/ (archived at https://perma.cc/62G6-YB24)

Mitchell, M, Wu, S, Zaldivar, A, Barnes, P, Vasserman, L, Hutchinson, B, Spitzer, E, Raji, I D, and Gebru, T (2019) Model Cards for Model Reporting, *Proceedings of the Conference on Fairness, Accountability, and Transparency (FAT)*, 220–229, doi.org/10.1145/3287560.3287596 (archived at https://perma.cc/H8EC-3W8U)

OECD (2020) OECD Principles on Artificial Intelligence, OECD, www.oecd.org/going-digital/ai/principles (archived at https://perma.cc/E57Z-ZTBT)

Raji, I D, Smart, A, White, R N, Mitchell, M, and Gebru, T (2020) Closing the AI Accountability Gap: Defining an End-To-End Framework for Internal Algorithmic Auditing, *Proceedings of the 2020 Conference on Fairness, Accountability, and Transparency (FAT)*, 33–44, doi.org/10.1145/3351095.3372873 (archived at https://perma.cc/WC3W-QX5R)

Salesforce (2020a) How Salesforce Infuses Ethics into Its AI, August 5, 2020, www.salesforce.com/news/stories/how-salesforce-infuses-ethics-into-its-ai/ (archived at https://perma.cc/JG9E-TDJA)

Salesforce (2020b) How Salesforce Is Building a Culture of Responsible Technology— and Why It Matters, August 4, 2020, www.salesforce.com/news/stories/how-salesforce-is-building-a-culture-of-responsible-technology-and-why-it-matters/ (archived at https://perma.cc/85ND-LRZ6)

Salesforce (2023a) Generative AI: 5 Guidelines for Responsible Development, February 7, 2023, www.salesforce.com/news/stories/generative-ai-guidelines/ (archived at https://perma.cc/3UKN-2ZXX)

Salesforce (2023b) Meet Salesforce's Trusted AI Principles, April 28, 2023, www.salesforce.com/blog/meet-salesforces-trusted-ai-principles/ (archived at https://perma.cc/3FY5-NLP6)

Salesforce Trailhead (n.d.) Define Ethics by Design, trailhead.salesforce.com/content/learn/modules/ethics-by-design/define-ethics-by-design (archived at https://perma.cc/VU2H-BU6Z)

Shevlin, H, Video interview with Nicole M. Alexander, November 22, 2024

UNESCO (2021) Recommendation on the Ethics of Artificial Intelligence, UNESCO, en.unesco.org/artificial-intelligence/ethics (archived at https://perma.cc/7URS-P36C)

PART FOUR

Leading with Integrity and Future-Proofing Marketing

9

Cultivating a Culture of Ethics

Implementing ethical AI in marketing requires more than governance frameworks and technical safeguards. It demands a cultural foundation that integrates shared values, beliefs, and behaviors into how organizations operate daily. Organizational culture determines whether ethical practices take root or falter, even in the presence of robust governance systems.

Studies consistently underscore the importance of culture. For instance, Deloitte's *State of Ethics and Trust in Technology* report highlights that while many companies are beginning to test or use generative AI, more than half (56 per cent) of respondents are uncertain if their organizations have ethical standards guiding its use. This uncertainty underscores the need for a strong ethical culture to navigate the complexities of AI implementation (Deloitte, 2023).

Similarly, research from *MIT Sloan Management Review* reveals that while many organizations are developing programs to manage AI tools responsibly, a significant number remain unprepared to address the risks posed by third-party and generative AI tools. This gap highlights the critical role of organizational culture in fostering ethical AI practices (MIT Sloan Management Review, 2023).

Building on the discussions from Chapter 8 on governance and Chapter 5 on the P.A.C.T. principles, this chapter offers actionable guidance for cultivating an ethical AI culture. It emphasizes leadership's role, cross-functional collaboration, comprehensive training, and embedding ethics into daily organizational systems. These strategies collectively lay the groundwork for sustained cultural transformation in the age of AI.

The Elements of Ethical AI Culture

Research in organizational behavior identifies several critical elements that distinguish companies with strong ethical AI cultures. A comprehensive study by MIT's Media Lab examining 150 organizations over three years found that successful ethical AI cultures share four key characteristics: clear values, psychological safety, distributed responsibility, and continuous learning.

Clear Values and Ethical Principles

One of the most critical elements of ethical AI culture is the establishment of clear values and principles that are actionable and integrated into daily operations. Best practices in organizational ethics consistently show that translating abstract principles into concrete behavioral expectations significantly improves their adoption in day-to-day decision-making. For example, Microsoft's AI ethics guidelines provide specific instructions for different roles, such as data minimization protocols for data scientists and transparency standards for marketing teams. These tangible guidelines help employees understand how to operationalize ethical principles in their roles.

Defining ethical behavior in practical terms ensures consistency and eliminates ambiguity. Ethical guidelines must not only outline what the organization stands for but also specify what employees should and should not do, thereby aligning ethical values with business goals.

Psychological Safety

Psychological safety—the belief that employees can voice concerns without fear of retribution—is a cornerstone of an ethical AI culture. In the context of ethical AI, this safety enables employees to raise ethical concerns proactively, which can prevent minor issues from escalating into major problems.

Stanford University's Human-Centered AI Institute found that organizations with formal mechanisms for escalating ethical concerns, such as anonymous reporting tools or structured feedback processes, identified and mitigated AI-related risks up to three months earlier than those without such systems (Stanford HAI, 2023). Companies like IBM have pioneered ethics escalation paths that ensure reported concerns are addressed promptly, fostering an environment of trust and collaboration.

Distributed Responsibility

Ethical AI culture cannot rest solely with leadership or ethics committees—it must permeate every level of the organization. According to a longitudinal study of Fortune 500 companies, organizations that distributed responsibility for ethical AI across all functions were 3.5 times more likely to avoid major controversies. Salesforce exemplifies this approach by embedding "ethics owners" within each product and marketing team, ensuring ethical considerations are addressed during every stage of development and deployment.

This decentralized model ensures that ethical accountability becomes a shared responsibility rather than a siloed function. When all employees understand their role in upholding ethical AI standards, ethical practices become a natural part of the organization's operations.

Commitment to Learning

Ethical AI requires a mindset of continuous learning. Organizations must view ethics as an evolving discipline, adapting to new challenges as they arise. Research from MIT Sloan Management Review found that companies investing at least 3 per cent of their AI budgets in ethics training and development significantly reduced ethical missteps and recovered more effectively from challenges (MIT Sloan Management Review, 2023).

Continuous learning initiatives include:

- regular ethics training programs
- real-world example discussions to analyze past successes and failures.
- cross-functional knowledge-sharing forums
- partnerships with academic institutions to access cutting-edge research.

By institutionalizing continuous learning, organizations create a workforce that is both knowledgeable and prepared to navigate the complexities of ethical AI.

Leadership's Role in Cultural Transformation

Leadership plays an outsized role in shaping an organization's ethical AI culture. Employees are 2.5 times more likely to report ethical concerns when they perceive their leaders as committed to ethical behavior (Ethics & Compliance Initiative, 2023). Leaders who prioritize ethics inspire trust, set the tone for cultural transformation, and model the behaviors they wish to see across their organizations.

Setting the Ethical Tone

Leaders influence ethical culture through direct communication, resource allocation, and behavioral modeling. A study by Edmondson and Chamorro-Premuzic (2021) demonstrated that organizations whose leaders actively modeled ethical decision-making were four times more likely to implement ethical AI practices successfully.

Satya Nadella, CEO of Microsoft, exemplifies this approach. Beyond making public commitments to responsible AI, Nadella has allocated substantial resources to ethical AI initiatives and reviews key projects through an ethical lens. This leadership has helped Microsoft develop one of the most comprehensive ethical AI frameworks in the technology industry.

Building Trust through Transparency

Transparency is a foundational element of ethical leadership. Leaders who openly discuss AI challenges and failures foster a culture of trust.

Adobe's leadership team has embraced this approach in their development of generative AI tools. By being upfront about the challenges they've encountered and the trade-offs made, they've cultivated trust among employees and stakeholders. This transparency has also encouraged greater participation in ethical decision-making processes throughout the organization.

Cross-Functional Collaboration

Ethical AI requires breaking down silos and fostering collaboration across marketing, technology, legal, and compliance teams. Research from MIT Sloan School of Management reveals that organizations with strong cross-functional collaboration are 2.8 times more likely to identify ethical issues early (2023).

Creating Integrated Teams

Cross-functional teams that bring together diverse perspectives are essential for ethical AI implementation. Research by Madaio et al. (2020) highlights how organizations benefit from involving representatives from multiple functions—such as product management, legal, data science, and ethics—in the AI development process. These integrated teams help ensure that fairness and ethical concerns are considered from the earliest stages, improving accountability and reducing the risk of harm. For example, IBM's cross-functional teams conduct ethics reviews throughout the development cycle to ensure responsible AI deployment.

Establishing Shared Goals and Metrics

Shared objectives help align cross-functional efforts. Research shows that organizations with integrated ethical and business metrics achieve significantly better compliance outcomes while maintaining strong business performance. These metrics might include measures of AI fairness, transparency, and trust alongside traditional KPIs.

For instance, IBM developed an "AI Ethics Index" that tracks metrics such as algorithmic bias, transparency scores, and user trust ratings. This integrated approach ensures that ethical considerations are prioritized across all functions.

Fostering Collaborative Problem-Solving

The Harvard Business Review's study of ethical AI implementation found that organizations using structured collaborative problem-solving methods were twice as likely to develop effective solutions to ethical challenges (Davenport and Miller, 2023). These methods include:

- regular cross-functional ethics reviews
- joint risk assessment protocols
- collaborative ethical impact assessments
- shared decision-making frameworks.

Training and Capability Building

Cultivating an ethical AI culture requires a comprehensive approach to building organizational capabilities. Training programs should go beyond basic compliance to develop ethical reasoning and technical literacy, equipping employees with the skills needed to navigate complex AI-related challenges.

Developing Ethical Decision-Making Capabilities

Traditional ethics training often falls short because it focuses solely on rules rather than cultivating decision-making skills. Organizations that employ case-based, experiential learning approaches consistently achieve better outcomes in ethical decision-making than those using standard compliance-focused methods.

Effective training programs incorporate:

- **Real-world scenarios:** Employees analyze actual cases that reflect ethical dilemmas they may encounter in their roles
- **Structured frameworks:** Participants use ethical frameworks to evaluate scenarios, encouraging critical thinking and reasoned decision-making
- **Guided feedback:** Facilitators provide tailored feedback to reinforce ethical reasoning skills.

For example, Mastercard's AI ethics training presents marketing teams with real-world dilemmas, such as determining the ethical use of sensitive demographic data for targeting. These exercises teach practical judgment and foster a deeper understanding of ethical principles.

Building Technical Literacy

Marketers need foundational technical knowledge to identify and address potential ethical risks in AI systems. Organizations providing basic AI literacy training to non-technical teams consistently identify more ethical issues during project planning than those without such training.

Key areas of focus for technical training include:

- understanding machine learning fundamentals
- recognizing common sources of algorithmic bias
- ensuring data privacy and security
- identifying the limitations of AI systems.

This technical literacy ensures that marketing professionals can collaborate effectively with technical teams, asking the right questions and flagging potential issues before they escalate.

Creating Ethical Awareness

Beyond formal training, organizations must develop ongoing methods for raising ethical awareness. Recent research shows companies implementing regular ethics discussions experience significant reductions in ethical incidents—with a 2024 study finding that organizations with consistent ethics workshops reported 70 per cent fewer security incidents compared to those relying solely on compliance-based training (Keepnet Labs, 2024).

Effective approaches include:

- **Ethics office hours:** Regular sessions where teams can discuss ethical concerns with experts
- **Real-world example reviews:** Monthly discussions of ethical AI successes and failures
- **Interactive workshops:** McKinsey's 2025 research shows 71 per cent of employees trust their employers to deploy AI ethically, highlighting the importance of employer-led discussions (McKinsey, 2025)
- **Practical simulations:** Security awareness studies indicate trained users are 30 per cent less likely to engage in risky technology behaviors when training includes realistic scenarios (Keepnet Labs, 2024).

Measuring Training Effectiveness

Traditional training metrics like completion rates provide little insight into actual behavior change.

Using multiple measurement approaches to assess training impact is optimal and includes:

- pre-/post-assessments of ethical reasoning skills
- behavioral observation in simulated scenarios
- analysis of actual decision-making patterns
- tracking of ethical issue reporting rates
- long-term monitoring of ethical outcomes.

Organizations that implement comprehensive measurement approaches are 2.4 times more likely to sustain improvements in ethical behavior compared to those using basic metrics alone.

Implementation Strategies

Successfully embedding ethical AI practices within an organization is a multi-pronged endeavor that demands careful attention to execution. While the principles and frameworks for ethical AI provide a foundational blueprint, the true impact lies in their practical application across all levels of the organization. The journey of integrating ethical considerations into the fabric of a company's culture and processes requires a strategic and thoughtful approach to implementation.

Creating a Roadmap for Change

While frameworks and roadmaps provide crucial structure, organizations must remain adaptable in their approach to cultural transformation. As we saw with Ipsos's adaptable governance structure in Chapter 8, organizations must build flexibility into their approaches to keep pace with rapidly evolving AI capabilities. This balance between structure and adaptability becomes particularly crucial when implementing cultural changes across diverse teams and markets. The key is to create "flexible framework" approaches that provide clear direction while allowing for adaptation based on team needs, market conditions, and emerging technologies. Just as Ipsos developed region specificity while maintaining global standards, organizations must find ways to promote consistent ethical practices while respecting local team dynamics and cultural nuances.

Successful ethical AI transformations have four critical phases that organizations must navigate:

- **Phase 1:** Foundation building (3–6 months)
  - o Assessing current cultural state
  - o Defining desired future state
  - o Identifying key stakeholders
  - o Establishing baseline metrics

- **Phase 2:** Initial implementation (6–12 months)
  - o Launching pilot programs
  - o Training key personnel
  - o Testing new processes
  - o Gathering early feedback
- **Phase 3:** Broad deployment (12–18 months)
  - o Rolling out organization-wide initiatives
  - o Scaling successful pilots
  - o Adjusting based on learnings
  - o Building momentum
- **Phase 4:** Reinforcement and refinement (ongoing)
  - o Embedding new practices
  - o Measuring progress
  - o Making adjustments
  - o Celebrating successes

Managing Resistance to Change

One of the most significant challenges in cultural transformation is overcoming resistance. Research on organizational change indicates that resistance to ethical AI initiatives typically stems from three primary sources (Kotter, 2023):

1 Fear of reduced performance or efficiency.

2 Uncertainty about new responsibilities.

3 Attachment to existing practices.

Successful organizations address these concerns through what change management scholars call the "Three E's":

- **Education:** Helping people understand why change is necessary.
- **Empowerment:** Giving them tools and authority to implement changes.
- **Encouragement:** Recognizing and rewarding progress.

Building Support Systems

A fundamental aspect of successfully embedding ethical AI within an organization is the establishment of robust support systems. It's widely understood that significant cultural transformations require these underlying structures to take root and thrive. These support systems often include interconnected elements designed to empower employees and facilitate the adoption of new practices. Key components involve actively engaged networks of change champions and readily accessible resource centers, both of which play distinct yet complementary roles in fostering a culture of ethical AI.

CHANGE CHAMPIONS NETWORK

Organizations that establish networks of change champions—influential employees who model and promote desired behaviors—achieve their cultural transformation goals 2.3 times more frequently than those relying solely on top-down directives. These networks should include:

- representatives from different levels and functions
- respected informal leaders
- technical experts
- ethics specialists.

RESOURCE CENTERS

Successful organizations create central repositories for:

- training materials
- decision frameworks
- use cases
- best practices
- tools and templates.

Companies with well-resourced ethics centers see 47 per cent higher engagement in ethical initiatives compared to those without dedicated resources.

Measuring Progress

Organizations must establish comprehensive metrics to evaluate their ethical AI initiatives. The *MIT Sloan Management Review* (2023) identifies three key categories of metrics that are essential for measuring progress:

- **Leading indicators:** Metrics such as employee engagement in ethics training, the frequency of reported concerns, and cross-functional collaboration levels serve as early warning signs of potential risks.
- **Behavioral metrics:** Tracking decision-making patterns, resource allocation, and communication practices helps assess whether ethical principles are being integrated into daily operations.
- **Outcome measures:** Indicators like customer trust scores, regulatory compliance rates, and ethical incident trends provide insights into the overall effectiveness of ethical AI programs.

Companies like IBM treat ethical audits with the same rigor as financial audits, regularly publishing findings and implementing corrective actions to address any gaps. This level of transparency builds trust among stakeholders and ensures accountability.

Sustaining Cultural Change

Creating an ethical AI culture is only the first step; maintaining it over time is the real challenge, especially in fast-paced marketing environments. For marketers, the stakes are high. The ethical reputation of AI systems not only affects internal culture but also directly impacts brand credibility, customer trust, and overall market positioning. Marketers must, therefore, adopt robust mechanisms to ensure that ethical AI practices are sustained well beyond the initial rollout of policies and training sessions.

The foundation for this sustained change lies in what organizational theorists describe as institutional embedding—integrating ethical principles so deeply into the fabric of operations that they become as routine as daily decision-making. For marketing professionals, this means that ethical considerations should be incorporated into every step of the campaign and product lifecycle, from the initial ideation of AI-powered customer segmentation to the execution of data-driven advertising campaigns. This integration is not just about compliance; it is about building long-term trust with customers and differentiating the brand in a crowded market.

One effective strategy is to weave ethical review processes into the decision-making fabric. For instance, just as leading tech firms have implemented formal ethics checkpoints for major AI projects, marketers can adopt a similar practice by requiring an ethics assessment as part of campaign approval processes. This ensures that ethical considerations are addressed early on, preventing potential crises that could damage a brand's reputation. As Peter Drucker's well-known adage reminds us, "what gets measured gets managed" (Drucker, 2007). In the marketing context, performance management must extend beyond traditional metrics like efficiency and revenue. Marketers need to develop new KPIs that capture ethical performance—such as transparency scores, fairness in data usage, and customer sentiment regarding ethical practices—which can be tracked over time to ensure the long-term success of ethical initiatives.

By combining conventional business metrics with ethical indicators, marketers can ensure that performance is evaluated holistically. For example, a campaign's success might be measured not only by its conversion rates but also by its impact on brand trust and public perception of the company's commitment to ethical practices. This dual focus reinforces the message that ethical behavior is integral to success, not an optional add-on.

Risk management is another critical aspect of sustaining ethical AI practices in marketing. In a field where rapid response to market changes is essential, establishing clear thresholds for intervention when ethical standards slip is vital. Techniques such as "premortem" analysis, where teams envision potential failures before they occur and work backward to design preventive measures, can be invaluable. These proactive strategies allow marketers to identify and mitigate risks—such as the misuse of consumer data or biased algorithmic recommendations—before they escalate into public relations crises.

Moreover, aligning individual and team incentives with ethical objectives can reinforce a culture that prioritizes long-term reputation over short-term gains. Marketers should look to integrate ethical behavior into performance evaluations and recognition programs. When employees are rewarded for ethical innovation and effective risk management, they are more likely to incorporate these practices into their everyday work. For marketing teams, this might involve celebrating campaigns that have effectively balanced commercial goals with ethical considerations or recognizing individuals who have championed ethical decision-making in high-pressure environments.

The process of sustaining an ethical culture also hinges on continuous measurement and reflection. Just as financial audits are a routine part of business, ethical audits should be conducted with equal rigor. Implementing a comprehensive measurement framework—one that tracks leading indicators (such as engagement with ethics training and early warnings from internal audits), behavioral metrics (like decision patterns and resource allocation), and outcome measures (including customer trust scores and compliance rates)—ensures that ethical performance remains visible and actionable. Regular reflection sessions, whether through quarterly ethics reviews or ad hoc debriefs after major projects, provide an opportunity to learn from successes and setbacks alike.

Finally, communication is the lifeblood of a sustained ethical culture. For marketers, transparent and regular communication about ethical initiatives not only reinforces internal alignment but also serves as a powerful signal to external stakeholders. Consistent messaging about the company's commitment to ethical AI can enhance customer engagement and foster a strong, trusted brand image. As research in organizational communication has shown, when employees and customers alike understand and support ethical priorities, the organization is far more resilient in the face of change.

Sustaining an ethical AI culture is not a one-time effort but a continuous journey—one that is particularly critical for marketing organizations tasked with shaping public perception and building lasting brand value. By institutionalizing ethical practices through integrated decision-making processes, comprehensive performance management systems, proactive risk management, and open communication, marketers can ensure that their ethical initiatives are not only implemented but also enduring. This approach not only mitigates risk but also positions the brand as a leader in ethical innovation—a significant competitive advantage in today's market.

Future-Proofing Ethical AI Culture

Organizations need to ensure their ethical cultures can adapt and grow with the changing technological landscape. Companies with forward-looking cultural practices are significantly more likely to successfully navigate emerging ethical challenges in AI implementation. These organizations understand that ethical AI is not a static achievement, but a dynamic, continuous journey requiring institutional agility and foresight.

The pace of AI advancement creates a foundational challenge: ethical frameworks developed for today's AI capabilities may quickly become obsolete as the technology evolves. Organizations that excel at ethical AI implementation approach this challenge systematically, building cultural practices that anticipate rather than merely react to emerging ethical issues. They cultivate workforces that value ethical considerations as integral to innovation rather than viewing ethics as a compliance hurdle.

This forward-looking approach involves embedding ethical thinking throughout the organization, from leadership strategy to daily operations. Companies that successfully navigate ethical challenges typically establish clear values that guide decision-making, invest in continuous ethical education, and create governance structures that adapt to emerging technologies. They recognize that building an ethical culture around AI isn't merely about preventing harm—it's about creating sustainable competitive advantage through responsible innovation that builds trust with customers, employees, and society.

Anticipating Future Challenges

Organizations need systematic approaches to identifying and preparing for emerging ethical issues. The *Journal of Business Ethics'* longitudinal study of AI-driven companies reveals three critical practices that help organizations stay ahead of ethical challenges: horizon scanning, scenario planning, and stakeholder engagement (Journal of Business Ethics, 2023).

HORIZON SCANNING

Regular assessment of emerging technologies and their ethical implications helps organizations prepare for future challenges. For example, Microsoft's AI ethics team conducts quarterly reviews of emerging AI capabilities, assessing potential ethical implications before they become pressing issues. This proactive approach has helped them develop ethical guidelines for new technologies like generative AI months before they reached widespread adoption.

SCENARIO PLANNING

Organizations that regularly engage in ethical scenario planning show greater adaptability when facing new challenges. This involves:

- creating detailed scenarios of potential ethical challenges
- testing current frameworks against these scenarios
- identifying capability gaps
- developing response strategies before they're needed.

Research shows that companies using structured scenario planning identify potential ethical issues 2.3 times faster than those using reactive approaches.

STAKEHOLDER ENGAGEMENT

Regular dialogue with diverse stakeholders helps organizations understand evolving ethical expectations. Research from Stanford's Human-Centered AI Institute shows that companies maintaining active engagement with ethics experts, advocacy groups, and consumers identify emerging ethical concerns 3.1 times more effectively than those operating in isolation.

Building Adaptive Capabilities

The ability to evolve ethical practices while maintaining core principles is crucial. Research from Harvard University's Edmond & Lily Safra Center for Ethics highlights that "values-based approaches are inherently flexible, allowing organizations to adapt ethical considerations to diverse situations and contexts." This flexibility enables organizations to respond quickly to emerging ethical challenges while promoting innovative solutions. The Center identifies four key capabilities that help organizations adapt their ethical cultures:

1 **Learning agility:** Organizations must develop systems for rapidly incorporating new ethical insights. This includes:

- regular ethics training updates
- rapid response protocols for new challenges
- flexible policy frameworks
- active learning networks
- cultural flexibility.

2 **Cultural flexibility:** While core ethical principles remain constant, their application must evolve. The Harvard research contrasts rigid principles-based approaches that "may struggle to address novel or unprecedented scenarios" with values-based approaches that "enable organizations to respond promptly to evolving ethical challenges and opportunities." Successful organizations maintain what scholars call "principled flexibility"—the ability to adapt practices while preserving fundamental values.

3 **Innovation integration:** Companies need processes for ethically evaluating new AI capabilities. The Harvard research emphasizes that values-based approaches "encourage innovation and creativity in ethical decision-making" by "empowering employees to apply ethical values creatively" when exploring solutions to complex ethical dilemmas.

4 **Collaborative problem-solving:** As ethical challenges become more complex, organizations need robust systems for bringing diverse perspectives together. The Harvard research underscores that values-based approaches "prioritize stakeholder engagement and inclusivity, ensuring that diverse perspectives are considered in

ethical decision-making processes," which "enhance the legitimacy and social responsibility" of technology initiatives (Saviano et al., 2023).

Measuring Success

Creating a sustainable ethical AI culture takes more than good intentions—it requires tracking our progress over time to make sure our values actually stick. Research shows we can measure how well this cultural shift is working at different stages, from the early days all the way to when these practices become second nature. Think of it as a journey with distinct phases that help us see how we're doing and what impact we're making as our culture evolves:

Short-Term Indicators (0–12 months)

- Employee engagement in ethical initiatives
- Use of ethical decision frameworks
- Reporting of ethical concerns
- Training completion and effectiveness

Medium-Term Measures (1–3 years)

- Changes in decision-making patterns
- Integration of ethics into processes
- Cross-functional collaboration levels
- Ethical incident rates and resolution

Long-Term Metrics (3+ years)

- Sustained behavioral change
- Cultural embedding of ethical practices
- Organizational reputation
- Stakeholder trust levels

Continuous Improvement and Adaptation

Establishing robust feedback loops and data-driven processes for continuous refinement is essential to sustaining an ethical AI strategy over time. This involves integrating both internal and external perspectives to identify areas for improvement.

Organizations must first focus on integrating feedback loops from cross-functional teams and customers. By collecting input from marketing, data science, legal, and compliance personnel, companies can surface emerging issues or unintended consequences with their AI systems. Similarly, implementing customer feedback mechanisms, such as surveys and online forums, allows them to gauge perceptions of AI-driven experiences and identify potential trust concerns. Analyzing employee sentiments through pulse checks and performance reviews can also shed light on their experiences with ethical AI implementation.

Complementing these feedback loops, organizations should also leverage data analytics for ongoing refinement. Advanced analytics can continuously monitor the performance and ethical alignment of AI systems, tracking key indicators like bias, fairness, and transparency. Utilizing data visualization tools helps surface trends and patterns that can inform iterative adjustments to AI models, data sources, and marketing workflows. Establishing a culture of data-driven decision-making ensures that these insights routinely trigger reviews and improvements to ethical AI practices.

It's crucial to align metrics with evolving ethical standards. As the technological, regulatory, and societal landscape continues to shift, marketing leaders must regularly review and update their KPIs. This may involve collaborating with industry groups and subject matter experts to stay informed of emerging ethical frameworks and best practices. Incorporating qualitative measures, such as customer trust surveys and employee sentiment, alongside traditional marketing metrics, helps ensure a well-rounded view of success.

By embedding continuous improvement mechanisms, organizations can adapt their ethical AI strategies in lockstep with evolving technology, consumer expectations, and regulatory landscapes. This nimble, data-driven approach is essential for maintaining the relevance and effectiveness of ethical AI initiatives over the long term.

Operationalizing Ethical AI in Marketing Workflows

While defining ethical principles and fostering awareness are critical, embedding these principles into daily workflows ensures their consistent application. Operationalizing ethical AI in marketing involves integrating ethics into campaign planning, cross-functional collaboration, and formal review processes.

EMBEDDING ETHICAL AI IN CAMPAIGN PLANNING

Integrating ethical considerations at the outset of campaign development prevents ethical missteps and builds accountability. Organizations like Google have made ethical impact assessments mandatory in their project planning phases, ensuring that privacy, transparency, and algorithmic fairness are evaluated at every stage (Google AI Principles, 2023).

For example, creating campaign checklists that include questions such as, "Does this initiative respect user privacy?" or "Are there potential biases in the data being used?" helps teams systematically address ethical concerns. Embedding these prompts into marketing and creative briefs encourages teams to consider the broader implications of their work from the beginning.

CROSS-FUNCTIONAL COLLABORATION FOR ETHICAL IMPLEMENTATION

Collaboration across marketing, legal, data science, and compliance teams ensures a comprehensive approach to ethical AI. Organizations with formal cross-functional working groups consistently identify ethical risks significantly faster than siloed teams.

These groups often meet regularly to:

- discuss ongoing projects and potential ethical dilemmas
- share updates on industry trends and regulatory changes
- establish shared protocols for addressing emerging challenges.

For instance, Salesforce convenes cross-functional ethics councils to align AI projects with their corporate values and ensure consistency across departments.

FORMAL APPROVAL AND REVIEW PROCESSES

Organizations must implement workflows that require ethical approval before launching AI-driven marketing campaigns. Periodic reviews of active campaigns assess their ethical alignment, enabling teams to make real-time adjustments as needed.

In addition, performance evaluations should incorporate ethical metrics alongside traditional KPIs. For example, IBM's "AI Ethics Index" measures factors such as algorithmic transparency, user trust ratings, and fairness across demographic groups. These metrics not only reinforce ethical priorities but also provide teams with clear benchmarks for success.

Building a Sustainable Ethical AI Culture

Cultivating an organizational culture that prioritizes ethical AI is essential for long-term success. This involves securing leadership commitment, empowering employees as ethical champions, and aligning incentives and recognition programs.

At the top, leadership commitment and modeling is crucial. Ensuring that senior executives visibly demonstrate their support for ethical AI principles and initiatives sets the tone for the entire organization. Incorporating ethical AI considerations into the company's mission, values, and strategic priorities further embeds these priorities into the fabric of the business. Allocating sufficient resources, including budget and personnel, to ethical AI implementation and continuous improvement signals the organization's dedication to this effort.

Complementing this top-down approach, employee training and development empowers individuals to become ethical champions. Providing comprehensive training programs educates all employees on ethical AI concepts, guidelines, and best practices. Encouraging cross-functional collaboration and knowledge-sharing fosters a shared understanding of ethical AI challenges and solutions across the organization. Ultimately, incorporating ethical AI competencies into performance management and career development frameworks reinforces their importance.

Incentivizing and recognizing ethical behavior sends a clear message about the organization's priorities. Establishing reward and recognition programs that celebrate teams and individuals who uphold ethical AI principles in their work demonstrates the value placed on responsible innovation. Considering the inclusion of ethical AI metrics into employee compensation and promotion criteria further aligns individual incentives with the organization's ethical goals. Showcasing ethical AI success stories and lessons learned helps inspire others within the company to follow suit.

By embedding ethical AI as a core cultural value, organizations can ensure that responsible innovation becomes a natural part of the marketing team's mindset and daily practices. This sustainable ethical AI culture serves as the foundation for long-term success and resilience.

Ensuring Long-Term Resilience

As the AI landscape continues to evolve rapidly, marketing organizations must cultivate the ability to anticipate and adapt to emerging ethical challenges. This requires a strategic, forward-looking approach to ethical AI governance.

The first step is scenario planning for emerging ethical challenges. By convening cross-functional teams to envision plausible future scenarios involving technological advancements, regulatory changes, and shifting consumer attitudes, companies can stress-test their existing ethical AI frameworks and practices. This process helps identify potential vulnerabilities and areas for improvement, allowing the organization to develop contingency plans and decision-making frameworks to guide its response to unexpected ethical dilemmas.

Complementing this scenario planning, horizon scanning and preparedness activities ensure the organization remains agile and responsive. Dedicating resources to continuously monitor emerging trends, technologies, and regulatory developments that could impact the ethical application of AI in marketing keeps the leadership team informed. Collaborating with industry peers, academic institutions, and policymakers allows the organization to stay at the forefront of the latest thinking and best practices in ethical AI governance. Allocating budget and personnel for ongoing research, experimentation, and piloting of innovative ethical AI solutions further bolsters the company's ability to adapt.

Ultimately, advocating for industry-wide standards is crucial for building long-term resilience. By actively participating in industry associations, working groups, and standard-setting bodies, organizations can shape the development of ethical AI guidelines and frameworks. Leveraging the company's thought leadership and influence to promote the adoption of responsible AI practices across the marketing ecosystem creates a rising tide that lifts all boats. Collaborating with policymakers and regulators to ensure that emerging legislation and regulations strike the right balance between innovation and ethical safeguards also secures the organization's long-term future.

By adopting a long-term, strategic mindset, marketing organizations can build resilient ethical AI frameworks that adapt to the rapidly evolving technological and regulatory landscape. This proactive, collaborative approach empowers companies to stay ahead of the curve and maintain their ethical edge in an increasingly AI-driven world.

Bringing It All Together

Cultivating an ethical AI culture in marketing organizations is a complex, multifaceted process that requires commitment, collaboration, and continuous learning. As we've explored in this chapter, there are several key insights for driving successful cultural transformation.

Ultimately, the path to a sustainable ethical AI culture is a journey of continuous learning and growth. By committing to the principles and practices outlined in this chapter, marketing organizations can not only mitigate the risks of irresponsible AI use but also unlock the full potential of this transformative technology to drive both business and societal value. The organizations that master this delicate balance will be the ones that thrive in the age of AI.

KEY TAKEAWAYS

- **Defining ethical behavior**: Clear values and behavioral expectations are essential for translating abstract ethical principles into concrete actions.
  Why it matters: Explicitly defining what ethical behavior looks like in practice helps employees understand how to apply ethical principles in their day-to-day work, reducing ambiguity and promoting consistency.

- **Fostering psychological safety**: Psychological safety is crucial for fostering an environment where employees feel comfortable raising concerns and speaking up about potential ethical issues.

> *Why it matters*: When employees feel safe bringing up ethical concerns, organizations can identify and address issues early before they escalate into major problems. This proactive approach is key to maintaining an ethical culture.
>
> - **Embedding ethical accountability**: Distributed responsibility for ethics, with ownership shared across all levels and functions, is more effective than relying solely on top-down control or siloed ethics teams.
>   *Why it matters*: Embedding ethical accountability throughout the organization ensures that ethics is treated as a fundamental part of everyone's job rather than an afterthought or the sole purview of a specific department.
>
> - **Prioritizing continuous learning**: Continuous learning, supported by robust training programs and knowledge-sharing initiatives, is essential for building ethical skills and staying ahead of evolving challenges.
>   *Why it matters*: In a rapidly changing technological and regulatory landscape, ongoing learning is crucial for ensuring that employees have the most up-to-date knowledge and capabilities needed to navigate complex ethical issues.

Looking Ahead

As we move into Chapter 10, "The Evolving Landscape of AI in Marketing," we'll explore the cutting-edge technologies and emerging trends that are set to transform the marketing landscape. From the rise of generative AI to the growing importance of emotional intelligence, we'll examine how these developments are reshaping the way marketing departments operate and engage with customers.

We'll also delve into the ethical implications and practical considerations that these new technologies present for marketing leaders. Building on the foundation of ethical AI culture explored in this chapter, we'll discuss strategies for proactively preparing your team to navigate this shifting terrain while staying true to your values and commitments.

Food for Thought

1 How can marketing organizations balance the need for ethical AI practices with the pressure to stay competitive?

2 Imagine you're leading the cultural transformation effort for ethical AI. What resistance might you encounter from different stakeholders, and how would you address their concerns?

3 How might the increasing use of AI in marketing impact consumer expectations around transparency, privacy, and control? What steps can organizations take now to build trust and prepare for these shifting expectations?

4 As AI becomes more sophisticated and autonomous, how might the role of human judgment evolve in marketing decision-making? What skills and capabilities will be most important for marketers to develop in this context?

References

Deloitte (2023) *State of Ethics and Trust in Technology: Insights into AI Preparedness*, www2.deloitte.com/content/dam/Deloitte/us/Documents/us-tte-annual-report-2023.pdf (archived at https://perma.cc/E7UA-C828)

Drucker, P F (2007) *Management Challenges for the 21st Century*, Harper Business, New York

Edmondson, A C and Chamorro-Premuzic, T (2021) Leadership in Times of Upheaval: The Rise of the Empathic Leader, *Social Scientists Confronting Global Crises*, edited by Jean M Bartunek, Routledge, Abingdon

Ethics & Compliance Initiative (2023) *Global Business Ethics Survey*, www.ethics.org (archived at https://perma.cc/Z6E4-2V6F)

Google AI Principles (2023) *Responsible AI Development at Scale*, ai.google/principles (archived at https://perma.cc/H4J7-GNNE)

Keepnet Labs (2024) 2024 security awareness training stats and trends, https://keepnetlabs.com/blog/2024-security-awareness-training-statistics (archived at https://perma.cc/8Q8E-86M7)

Kiron, D, Schrage, M, Candelon, F, Khodabandeh, S, and Chu, M (2023) Governance for smarter KPIs, MIT Sloan Management Review, https://sloanreview.mit.edu/article/governance-for-smarter-kpis/ (archived at https://perma.cc/E9NG-ADVC)

Kotter, J P (2022) The 8-Step Process for Leading Change, www.kotterinc.com/methodology/8-steps/ (archived at https://perma.cc/VU9C-YU9B)

Madaio, M A, Stark, L, Wortman Vaughan, J, and Wallach, H (2020) Co-designing Checklists to Understand Oranizational Challenges and Opportunities Around Fairness in AI, *CHI'20: Proceedings of the 2020 CHI Conference on Human Factors in Computing Systems*, 1–14, https://dl.acm.org/doi/10.1145/3313831.3376445 (archived at https://perma.cc/RNT9-LTKG)

McKinsey (2025) AI in the workplace: A report for 2025, www.mckinsey.com/capabilities/mckinsey-digital/our-insights/superagency-in-the-workplace-empowering-people-to-unlock-ais-full-potential-at-work (archived at https://perma.cc/73YR-9DWY)

Saviano, J, Hack, J, Okonkwo, V, and Huo, S (2023) Reimagining AI ethics, moving beyond principles to organizational values, Edmond & Lily Safra Center for Ethics, Harvard University, www.ethics.harvard.edu/blog/post-5-reimagining-ai-ethics-moving-beyond-principles-organizational-values (archived at https://perma.cc/L5Z4-REG6)

10

The Evolving Landscape of AI Tools and Applications

The marketing landscape is undergoing a profound transformation, propelled by the relentless advancement of AI. From hyper-personalized customer experiences and predictive analytics to the tantalizing prospect of autonomous decision-making, AI is reshaping every facet of how brands engage with consumers. Yet, amidst this exhilarating wave of innovation, a critical imperative emerges: to harness the power of AI responsibly, ethically, and in service of genuine human values.

This chapter embarks on a journey to the cutting edge of AI, exploring the technologies and trends poised to define the future of marketing. We'll navigate the exciting possibilities and the novel ethical challenges that demand our attention. Building upon the foundations of ethical AI principles, governance frameworks, and organizational culture discussed in previous chapters, we'll equip marketers with practical strategies to proactively navigate this evolving landscape.

Foundation Models: The New Infrastructure

Foundation models, also known as LLMs, have introduced unprecedented capabilities in NLP, understanding, and generation. To clarify for a broader audience, NLP is a branch of AI that focuses on enabling computers to understand, interpret, and generate human language. Trained on vast amounts of data, these models can perform a wide range of language tasks with remarkable accuracy and fluency.

In the marketing context, foundation models are being used to power a variety of applications, from content creation and personalization to customer service and sentiment analysis. For example, OpenAI's latest model has been used by companies like Microsoft and Salesforce to generate marketing copy, product descriptions, and even computer code.

The impact of generative AI models on marketing efficiency and effectiveness has proven to be profound. The overwhelming majority of organizations are now utilizing generative AI in some capacity, with many actively investing in and adopting it enterprise-wide, while most others are experimenting with the technology across various departments. The productivity gains are substantial. Enterprises leveraging generative AI for content creation and other tasks have reported significant cost reductions and revenue increases, highlighting the potential of this technology in marketing operations.

However, the use of foundation models also raises important ethical considerations. Because these models are trained on vast internet datasets, they can inherit biases and generate inappropriate or misleading content if not carefully controlled. Research has shown that even advanced models can reproduce societal stereotypes and occasionally generate content that doesn't align with brand standards or values. Marketers should be steadfast in monitoring and testing model outputs to ensure they align with brand values and avoid potential harms, implementing appropriate guardrails and human oversight in their AI workflows.

Generative AI: Reimagining Content Creation

The future of content creation stands at a fascinating inflection point. As COLLINS co-founder Brian Collins observes, "Soon, it will not be the AI systems making things for you and me. It's the AI systems making things for other AI systems... Marketing is going to be AI talking to other marketing AIs and letting us do other stuff" (Collins, 2024). This prediction highlights a crucial shift: AI won't just assist human creators—it will reshape how content flows through marketing ecosystems.

Already, we're seeing AI systems that can generate entire marketing campaigns, autonomously A/B test content variations, and optimize messaging in real time. But the real transformation lies ahead, where AI systems will increasingly communicate with each other to orchestrate content creation, distribution, and optimization. Imagine AI content generators working in concert with AI audience analysis tools, creating and refining content based on real-time performance data without human intervention.

This evolution raises critical questions about the role of human creativity and oversight. While AI can generate content at unprecedented scale and speed, successful organizations will need to maintain the delicate balance between automation and authentic human connection. The key lies in using AI to augment rather than replace human creativity, focusing human efforts on strategy, emotional resonance, and ethical governance while letting AI handle optimization and scale.

However, generative AI also presents complex ethical and legal challenges around intellectual property rights, content authenticity, and potential misuse. For instance, in early 2024, a legal dispute arose regarding the use of AI-generated images in the promotional materials for the film *Late Night With the Devil*. The filmmakers acknowledged using AI to create three still images that were briefly shown in the movie. This sparked controversy, with some arguing that the use of AI undermines the work of human artists and raises questions about the authenticity of creative works in the film industry (Earl, 2024). This case highlights the ongoing debate surrounding the ethical and legal implications of using AI in creative fields. As these tools become more accessible and powerful, marketers will need robust frameworks to ensure responsible use.

THE EVOLUTION OF CREATIVE OPTIMIZATION

While generative AI presents immense opportunities, early implementations have faced significant challenges. As Ally Financial's CMO Andrea Brimmer observes, "We've all talked about DCO, right? The dynamic creative optimization. I've never seen it be good or work the way it was intended. I've seen these crazy systems built and everybody promises you the world, and they're all lame and have failed" (2025). However, Brimmer sees this changing with new AI capabilities, suggesting we're on the cusp of a renaissance in creative optimization.

Transformative Technologies Reshaping AI

The marketing landscape stands at the threshold of several transformative technologies that promise to reshape how we engage with customers. These advances extend far beyond incremental improvements in existing capabilities—they represent quantum leaps that will redefine what's possible in marketing. Let's explore these groundbreaking technologies and their implications for the future of marketing.

Quantum Computing: Marketing's Next Computational Frontier

Imagine being able to analyze every possible combination of customer behaviors, preferences, and interactions simultaneously. This is the promise of quantum computing in marketing. Unlike classical computers that process information in binary bits (0 or 1), quantum computers harness quantum mechanical properties like superposition and entanglement to perform certain calculations exponentially faster.

For marketers, this computational leap will transform how we understand and serve our customers. Consider customer segmentation, traditionally limited by the processing power needed to analyze multiple variables across large populations. Quantum algorithms could simultaneously analyze thousands of behavioral attributes across millions of customers in real-time, uncovering hidden patterns and micro-segments that traditional approaches would miss. For example, a retail bank could identify highly specific product opportunities by analyzing the interplay between transaction histories, life events, digital behavior, and countless other variables—all in the time it currently takes to run basic demographic analysis.

Campaign optimization represents another frontier where quantum computing could revolutionize marketing practices. Today's marketers face tough trade-offs when optimizing campaigns, often forced to limit the variables they consider due to computational constraints. Quantum computing could eliminate these limitations, allowing simultaneous optimization of timing, channel mix, creative elements, and audience targeting while respecting budget constraints and brand guidelines.

However, organizations should temper their excitement with practical considerations. Most experts agree that widespread marketing applications of quantum computing remain several years away. The next few years will likely be characterized by early experimentation, primarily in research settings. The first commercial applications in specific marketing use cases may emerge between 2026 and 2028, with broader adoption following as the technology matures.

AI Agents: The Evolution of Autonomous Marketing

Marketing tech is shifting from basic automation to truly autonomous AI agents. These agents aren't just following predetermined playbooks; they're making independent decisions, learning continuously, and adapting strategies in real-time based on market conditions and performance data.

The true game-changer for marketers is the emergence of AI as the new decision layer. As Brimmer notes, "We're going to have to start thinking about marketing to Nicole's agents… if you're going to be influenced by artificial intelligence… you might not ever even see me as an option as a result" (Brimmer, 2025). These AI intermediaries are rapidly becoming the new gatekeepers of consumer attention, filtering options before humans ever see them.

This shift is exemplified by the rise of agentic marketing ecosystems—where specialized AI agents operate in coordinated systems. Picture a marketing operation where one agent optimizes creative assets, another orchestrates budget allocation across channels, and a third dynamically segments and targets audiences. These aren't isolated tools but an interconnected network sharing intelligence and continuously refining strategies based on collective performance.

However, the most successful implementations are mastering the human-AI collaboration dynamic. While these agents excel at data processing, pattern recognition, and tactical execution, human marketers remain essential for strategic direction, creative inspiration, and ethical oversight. Forward-thinking organizations are establishing clear frameworks for this partnership—defining specific handoff points, implementing regular human review processes, and creating explicit protocols for when decisions require human judgment.

The cutting edge of AI agent development in marketing now centers on autonomous experimentation and learning. Modern marketing agents don't just execute—they proactively test hypotheses, identify new opportunities, and build institutional knowledge that compounds over time. This represents a fundamental shift from tools that simply automate existing processes to systems that continuously discover and implement new strategies.

For marketers navigating this landscape, the competitive advantage lies in leveraging agent orchestration platforms that coordinate these specialized AI systems while maintaining centralized control and visibility. The organizations seeing the greatest ROI aren't just deploying individual agents but creating integrated systems where agents collaborate toward common business objectives while operating within clearly defined constraints and ethical guidelines.

Neural Interfaces: The Direct Connection

As brain-computer interface technology advances, we stand at the cusp of a new era in marketing—one where direct neural feedback could transform how we understand and engage with consumers. This technology extends far beyond traditional neuro-marketing techniques, offering unprecedented insight into emotional responses and cognitive processing of marketing stimuli. To illustrate, companies like Neuralink are developing implantable devices, while others like Emotiv offer non-invasive headsets that measure brain activity.

Modern neural interface technologies enable real-time monitoring of emotional reactions at a level of detail previously impossible. Rather than relying on surveys or behavioral proxies, marketers could potentially understand exactly how consumers *feel* when encountering their brand, products, or marketing messages. This capability extends to detecting subconscious preferences and measuring genuine engagement, cutting through the noise of self-reported data.

However, the intimate nature of neural data raises serious ethical considerations that marketers must address proactively. Organizations must implement robust encryption protocols for neural data, establish strict access controls, and maintain detailed audit trails. Perhaps most importantly, the industry must develop clear ethical guidelines around neural marketing practices, including explicit prohibitions on manipulative techniques and strong protections for mental autonomy.

Advanced Cognitive Architectures: Moving Toward True Understanding

The evolution of cognitive architectures in AI represents a fundamental shift from pattern matching to genuine understanding. While early marketing AI excelled at identifying correlations in customer data, advanced cognitive architectures aim to comprehend customer intent, context, and emotional state in ways that more closely mirror human cognition.

At the heart of this evolution lies the development of more sophisticated natural language understanding. Modern cognitive architectures can now grasp nuance, context, and even implied meaning in customer communications. Consider how this transforms customer service interactions. Where traditional chatbots might struggle with complex queries or become confused by colloquialisms, advanced cognitive systems can maintain coherent conversations across multiple topics, remember context from earlier interactions, and even detect subtle emotional undertones in customer messages.

These advances in cognitive architecture extend beyond language processing to decision-making capabilities. Today's systems are developing what we might call "marketing intuition" —the ability to make nuanced decisions based on incomplete or ambiguous information. For instance, a cognitive system might notice subtle changes in customer behavior patterns that suggest an impending shift in brand loyalty, allowing for proactive intervention before traditional metrics would raise any red flags.

Perhaps most significantly, advanced cognitive architectures are beginning to demonstrate capabilities in analogical reasoning—the ability to apply lessons learned in one context to novel situations. This means marketing AI can now adapt successful strategies from one market or customer segment to another, making appropriate adjustments for different contexts rather than simply applying rigid rules.

Biomimetic AI Systems: Learning from Nature's Intelligence

Nature has spent billions of years evolving sophisticated solutions to complex problems. Biomimetic AI systems aim to harness this evolutionary wisdom by mimicking natural intelligence processes in artificial systems. This approach is yielding particularly promising results in marketing applications where adaptability and resilience are crucial.

Evolutionary algorithms, inspired by natural selection, are revolutionizing how we optimize marketing campaigns. Instead of relying on predetermined rules, these systems generate multiple variations of marketing approaches and allow the most successful ones to "survive" and influence future iterations. This creates a dynamic optimization process that can adapt to changing market conditions much like natural organisms adapt to their environments.

Consider how this works in practice. A biomimetic system running an email marketing campaign might start with a diverse "population" of subject lines, layouts, and calls to action. As the campaign runs, the system observes which combinations perform best and uses those insights to generate new variations, each potentially better suited to engaging target audiences. This process continues automatically, with the campaign evolving to become more effective over time.

Neural networks inspired by brain architecture are also transforming how we process and understand customer data. These systems mirror the way biological brains learn from experience, forming and strengthening connections based on successful outcomes. This allows for more natural and intuitive pattern recognition in customer behavior analysis. For example, a neural network might identify subtle combinations of behaviors that indicate a customer is ready for an upgrade, even if those patterns weren't explicitly programmed into the system.

The integration of biological computing elements represents the next frontier in biomimetic AI. Early experiments with DNA-based storage and processing suggest the possibility of marketing systems that can store and process vast amounts of customer data with unprecedented efficiency. While these technologies remain largely experimental, they point toward a future where marketing systems might operate with the sophistication and efficiency of biological intelligence.

These biomimetic approaches offer particular promise in developing more sustainable AI marketing systems. By mimicking the energy efficiency of natural intelligence, we may be able to create systems that deliver powerful capabilities while minimizing environmental impact—a growing concern as AI becomes more central to marketing operations.

Infrastructure and Platform Evolution

The future of AI marketing depends heavily on advances in digital infrastructure. Edge computing represents one of the most significant developments in this space, bringing AI processing closer to data sources and enabling new capabilities in personalization and autonomous decision-making. Edge computing, in simple terms, means processing data closer to where it's generated (like on a smartphone or a sensor) instead of sending it to a central server.

By processing data closer to its source, edge computing dramatically reduces latency in customer interactions while enhancing privacy through local data processing. Consider a retail environment where AI-driven personalization happens instantly as customers move through the store, with all processing occurring on-site rather than being sent to distant servers. This not only improves the customer experience but also addresses growing privacy concerns about data transmission and storage.

The rollout of 6G networks will further transform what's possible in AI marketing. With unprecedented bandwidth and near-zero latency, 6G will enable truly immersive brand experiences, including high-fidelity holographic marketing and seamless integration of AI across physical environments. Marketers will be able to create rich, interactive demonstrations that blend digital and physical elements in ways previously confined to science fiction.

Zero-Trust Security: Safeguarding AI Marketing Systems

As marketing AI systems become more distributed and autonomous, traditional security perimeters no longer suffice. The zero-trust security model has emerged as the new paradigm for protecting AI marketing infrastructure, operating on the principle that no component, user, or process should be inherently trusted—even within the organization's network.

This approach transforms how we secure AI marketing systems through continuous verification and monitoring. Every interaction between system components, every data transfer, and every AI decision must be authenticated and authorized. Think of it as creating a digital equivalent of airport security—where even authorized personnel must present credentials and undergo screening at multiple checkpoints, rather than simply flashing a badge once at the entrance.

The implications for marketing operations are significant. When an AI system makes a decision about customer segmentation or campaign optimization, the zero-trust framework verifies not only the authenticity of the data inputs but also the integrity of the AI model itself. This continuous validation helps prevent both external attacks and internal misuse, ensuring that marketing AI systems remain reliable and trustworthy.

Convergence Trends

Bio-Digital Convergence: The Next Marketing Frontier

The convergence of biological and digital systems represents perhaps the most fascinating frontier in AI marketing. As biosensors become more sophisticated and ubiquitous, marketers gain unprecedented ability to understand and respond to consumers' physical and emotional states in real time.

Consider a retail environment where AI systems can detect subtle changes in a customer's physiological state—heart rate, skin conductance, even microscopic facial expressions—and adjust the shopping experience accordingly. This might mean automatically adjusting lighting and music to reduce stress, or offering timely assistance when confusion is detected. While such capabilities raise important ethical considerations, they also offer the potential for truly empathetic, responsive marketing experiences.

The integration of AI with AR creates another dimension of bio-digital convergence. Marketing experiences can now adapt not just to what consumers do, but to how they perceive and interact with their environment. This creates opportunities for immersive brand experiences that feel natural and intuitive, blending seamlessly with the physical world while respecting personal boundaries and preferences.

Competitive Dynamics in the AI Era

The integration of AI into marketing requires more than just technological adoption—it demands fundamental changes in how marketing teams are structured, skilled, and led. This transformation challenges traditional marketing organizational models that were built for a more predictable, less data-intensive era.

Consider how the role of the marketing strategist has evolved. Where once these professionals relied primarily on market research and creative intuition, they now must synthesize insights from AI systems while maintaining their strategic and creative vision. The most effective strategists have become adept at what we might call "augmented thinking" —combining human creativity and judgment with AI-driven insights to create more compelling and effective marketing strategies.

The composition of marketing teams is also changing dramatically. Traditional skill divisions between creative, analytical, and technical roles are blurring. Today's marketing professionals increasingly need to understand both the creative and technical aspects of their work, even if they specialize in one area. A content creator, for example, should understand how AI content optimization works to create effectively for digital channels, while a data analyst needs to appreciate creative principles to make their insights actionable.

Strategic Differentiation

In the AI-driven future, a company's mastery of AI technologies will become a core competitive advantage. Marketers will need to decide whether to pursue first-mover advantages by pioneering new AI applications or adopt fast-follower strategies to learn from others' successes and failures. Innovation leadership in AI will become a key point of differentiation, with brands striving to position themselves at the fore-front of AI adoption in their industries. The choice of technology stack and partnerships will also play a critical role in differentiation, as companies seek to build unique AI capabilities that set them apart from rivals.

Industry Transformation

The impact of AI will vary across industries, with some sectors facing more rapid and profound disruption than others. Marketers must understand the specific disruption patterns in their industry, such as changes to value chains, the emergence of new competitors, and the restructuring of ecosystem relationships. The rise of AI-powered platforms and marketplaces will reshape the economics of many industries, requiring marketers to adapt their strategies for a world of network effects, data-driven winner-take-all dynamics, and platform-mediated customer relationships.

The impact on traditional agency relationships is particularly notable. "The future of agency remits is going to be heavily influenced by AI—both media planning, buying, creative, I mean, honestly, all of it," observes Brimmer (2025). While early attempts at AI-driven creatives have met mixed results—"Coke took flak over their holiday ad where they used AI," she notes—"that's now. It's not going to be forever." Brimmer is referring to Coca-Cola's 2024 holiday campaign, which included an AI generated ad, which faced criticism as some viewers found the AI-generated imagery in the commercial to be "creepy" or "uncanny," with some elements appearing distorted or out of place. This sparked a debate about the limitations of AI in crea-tive endeavors and the importance of maintaining a human touch in advertising, particularly for a brand known for its emotionally resonant campaigns (Whitten, 2023). This perspective highlights how AI may fundamentally restructure agency value propositions and service models.

Business Model Innovation

To stay competitive in the age of AI, marketers will need to embrace business model innovation. This may involve developing entirely new, AI-native business models that are built around the unique capabilities of AI, such as hyper-personalization, predictive analytics, and autonomous decision-making. Existing business models will also need to be transformed to incorporate AI, whether through incremental improvements or more radical overhauls. Hybrid approaches that combine elements of traditional and AI-driven models may offer a path forward for many companies. As AI reshapes industries, marketers must also be prepared for the potential obsoles-cence of certain business models and revenue streams.

Competitive Risk Management

Navigating the competitive landscape in the age of AI will require active risk manage-ment. Marketers must carefully consider the timing of their technology adoption, balancing the risks of being left behind with the challenges of being an early adopter in a rapidly evolving space. Capability development, whether through internal upskilling, talent acquisition, or partnerships, will be critical to staying competitive. Collaboration and co-opetition strategies, such as joining AI industry consortia or forming data-sharing agreements with partners, can help mitigate risks and acceler-ate learning. Marketers will also need to continually assess their market positioning and make bold bets to stay ahead of the curve.

Investment Prioritization: Making Strategic Choices

The expanding landscape of AI marketing capabilities forces organizations to make careful choices about where to invest their resources. The challenge isn't just finan-cial—it's about allocating attention and organizational energy to the initiatives that will create the most value while maintaining ethical alignment.

Leading organizations are adopting portfolio approaches to AI investment, balancing "sure bets" that enhance existing capabilities with more experimental initiatives that could unlock new opportunities. They're also considering longer time horizons than traditional marketing investments, recognizing that building robust AI capabilities often requires sustained commitment over several years.

The most successful organizations maintain flexibility in their investment strategies, ready to adjust as technologies mature and new opportunities emerge. They've learned to distinguish between genuine breakthroughs and temporary hype, focusing their resources on capabilities that create lasting competitive advantage while upholding their ethical principles.

Environmental and Social Dimensions

Environmental Impact

The environmental footprint of AI marketing systems has become impossible to ignore. The energy consumption required to train and operate sophisticated AI models poses a growing sustainability challenge that forward-thinking marketing leaders must address.

Progressive organizations are adopting green AI development practices that optimize for both performance and energy efficiency. This might mean choosing smaller, more efficient models over larger ones when the performance difference is marginal, or scheduling intensive AI training during periods when renewable energy is most available. Some companies have begun incorporating carbon impact into their AI model selection criteria, weighing environmental costs alongside traditional metrics like accuracy and speed.

The drive for sustainability has also sparked innovation in AI infrastructure. Marketing teams are experimenting with new approaches to distributed computing that reduce energy consumption while maintaining performance. For instance, some organizations have developed systems that dynamically adjust their computational intensity based on task urgency and available renewable energy, much like a smart power grid balances supply and demand.

Social Responsibility

The societal implications of AI will also demand attention from marketers. Ensuring inclusive and equitable access to AI-driven products, services, and experiences will be critical. This will require thoughtful consideration of demographic differences, cultural nuances, and accessibility needs in AI design and deployment. Marketers should strive to create AI experiences that are inclusive and sensitive to the diversity of human experiences, adopting universal design principles that accommodate a wide range of user needs and preferences.

Digital Inclusion

As AI becomes increasingly central to marketing operations, the risk of excluding significant portions of the population grows more acute. The digital divide—the gap between those who can fully participate in the digital economy and those who cannot—threatens to create a two-tiered marketing ecosystem where some consumers enjoy highly personalized, AI-driven experiences while others remain on the margins.

Forward-thinking marketing leaders are taking proactive steps to address this challenge. Some organizations have developed simplified versions of their AI-driven interfaces that work effectively on lower-end devices or slower internet connections. Others are creating hybrid approaches that combine AI-driven personalization with traditional marketing methods, ensuring they can reach and serve all segments of their market effectively.

Educational initiatives play a crucial role in this effort. Many companies are investing in digital literacy programs that help consumers understand and engage with AI-driven marketing tools. These programs range from basic tutorials on using digital interfaces to more sophisticated education about data privacy and AI personalization preferences.

Sustainable AI Practices

To ensure the long-term viability and positive impact of AI, marketers must embrace sustainable AI practices. This includes developing energy-efficient algorithms, using renewable energy sources for AI infrastructure, and exploring the potential of AI for circular economy applications. Robust impact measurement frameworks will be essential to assess the social and environmental consequences of AI deployments over time. Long-term sustainability planning should be integrated into AI strategies from the outset, considering the entire lifecycle of AI systems and their broader societal implications.

Market and Consumer Evolution

The proliferation of AI in marketing isn't just changing how companies operate—it's fundamentally reshaping consumer behavior and expectations. Today's consumers interact with brands through an increasingly complex web of AI-mediated touchpoints, from virtual assistants handling customer service to recommendation engines guiding purchase decisions. This new reality demands a profound rethinking of traditional marketing approaches.

Consumer privacy attitudes have evolved particularly dramatically. The initial era of digital marketing was characterized by relatively free data collection, but today's consumers demonstrate sophisticated understanding of their data rights and value. They expect granular control over their information and transparency about its use. Organizations that treat privacy as a fundamental right rather than a regulatory burden are finding themselves at a competitive advantage, building deeper trust with their audiences.

The nature of brand relationships is also transforming. AI-driven personalization has created expectations of highly relevant, contextual interactions, but consumers increasingly seek authenticity in these exchanges. They can readily distinguish between genuine personalization that adds value and superficial attempts at customization. This has led to the emergence of what we might call "authentic personalization"—AI-driven experiences that respect individual preferences while maintaining genuine human connection.

Industry-Specific Applications

While the fundamental principles of AI marketing remain constant across industries, their application varies significantly by sector. Understanding these variations helps organizations adapt general best practices to their specific context.

In retail, for example, AI marketing applications often focus on creating seamless omnichannel experiences. Physical stores are being transformed into data-rich environments through the integration of sensors, computer vision, and edge computing. This allows retailers to bring the personalization capabilities of digital commerce into the physical world, creating what some call "responsive retail environments" that adapt to customer behavior in real time.

Financial services organizations, on the other hand, often prioritize using AI for risk management and compliance alongside marketing objectives. They're developing sophisticated systems that can personalize marketing offers while simultaneously assessing risk and ensuring regulatory compliance. This has led to the emergence of what we might call "compliance-aware AI" that builds regulatory considerations into its decision-making processes.

Healthcare organizations face unique challenges in balancing personalization with privacy. They're pioneering approaches to AI marketing that maintain strict HIPAA compliance while still delivering relevant, personalized communications. This has led to innovations in privacy-preserving AI techniques that could benefit other industries as privacy regulations become more stringent.

Strategic Planning

The rapid evolution of AI capabilities requires a new approach to strategic planning in marketing. Traditional annual planning cycles are giving way to more dynamic, adaptive frameworks that can respond to technological changes and emerging opportunities in real time.

Technology adoption frameworks have become particularly crucial. Leading organizations are developing sophisticated models for evaluating new AI capabilities, considering not just technical performance but also ethical implications, resource requirements, and organizational readiness. These frameworks often incorporate staged implementation approaches, allowing organizations to test and refine new technologies before full-scale deployment.

Risk assessment has also evolved beyond traditional metrics. Modern risk models must consider a broader range of factors, including algorithmic bias, privacy vulnerabilities, and potential reputational impacts. Many organizations are adopting scenario-planning approaches that help them anticipate and prepare for various potential outcomes of AI adoption.

Partnership strategies have become increasingly important as the AI ecosystem grows more complex. Few organizations can develop all required capabilities internally, leading to the emergence of sophisticated partnership networks. These might include technology providers, data partners, and even competitors in certain areas. The key is identifying which capabilities to build internally versus access through partnerships, always considering both strategic control and ethical alignment.

Skill Development: The New Marketing Competencies

The evolution of AI marketing capabilities has created demand for new skills and competencies that many marketing professionals never anticipated needing. This shift goes beyond technical literacy—it requires a fundamental rethinking of what it means to be a marketing professional in the AI age.

Data literacy has become as fundamental to marketing as writing skills. However, this doesn't mean every marketer needs to become a data scientist. Rather, they need what we might call "data fluency"—the ability to understand, interpret, and communicate effectively about data and AI-driven insights. This includes understanding basic statistical concepts, recognizing the limitations and potential biases in data, and knowing how to ask the right questions of data analysts and AI systems.

Ethical reasoning capabilities have also become crucial. Marketing professionals must develop the ability to identify and navigate the ethical implications of AI-driven marketing decisions. This includes understanding concepts like algorithmic bias, data privacy, and the potential societal impacts of marketing actions. The most effective marketing leaders have developed frameworks for ethical decision-making that help their teams navigate these complex issues consistently.

Prioritizing Technologies by Time Horizon

While the future of AI in marketing is rich with possibilities, not all innovations will mature at the same pace. Distinguishing between near-term and mid-term time horizons can help marketing leaders make more informed investment decisions, focus on the most impactful capabilities, and stay agile amid ongoing change.

NEAR-TERM (1–2 YEARS)

In the immediate future, foundational AI applications—such as generative text and image models, advanced personalization engines, and integrated customer analytics tools—will continue to mature rapidly. Many of these solutions are already entering mainstream marketing workflows, bolstered by readily available platforms and growing industry expertise. Over the next one to two years, marketers should concentrate on strengthening their existing AI infrastructure, refining their data pipelines, and enhancing model oversight and bias detection. This incremental approach ensures that near-term initiatives deliver quick wins—like more relevant content recommendations or streamlined creative production—while reinforcing ethical safeguards already discussed in earlier chapters.

MID-TERM (3–5 YEARS)

Looking three to five years out, emerging technologies such as quantum computing for campaign optimization, sophisticated autonomous AI agents orchestrating end-to-end customer journeys, and early-stage neural interface experimentation may begin to transition from research labs and niche pilots into more accessible tools. Although these advancements remain on the horizon, marketers can prepare by monitoring industry consortia, engaging with academic and startup partners, and allocating modest "innovation budgets" to pilot next-generation solutions. This forward-looking posture allows organizations to build capabilities and expertise in advance, so when the technology matures, they are ready to scale quickly while maintaining ethical, culturally aligned principles.

By categorizing capabilities into near-term and mid-term horizons, marketing leaders can construct balanced portfolios of AI initiatives. The goal is to deliver tangible value in the short run—improving efficiency, personalization, and trust—while simultaneously cultivating the foresight and capacity to embrace more disruptive, transformative technologies as they come of age. This dual time-horizon approach not only enhances strategic clarity but also ensures that ethical considerations remain central, even as the field evolves from today's practical innovations to tomorrow's groundbreaking possibilities.

Bringing It All Together

Throughout this chapter, we've surveyed the rapidly evolving AI marketing landscape, examining transformative technologies, converging trends, and the expanding range of infrastructure and platform solutions that promise new levels of personalization, efficiency, and consumer engagement. As AI capabilities push deeper into creative, strategic, and even cognitive domains, marketers face not only unprecedented opportunities but also heightened responsibilities.

KEY TAKEAWAYS

- **Emerging technologies**: From foundation models and generative AI to quantum computing and biomimetic systems, the future of AI in marketing extends well beyond incremental improvements.

Why it matters: Understanding these innovations—especially which will have near-term versus mid-term impacts—enables marketers to prioritize investments that deliver immediate value while preparing for more revolutionary changes on the horizon.

- **Infrastructure and platforms**: The rise of edge computing, 6G networks, and ambient intelligence will transform how customers interact with brands, demanding agility and secure, real-time engagement.
  Why it matters: As these infrastructures mature, marketers must integrate ethical and strategic considerations into system design, ensuring that responsiveness and scalability never come at the expense of trust and fairness.

- **Technological convergence**: The intersection of AI with IoT, extended reality, and biometric data is redefining the boundaries of consumer experiences.
  Why it matters: Anticipating how these convergences evolve over a 1–2-year versus a 3–5-year timeframe helps marketers allocate resources effectively, ensuring short-term gains do not distract from building capacity for more disruptive medium-term opportunities.

- **Competitive AI landscape**: In an environment where differentiation hinges on AI mastery, marketers must make strategic choices about timing, capability development, and partnerships.
  Why it matters: A time-horizon approach—focusing first on near-term, readily adoptable technologies while monitoring and planning for future breakthroughs—empowers marketers to stay ahead of competitors and adapt as markets and regulatory standards shift.

Looking Ahead

In Chapter 11, we'll delve into the continuous learning and adaptive strategies that marketers will need to thrive. We'll explore how to develop robust sensing and foresight capabilities, foster a culture of experimentation and agile learning, and cultivate the skills and mindsets needed for long-term success in a world of perpetual change. As we've seen throughout this book, the future of marketing belongs to those who can harness the power of AI while staying grounded in human values and experiences. With the right mix of technical savvy, creative vision, and ethical judgment, marketers can chart a course toward a future where AI enhances and enriches the art and science of marketing for the benefit of companies, customers, and societies.

Food for Thought

1 How do you anticipate the emerging technologies discussed in this chapter, such as quantum computing or neural interfaces, impacting your industry and marketing

practices in the coming years? What steps can you take now to start preparing for these transformations?

2   Consider the potential convergence of AI with other technologies, such as IoT or extended reality, in your market. What new opportunities and challenges do you foresee for engaging customers and creating value in this hybrid, multi-modal environment?

3   Reflect on the competitive landscape in your industry. How might the adoption of AI change the bases of competition, the key success factors, and the dominant business models in your market? What strategies and capabilities will be most critical for your organization to stay ahead of the curve?

4   As AI becomes more deeply embedded in marketing and society, what role do you believe marketers should play in shaping the responsible development and deployment of these technologies? How can marketing leaders balance the imperatives of business performance with the need for ethical, socially beneficial innovation?

References

Brimmer, A, Video interview with Nicole M. Alexander, January 27, 2025

Earl, W (2024) "Late Night With the Devil" Directors Explain Using AI Art in the Film, Say They "Experimented" With Three Images Only (EXCLUSIVE), March 21, *Variety*, variety.com/2024/film/news/late-night-with-the-devil-ai-images-clarifica-tion-1235947599/ (archived at https://perma.cc/H6BB-AATP)

Whitten, S (2023) Coca-Cola Causes Controversy with AI-made Ad, *NBC News*, www.nbcnews.com/tech/innovation/coca-cola-causes-controversy-ai-made-ad-rcna180665 (archived at https://perma.cc/4GH6-G4DT)

Navigating the Horizon: Continuous Learning and Adaptive Strategies

The rapid evolution of AI in marketing, as explored in the previous chapter, demands a systematic approach to continuous learning and adaptation. Organizations can no longer rely on static strategies or traditional change management approaches. Instead, they should develop dynamic capabilities that allow them to sense, respond to, and shape the future of ethical AI in marketing.

This chapter builds on the cultural foundations discussed in Chapter 9 and the technological landscape outlined in Chapter 10 to provide a practical framework for sustainable success in ethical AI marketing. We'll explore how organizations can build the adaptive capabilities, learning systems, and cultural elements needed to thrive in an increasingly AI-driven world while maintaining strong ethical principles.

Building Adaptive Capabilities

Succeeding with ethical AI in marketing transcends mere technological adoption. It necessitates cultivating robust organizational capabilities that enable continuous adaptation in a rapidly evolving landscape. Research demonstrates a strong positive correlation between organizational adaptability and the successful implementation of ethical AI initiatives. Organizations possessing robust adaptive capabilities are significantly better positioned to navigate the complexities of ethical AI deployment compared to their counterparts focused solely on technological acquisition. This underscores the critical role of systematic organizational learning and adaptation in the ethical AI journey.

Adaptability in ethical AI marketing hinges on three interconnected and mutually reinforcing principles: robust sensing capabilities, response flexibility, and learning integration. These principles, working in concert, create a responsive and ethically minded organization capable of navigating the multifaceted challenges and opportunities presented by AI.

Developing Sensing Mechanisms

Organizations require sophisticated systems to monitor and interpret the dynamic ethical AI landscape. Effective organizations adopt a holistic approach, integrating traditional market intelligence with specialized monitoring of AI ethics developments (Deloitte, 2023). This involves establishing structured processes for gathering and analyzing information from diverse sources, including stakeholder feedback (customers, employees, advocacy groups), evolving regulatory changes (local, national, international), rapid technological advancements in AI, and shifting consumer expectations regarding data privacy and algorithmic transparency.

Leading organizations move beyond passive monitoring to actively engage with their stakeholder communities. They conduct regular dialogues, surveys, and focus groups with customers, employees, and recognized ethical experts to understand emerging concerns, anticipate potential societal impacts, and identify opportunities for ethical innovation. This proactive approach enables organizations to anticipate and address potential ethical challenges before they escalate into reputational crises or regulatory interventions. This proactive stance is particularly crucial in the rapidly evolving field of AI ethics, where public perception and regulatory scrutiny can significantly impact an organization's long-term viability.

Integrating with Existing Marketing Workflows

Integrating adaptive capabilities seamlessly into existing marketing operations presents a significant challenge. Ethical considerations and adaptive learning must become an integral part of the natural workflow, not an added burden or a separate, siloed activity. This requires careful attention to both process design and cultural change management.

Successful organizations embed ethical checkpoints and learning mechanisms into their standard marketing processes without creating excessive bureaucracy. This might involve incorporating ethical impact assessments into campaign planning processes, establishing regular ethics review cycles for AI-driven marketing initiatives, or developing automated monitoring systems that flag potential ethical concerns (bias in algorithms, discriminatory targeting) for human review. This seamless integration fosters a culture of ethical awareness and proactive risk management, ensuring that ethical considerations are embedded in every stage of the marketing lifecycle.

Fostering Cross-Functional Team Development

Building truly adaptive capabilities necessitates breaking down traditional organizational silos and fostering collaboration across different functional areas. Strong cross-functional integration is essential for maintaining ethical compliance while simultaneously driving innovation in AI initiatives. Cross-functional teams, composed of individuals with diverse expertise (e.g. marketing, technology, legal, ethics), bring a broader range of perspectives to the table, enabling a more comprehensive assessment of ethical implications and a more agile response to emerging challenges. This collaborative approach facilitates a shared understanding of ethical principles, promotes a culture of shared responsibility for ethical AI development and deployment, and helps to avoid the pitfalls of "ethical silos" where responsibility for ethical considerations is diffused or unclear.

Continuous Learning Framework

Building adaptive capabilities is essential, but it's only the starting point. To truly thrive in the rapidly evolving world of AI marketing, organizations need a robust engine for continuous learning—a system that fuels ongoing knowledge acquisition, integration, and application. This goes far beyond traditional training programs or occasional reviews; it requires a comprehensive, organization-wide framework that fosters a culture of continuous improvement.

Building a Knowledge Pipeline

The rapid evolution of AI technology and its associated ethical considerations necessitates a structured approach to knowledge management within organizations. A study by Boston Consulting Group and MIT Sloan Management Review (2022) highlights that while 84 per cent of companies believe responsible AI should be a top management priority, only 25 per cent have fully mature, responsible AI programs in place. This disparity underscores the importance of proactively establishing comprehensive learning frameworks to effectively navigate AI's ethical complexities. It's not merely about reacting to emerging issues; it's about building a robust knowledge infrastructure that positions the organization ahead of the curve (World Economic Forum, 2021a).

To build an effective knowledge pipeline, organizations should focus on three key streams:

1 **Technical proficiency:** Maintaining a deep understanding of AI's capabilities is fundamental. This involves staying abreast of new algorithms, platforms, and applications, and understanding how they can be applied in marketing contexts.

2 **Ethical awareness:** Equally important is a keen awareness of the ethical implications of these technologies. This includes understanding potential biases, privacy concerns, and societal impacts.

3 **Stakeholder insights:** Organizations must understand the evolving expectations of their stakeholders—customers, employees, regulators, and the broader public.

This requires actively listening to their concerns and incorporating their feedback into the learning process.

Microsoft offers a compelling example of this integrated approach. The company established the Responsible AI Standard, a framework outlining steps that teams must follow to support the design and development of responsible AI systems. This standard ensures that technical learning is aligned with ethical considerations from the outset, fostering a more responsible and sustainable approach to AI innovation (World Economic Forum, 2021b)

By focusing on these streams and learning from industry leaders, organizations can proactively build knowledge pipelines that not only keep pace with technological advancements but also anticipate and address ethical challenges in AI.

Data Collection and Analysis Processes

Simply collecting data isn't enough; the real power lies in turning that data into actionable insights that drive ethical decision-making. As Brian Collins, co-founder of COLLINS, aptly put it, "Data without context is just noise. The real value comes from understanding what the data tells us about human experiences and ethical implications" (Collins, 2024). This understanding is crucial for navigating the complexities of AI in marketing.

To achieve this, organizations need to develop robust capabilities for analyzing both quantitative and qualitative data related to their AI initiatives. This involves gathering information from various sources:

- **Technical performance metrics:** These metrics track the efficiency and effectiveness of AI systems, such as accuracy rates, processing speed, and resource utilization.
- **Ethical compliance indicators:** These indicators measure adherence to ethical guidelines and principles, such as fairness metrics, bias detection rates, and privacy safeguards.
- **Stakeholder feedback:** This qualitative data provides valuable insights into how stakeholders perceive and experience AI-driven marketing interactions.

Leading organizations are creating integrated dashboards that bring these diverse data streams together. These dashboards provide a holistic view of AI initiatives, allowing organizations to identify trends, detect potential issues, and make informed decisions that balance performance with ethical considerations.

Feedback Loops and Iteration Cycles

Effective feedback mechanisms are crucial for refining AI systems and addressing ethical challenges. Research indicates that integrating ethical principles throughout the AI lifecycle enhances the system's ability to identify and mitigate ethical issues more efficiently. Embedding these principles at every stage is essential for ensuring that AI systems operate responsibly and align with human values.

Effective feedback loops operate at multiple levels, creating a dynamic system of continuous improvement:

- **Operational feedback:** At this level, AI systems are continuously monitored for performance and ethical compliance. Adjustments are made in real time to optimize performance and address any immediate issues.

- **Tactical feedback:** This level focuses on analyzing patterns and trends emerging from the operational data. These insights inform short-term strategy adjustments and help organizations adapt to changing circumstances.

- **Strategic feedback:** This higher-level feedback loop helps organizations understand the long-term implications of their AI initiatives. It informs their overall approach to ethical AI and shapes their strategic direction.

By establishing robust feedback loops at each of these levels, organizations create a closed-loop system of learning and adaptation, ensuring that their AI marketing practices remain both effective and ethical.

Learning from Failures and Successes

One of the most valuable sources of learning comes from analyzing both failures and successes in ethical AI implementation. As Stephanie Bannos-Ryback of Ipsos emphasizes in our interview, "Every misstep is an opportunity to strengthen our ethical framework, provided we're willing to learn from it openly and honestly" (Bannos-Ryback, 2024).

Organizations must create environments where teams feel safe discussing and learning from failures. This involves more than just post-mortem analyses of major incidents; it requires ongoing attention to near-misses, unexpected outcomes, and successful interventions. The most effective organizations maintain detailed case libraries of both failures and successes, using these as teaching tools for continuous improvement.

AI Ethics Monitoring and Assessment

MAINTAINING ETHICAL VIGILANCE

Given the constantly evolving landscape of AI ethics, organizations need dedicated monitoring and assessment systems to ensure ongoing ethical compliance. Research from the Partnership on AI underscores the importance of this vigilance, revealing that organizations with dedicated ethics monitoring systems are three times more likely to maintain stakeholder trust (Partnership on AI, 2024). This proactive approach is crucial for building and preserving public confidence.

COLLABORATING FOR COLLECTIVE PROGRESS

The complexities of ethical AI often surpass the resources and expertise of any single organization. Recognizing this, forward-thinking companies are increasingly engaging in industry collaborations and knowledge-sharing networks. These partnerships accelerate learning, facilitate the development of best practices, and foster a more responsible approach to AI development and deployment.

Menaka Gopinath, CMO of PMI, highlights the value of this collaborative approach: "We've found that collaborative learning accelerates our ability to identify and address ethical challenges before they become significant issues" (Gopinath, 2024). This shared learning environment is essential for navigating the uncharted territory of ethical AI.

These collaborations take many forms, from formal industry consortia to informal networks of experts. The Content Authenticity Initiative, previously discussed in Chapter 7, serves as a prime example. With over 3,000 members sharing insights and best practices, this initiative has played a key role in establishing new standards for transparency and accountability in AI-generated content. This demonstrates the power of collective action in driving meaningful progress in ethical AI implementation.

Risk Management and Mitigation

As AI systems become more sophisticated and autonomous, the nature of risks evolves correspondingly. Organizations must develop comprehensive approaches to identifying, assessing, and mitigating both existing and emerging risks.

Identifying Emerging Risks

ANTICIPATING THE UNFORESEEN

Traditional risk management frameworks often fall short in addressing the dynamic challenges posed by AI. To bridge this gap, organizations are adopting comprehensive strategies that anticipate potential issues before they arise.

One such initiative is the AI Risk Repository developed by MIT, which consolidates over 1,000 AI risks extracted from 56 existing frameworks. This extensive database categorizes risks based on their causes and domains, providing organizations with a robust framework to understand and mitigate AI-related risks effectively. By utilizing such predictive risk identification methods, organizations can proactively address potential ethical issues, thereby minimizing incidents and fostering responsible AI deployment (AI Risk Repository, 2024).

Leading organizations are enhancing their risk management by integrating traditional assessment methods with AI-specific considerations. This involves a "horizon scanning plus" approach, which encompasses monitoring a broad spectrum of potential risks:

- **Technical risks:** Issues such as algorithmic bias, data privacy vulnerabilities, and system failures.
- **Societal risks:** Concerns including unintended discrimination, manipulation, or erosion of public trust.

By actively scanning for both technical and societal risks, organizations can address potential issues proactively, thereby minimizing negative impacts and promoting ethical AI practices in marketing.

Contingency Planning

AI-related issues can escalate rapidly, making robust contingency plans essential. Organizations must be prepared to respond swiftly and effectively to a range of potential scenarios, from technical malfunctions to ethical breaches.

Effective contingency plans go beyond simply addressing the immediate technical problem. They should encompass several key elements:

- **Technical response:** Clear procedures for addressing technical failures, system outages, and data breaches.
- **Stakeholder communication:** Pre-prepared communication strategies for informing affected stakeholders, including customers, employees, and the media.
- **Reputation management:** Strategies for mitigating reputational damage and rebuilding trust.
- **Remediation strategies:** Plans for rectifying the situation, compensating affected parties, and preventing future occurrences.

Leading organizations regularly test these plans through simulations and drills. This proactive approach ensures that teams are well-prepared to execute the plans effectively when a real crisis occurs, minimizing disruption and protecting the organization's reputation.

Algorithmic Bias Monitoring

Algorithmic bias poses a significant challenge, particularly in marketing, where AI-driven decisions can have a profound impact on consumer experiences and opportunities. To mitigate this risk, organizations should implement robust monitoring systems to detect and address bias in their AI systems.

Enterprises typically employ a multi-layered approach to bias monitoring, incorporating the following key strategies:

- **Automated testing:** Regular automated testing of AI systems against established fairness metrics provides a first line of defense against obvious biases.

- **Deep-dive analysis:** Periodic in-depth analysis helps uncover more subtle forms of bias that may not be detected by standard metrics. This often involves human review and expert analysis.

- **Stakeholder feedback:** Maintaining open channels for stakeholder feedback provides valuable insights into real-world experiences and can reveal biases that may not be apparent through testing alone.

Privacy Risk Evolution

As AI marketing systems become more sophisticated in their data collection and analysis capabilities, privacy risks continue to evolve in complexity and scope. Recent developments in consumer privacy regulations, coupled with advancing AI capabilities, have created new challenges for organizations seeking to balance personalization with privacy protection. Bannos-Ryback, who serves as Ipsos's EVP and Head of Experience Practice, emphasizes this evolution in our interview: "Privacy is no longer just about data protection—it's about respecting human dignity in an age of increasingly intimate consumer insights" (Bannos-Ryback, 2024).

The evolution of privacy risks extends beyond traditional concerns about data breaches or unauthorized access. Organizations must now grapple with "inference privacy"—the ability of AI systems to deduce sensitive personal information from seemingly innocuous data points. Regulatory bodies, such as the U.K.'s ICO, highlight that AI systems can be used to make inferences about individuals by analyzing and finding correlations between datasets. This can lead to the categorization, profiling, or prediction of details about someone, potentially revealing sensitive information, even if that information wasn't directly provided (ICO, n.d.). This capability of AI systems to infer personal characteristics, behaviors, and even health conditions from various data sources, including marketing data, raises new ethical challenges for responsible marketers.

Regulatory Compliance Adaptation

The regulatory landscape surrounding AI in marketing continues to evolve rapidly, requiring organizations to develop adaptive compliance capabilities. Rather than viewing compliance as a fixed target, successful organizations approach it as a dynamic process requiring continuous monitoring and adjustment.

Effective regulatory compliance adaptation requires organizations to develop "regulatory intelligence"—the ability to not just track but anticipate and prepare for regulatory changes. This involves maintaining close relationships with regulatory bodies, participating in policy discussions, and building flexible compliance frameworks that can adapt to new requirements without disrupting core operations.

Innovation Management

Innovation in ethical AI marketing requires a delicate balance between pushing technological boundaries and maintaining strong ethical guardrails. Organizations must develop sophisticated approaches to managing this tension productively.

Balancing Innovation with Ethical Considerations

The drive for innovation in AI marketing must be tempered by careful consideration of ethical implications. Research from the MIT Media Lab shows that organizations integrating ethical assessment into their innovation processes from the outset are significantly more likely to develop successful, sustainable AI marketing solutions (MIT Sloan Management Review, 2022). This finding challenges the common assumption that ethical considerations inherently slow innovation.

The most successful organizations have developed "ethics-forward innovation"—an approach that treats ethical considerations not as constraints but as creative challenges that drive more thoughtful and sustainable innovation. This approach requires close collaboration between technical teams, ethicists, and marketing strategists from the earliest stages of development.

Human-AI Collaboration Models

As AI systems become more sophisticated, the nature of human-AI collaboration in marketing continues to evolve. The most effective organizations have moved beyond simple automation to develop "augmented intelligence" approaches—models that leverage the unique strengths of both human and AI. This evolution reflects a growing understanding that the future of marketing lies not in AI replacement of human capabilities but in thoughtful integration of human and machine intelligence.

Experimental Approaches and Pilot Programs

The complexity of ethical AI in marketing necessitates rigorous experimental approaches prior to full-scale implementation. Organizations must develop systematic methods for testing new ideas while managing potential risks. These experimental approaches serve as crucial learning environments where organizations can refine both technical capabilities and ethical safeguards.

Intel exemplifies this approach through its commitment to responsible AI development. The company emphasizes the importance of designing AI that lowers risks and optimizes benefits for society. While specific details about "ethical sandboxes" are not publicly disclosed, Intel's comprehensive approach to responsible AI involves creating controlled environments to test AI marketing initiatives with real consumers under strict ethical oversight. This strategy allows for rapid iteration and learning while safeguarding consumer interests. As a result, initiatives tested through such meticulous experimentation have demonstrated higher success rates upon full deployment (Intel, 2024).

Organizations employing experimental approaches to AI integration are better positioned to navigate uncertainties and achieve successful outcomes. A study by MIT Sloan Management Review and Boston Consulting Group (2024) highlights that companies combining organizational learning with AI-specific training are more effective in managing uncertainties associated with AI deployment. This underscores the value of experimental methods in refining AI applications before broader implementation.

By adopting such experimental approaches, organizations can enhance their technical proficiency and ethical awareness, leading to more responsible and effective AI applications in marketing.

Scaling Successful Initiatives

The journey from pilot to full-scale implementation represents a critical inflection point in any AI initiative—one where even the most promising ethical frameworks can begin to show stress fractures. Just as a recipe that works perfectly for a family dinner might fail spectacularly when scaled up to serve a thousand, ethical AI systems that function beautifully in controlled pilots can encounter unexpected challenges at scale.

"The ethics of AI scaling isn't linear—it's exponential," explains Dr. Elizabeth M. Adams, Chief AI Ethics Advisor at Paravision. "Each order of magnitude increase in deployment introduces new ethical complexities. When you go from affecting hundreds of decisions to millions, you're not just dealing with more of the same ethical considerations—you're encountering entirely new categories of ethical risk" (Adams, 2024).

Successful organizations have learned to approach scaling through what experts call "ethical stage-gating"—a systematic process where AI initiatives must clear increasingly rigorous ethical reviews as they expand in scope and impact. This approach typically involves:

- defined ethical thresholds that trigger new levels of review
- cross-functional assessment teams that expand with scale
- enhanced monitoring systems for detecting emergent ethical issues
- regular reassessment of ethical frameworks against actual outcomes.

The key is maintaining ethical integrity while managing the complexity that comes with scale. As Dr. Adams notes, "At scale, you're not just protecting against known ethical risks—you're building systems capable of identifying and responding to emerging ethical challenges before they become critical issues."

Managing Innovation Portfolios

Organizations must develop sophisticated approaches to managing diverse portfolios of AI marketing initiatives, each with varying risk profiles and ethical considerations. The most successful organizations maintain "ethical innovation portfolios"—balanced collections of initiatives that span different time horizons and risk levels while ensuring strong ethical alignment.

Recent industry reports from firms like Accenture and McKinsey suggest that organizations adopting coordinated, ethics-aligned AI innovation portfolios outperform their peers by up to 40–50 per cent in AI-driven business outcomes. These portfolios enable a strategic balance of risk, experimentation, and long-term value creation through ethical oversight, centralized governance, and cross-functional collaboration (Accenture, 2023; McKinsey & Company, 2023).

For instance, Accenture's 2023 report on AI maturity found that "AI Achievers"—the top 12 per cent of organizations with mature, integrated AI practices—realized 50 per cent greater revenue growth compared to their peers. These outperformers were more likely to embed responsible AI principles, scale innovation effectively, and manage risk through a balanced portfolio approach (Accenture, 2023).

The emergence of ethics-driven innovation represents a critical evolution in how organizations develop and deploy AI marketing solutions. Rather than treating ethics as a constraint, leading companies are discovering how ethical considerations—such as transparency, inclusivity, and fairness—can serve as a catalyst for creative problem-solving, sustainable innovation, and stakeholder trust.

Stakeholder Engagement

The success of ethical AI marketing initiatives ultimately depends on meaningful engagement with diverse stakeholder groups. Organizations must develop sophisticated approaches to building and maintaining these relationships over time.

Building Long-Term Relationships

Creating lasting stakeholder relationships in the context of AI marketing requires more than traditional engagement approaches. Organizations must develop dynamic trust frameworks—systems that can adapt to evolving stakeholder concerns while maintaining consistent ethical principles.

Organizations that take a systematic and proactive approach to stakeholder relationship management are significantly more likely to sustain trust, especially during periods of scrutiny or controversy related to AI. Rather than relying on reactive crisis responses, leading companies prioritize continuous engagement, clarity, and accountability as part of their long-term strategy.

Effective stakeholder relationship management in the AI era requires adaptive transparency—the ability to share appropriate information at the right level of detail for different stakeholder groups while maintaining consistent ethical principles. Organizations must develop sophisticated approaches to communicating complex technical concepts in ways that resonate with various audiences while demonstrating genuine commitment to ethical practices.

Communication Strategies

The complexity of AI marketing systems demands new approaches to stakeholder communication. Traditional corporate communications often prove insufficient for explaining AI-driven decisions and their ethical implications. As Brian Collins emphasizes in our interview, "We need to move beyond simple transparency to what I call 'meaningful clarity'—helping stakeholders understand not just what our AI systems do, but why and how they align with shared values" (Collins, 2024).

Successful organizations have developed multi-layered communication frameworks that can adapt to different stakeholder needs while maintaining consistency in core messaging. This might involve creating different levels of technical detail for various audiences, using visual explanations for complex concepts, and maintaining regular dialogue about ethical considerations.

Consumer Trust Building

Building and maintaining consumer trust in AI-driven marketing requires a deliberate and sustained effort. As AI systems increasingly shape how brands interact with consumers—from personalized content to automated decision-making—trust becomes a critical currency. But in today's environment, trust is not granted automatically; it must be actively earned through transparency, ethical consistency, and ongoing engagement.

Recent Salesforce (2023) research reveals that only 45 per cent of consumers trust companies to use AI ethically, signaling a significant trust gap that marketers must address. In parallel, the Edelman Trust Barometer (2023) emphasizes that consumers expect brands to move beyond transactional interactions and demonstrate a commitment to responsible practices and open communication. Organizations that meet these expectations—by proactively clarifying how AI is used, protecting consumer data, and responding to concerns—are far more likely to establish enduring trust.

One of the most effective strategies for trust-building is progressive disclosure: the thoughtful, staged sharing of information about AI systems, tailored to the consumer's level of understanding. Rather than overwhelming users with technical details, this approach enables them to build confidence gradually. It recognizes that trust is not a one-time achievement but an evolving relationship, strengthened through consistent ethical behavior, transparent communication, and a demonstrated respect for consumer autonomy.

Employee Upskilling and Reskilling

The evolution of AI marketing creates new demands for employee capabilities at all organizational levels. Our interview with Henry Shevlin reveals the importance of comprehensive skill development: "We're not just training people to use new tools— we're developing their capacity for ethical reasoning in an AI-driven world" (Shevlin, 2024).

Organizations must develop sophisticated approaches to workforce development that combine technical training with ethical awareness building. This often involves creating "ethical competency frameworks"—structured approaches to developing both technical and ethical capabilities across different organizational roles.

Future-Proofing Strategies

The rapid evolution of AI technology and shifting ethical expectations require organizations to develop robust strategies for future-proofing their marketing operations. Traditional strategic planning approaches—typically based on three-to-five-year cycles—are often inadequate for addressing the long-term implications of AI in marketing. Instead, organizations must adopt adaptive foresight, a strategic approach that combines long-term vision with the flexibility to adjust as technology and ethical standards evolve.

Long-Term Planning Approaches

The acceleration of AI technology development necessitates planning frameworks that are both proactive and dynamic. Research from the MIT Sloan Management Review (2022) indicates that organizations leveraging adaptive foresight—a structured method of forecasting technological and ethical shifts—demonstrate 65 per cent greater preparedness for emerging AI-related ethical challenges compared to those relying on static strategic plans. These organizations employ horizon scanning techniques, integrating technological trend analysis with deep ethical foresight to anticipate risks and opportunities (MIT Sloan Management Review, 2022).

Scenario Planning and Forecasting

Organizations must move beyond traditional forecasting methods and adopt ethical scenario matrices—frameworks that evaluate AI's potential future developments alongside evolving societal expectations and regulatory shifts. As Bannos-Ryback explains: "We're not just planning for different technological futures—we're preparing for fundamental shifts in how society views the relationship between AI and human agency" (Bannos-Ryback, 2024).

By employing scenario-based strategic planning, companies can prepare for various AI futures, ensuring that ethical considerations remain central to their decision-making. Leading firms use multi-stakeholder scenario planning to incorporate diverse perspectives, aligning AI development with societal values and regulatory landscapes.

Building Sustainable Competitive Advantages

In an era where AI advancements quickly become commoditized, sustainable competitive advantage increasingly hinges on an organization's ability to maintain ethical leadership while driving innovation. Companies that proactively integrate ethical AI principles establish "ethical moats"—sustainable advantages built on deep stakeholder trust and demonstrated ethical responsibility.

For instance, Microsoft has positioned itself as a leader in responsible AI by embedding ethical principles into its AI governance, establishing trust with regulators, customers, and partners. Similarly, IBM's AI Ethics Board serves as a governance model that differentiates the company in an increasingly regulated AI landscape.

Environmental Sustainability Considerations

The environmental impact of AI has emerged as a crucial consideration in future-proofing strategies. As AI systems become deeply embedded in marketing and society, organizations must develop approaches that optimize for both performance and environmental impact.

THE CARBON FOOTPRINT OF AI-POWERED MARKETING

While AI significantly enhances marketing efficiency—enabling real-time personalization, audience targeting, and generative content creation—its energy demands are substantial and growing. As organizations scale their use of AI technologies in marketing, the environmental implications are becoming impossible to ignore.

Training large AI models requires massive computational resources. For instance, training OpenAI's GPT-3 model consumed approximately 1,287 megawatt hours of electricity, resulting in 502 metric tons of CO_2 emissions—roughly equivalent to the annual emissions of 112 gasoline-powered cars (Columbia Climate School, 2023). And that's just the training phase.

Once deployed, these systems continue to draw energy through inference—i.e. making predictions or generating content. For GPT-3, inference emissions are estimated at about 8.4 metric tons of CO_2 per year, even without accounting for the emissions tied to millions of daily users.

As demand for AI accelerates, the International Energy Agency warns that data center electricity usage, largely driven by AI workloads, could more than double between 2022 and 2026, potentially consuming as much power as the entire nation of Japan (Greenly, 2024).

This has direct implications for marketing use cases, where AI models are continuously running behind:

- programmatic advertising platforms processing millions of impressions per second
- generative content engines creating personalized video, images, or text at scale
- personalization algorithms delivering real-time recommendations and dynamic experiences.

To mitigate this footprint, marketers must consider not just what AI can do—but how it's done. Integrating sustainability into AI strategy is no longer optional; it's essential to future proofing both environmental and brand integrity.

SUSTAINABLE AI STRATEGIES FOR MARKETING

To balance AI-driven marketing efficiency with sustainability, forward-thinking organizations are developing "sustainable AI architectures"—approaches that optimize for both performance and environmental impact while maintaining strong ethical foundations:

- **Energy-efficient AI for targeting and personalization:** Reducing unnecessary AI-driven impressions by prioritizing quality over quantity in digital placements helps minimize environmental impact. Many organizations are adopting lightweight AI models for personalized recommendations instead of energy-intensive deep learning models when appropriate. Leading platforms like Google and Meta now incorporate carbon-aware optimization to reduce energy-intensive ad auctions.

- **Sustainable customer engagement:** Optimizing AI-powered chatbots to run on smaller, more efficient models can significantly reduce energy consumption. Batch-processing AI-driven insights (like customer sentiment analysis or churn prediction), rather than running them in real time unnecessarily, further reduces the carbon footprint. Using predictive engagement models to trigger marketing messages only when users are most likely to respond eliminates redundant AI computations.

- **Carbon-neutral AI infrastructure:** Choosing cloud providers committed to sustainability, such as those offering 100 per cent renewable energy-powered AI operations, can dramatically reduce environmental impact. Some marketing organizations are moving certain AI computations from centralized data centers to edge computing, reducing energy use significantly (MIT News, 2023). According to MIT research, shifting to edge devices not only improves computation efficiency but also reduces transmission costs by processing data closer to where it's collected and used, leading to substantial energy savings. Implementing AI energy-monitoring systems allows teams to track and optimize their marketing AI's environmental impact.

Ethical AI Governance Evolution

As AI systems become more autonomous and sophisticated, governance frameworks must evolve dynamically to ensure ethical oversight without stifling innovation. Organizations must implement adaptive AI governance models, which continuously update policies based on emerging risks, regulatory changes, and stakeholder expectations.

The EU AI Act and the U.S. AI Bill of Rights signal an increasing push for transparent and accountable AI. Leading companies are already adapting by:

- establishing internal AI ethics boards to oversee AI development (e.g. Google's AI Principles)

- implementing third-party AI audits to ensure compliance with evolving regulations

- developing "explainability frameworks," ensuring AI decisions remain interpretable and trustworthy for consumers and regulators alike.

By prioritizing adaptive foresight, ethical scenario planning, sustainable AI development, and governance innovation, organizations can future-proof their marketing strategies while maintaining ethical leadership in an AI-driven world.

Measuring Progress and Success

The challenge of measuring progress in ethical AI implementation extends beyond traditional marketing metrics. Organizations must develop sophisticated approaches to assessing both technical performance and ethical alignment over time.

Defining Success Metrics

Success in ethical AI marketing requires a multidimensional approach to measurement. Traditional marketing metrics like conversion rates and ROI must be complemented by new measures that capture ethical performance and stakeholder trust. The challenge of measuring ethical AI implementation extends beyond traditional marketing metrics. Dr. Henry Shevlin, from the Leverhulme Centre for the Future of Intelligence, offers a compelling perspective on this evolution: "Organizations often approach measurement through a purely quantitative lens. But measuring ethical AI implementation requires us to think more deeply about qualitative indicators and long-term impacts on human behavior and organizational culture. When we measure success in ethical AI, we're really measuring our ability to create sustainable, human-centered systems that can adapt and learn."

Organizations at the forefront of ethical AI marketing have developed what we might call "integrated success frameworks" that combine traditional performance metrics with ethical indicators. These frameworks typically assess performance across three key dimensions: technical effectiveness, ethical alignment, and stakeholder impact. This approach recognizes that true success in AI marketing requires excellence across all these areas rather than optimization of any single dimension.

Measuring Stakeholder Satisfaction

Understanding stakeholder satisfaction in the context of AI marketing requires more nuanced approaches than traditional customer satisfaction metrics. Organizations must develop methods for assessing not just immediate satisfaction with AI interactions but deeper trust and comfort with AI-driven marketing practices.

The most effective organizations have developed what we might call "trust velocity metrics"—measures that track not just current trust levels but the rate and direction of trust development over time. These metrics help organizations understand how their ethical AI practices influence stakeholder relationships and identify areas requiring additional attention.

Assessing Long-Term Impact

The true impact of ethical AI marketing practices often emerges only over extended periods. Organizations must develop approaches to measuring long-term effects across multiple stakeholder groups and society at large. This might involve tracking what we call "ethical ripple effects"—the broader societal impacts of AI marketing practices beyond immediate business outcomes.

Our interview with Henry Shevlin provides insight into this challenge: "We need to think beyond quarterly results to understand how our AI practices are shaping social norms and expectations around technology use" (Shevlin, 2024). This perspective requires organizations to develop new approaches to impact assessment that can capture both immediate and long-term effects of their AI marketing practices.

Building a Learning Culture

The success of ethical AI initiatives ultimately depends on creating organizational cultures that support continuous learning and ethical development. As Shevlin explains, "We're not just training people to use new tools—we're developing their capacity for ethical reasoning in an AI-driven world" (Shevlin, 2024).

Encouraging Knowledge Sharing and Collaboration

One of the most effective ways to cultivate a learning culture is to encourage and facilitate knowledge sharing among team members. This can be done through:

- establishing regular "brown bag" sessions or lunch-and-learns where employees can present on interesting AI ethics topics or share real-world examples
- creating an internal wiki or knowledge base where team members can document learnings, best practices, and resources related to ethical AI
- fostering a culture of "working out loud" where individuals share works-in-progress to get feedback and input from colleagues
- providing collaboration tools and spaces (both virtual and physical) that make it easy for employees to connect and share ideas.

Marketing leaders should model the behavior they want to see, openly sharing their own learnings and insights. They should also recognize and reward employees who actively contribute to the organization's collective knowledge.

Embracing Failure as a Learning Opportunity

In a rapidly evolving field like AI ethics, failures and missteps are inevitable. What distinguishes learning organizations is how they respond to these setbacks. Rather than assigning blame or sweeping issues under the rug, learning cultures treat failures as valuable opportunities for growth.

This requires a fundamental shift in mindset. Leaders must create an environment where it's psychologically safe to admit mistakes and discuss them openly. One way to do this is by conducting regular "blameless postmortems" after any AI ethics incidents. These sessions focus on understanding what happened, why it happened, and what can be learned to prevent similar issues in the future—not on pointing fingers.

Some organizations even celebrate failures as a mark of innovation and risk-taking. Etsy, for example, gives out an annual "Oopsies Award" to employees who made a significant mistake but handled it well and learned from it. This sends a powerful message that the company values learning and growth over perfection.

Investing in Formal and Informal Learning Opportunities

A robust learning culture supports both formal and informal learning. On the formal side, this might include:

- providing access to online courses, workshops, and certification programs related to AI ethics
- bringing in external experts to conduct training sessions or talks
- sponsoring employees to attend industry conferences and events
- offering tuition reimbursement for relevant degree programs.

Just as important, however, are the informal learning opportunities that occur through everyday work experiences. Leaders can encourage this type of learning by:

- giving employees stretch assignments that push them out of their comfort zone
- encouraging cross-functional collaboration and job shadowing to expose individuals to new perspectives
- providing time and space for self-directed learning and experimentation
- fostering a culture of continuous feedback where employees regularly give and receive constructive input.

The most effective learning organizations blend both structured and unstructured learning, understanding that growth happens both in and out of the classroom.

Measuring and Rewarding Learning

To truly embed learning into the cultural fabric of an organization, it needs to be measured and rewarded. This starts with setting clear learning objectives at both the individual and organizational level. What skills and knowledge do the company need to develop to stay ahead of the curve on AI ethics? What does growth look like for each employee given their role and career stage?

Next, organizations need to put systems in place to track progress against these objectives. This might include:

- conducting regular skills assessments to identify gaps and growth areas
- using learning management systems to monitor course completion and certification
- tracking participation in knowledge-sharing activities
- measuring the impact of learning on business outcomes (e.g. reduction in AI ethics incidents, improvement in customer trust scores).

Finally, learning needs to be explicitly tied to performance management and career advancement. Employees who demonstrate a commitment to continuous learning and actively contribute to the organization's AI ethics knowledge base should be recognized and rewarded. This could be through formal mechanisms like performance bonuses and promotions, or informal recognition like shout-outs in team meetings and company newsletters.

By measuring and incentivizing learning, organizations send a clear message that growth and development are valued and expected. This helps make learning an integral part of the company culture rather than just a side activity.

Integrating these strategies—encouraging knowledge sharing, embracing failure, investing in formal and informal learning, and measuring and rewarding growth—can help marketing organizations cultivate the learning culture needed to stay ahead in the fast-moving world of AI ethics. But building this kind of culture is an ongoing journey, not a one-time initiative. It requires consistent effort, resources, and leadership commitment. The payoff, however, is an organization that is continuously evolving, innovating, and staying at the forefront of responsible AI practices.

Bringing It All Together

As we've seen throughout this chapter, cultivating an ethical AI culture in marketing is a multifaceted endeavor that requires commitment, collaboration, and continuous learning. The key elements of clear values, psychological safety, distributed responsibility, and a growth mindset form the foundation upon which responsible AI practices can flourish.

KEY TAKEAWAYS

- **Leadership sets the ethical tone**: Leaders play a pivotal role in shaping an organization's ethical AI culture through their communication, resource allocation, and modeling of desired behaviors.
  Why it matters: When leaders visibly prioritize and invest in ethical AI practices, it sends a powerful signal throughout the organization that ethics is not just a nice-to-have but a core business imperative. This leadership commitment is the bedrock upon which an ethical AI culture is built.

- **Cross-functional collaboration is critical**: Building ethical AI systems requires close collaboration across technical, business, and ethical perspectives. Integrated, diverse teams are better equipped to spot and address ethical blind spots.
  Why it matters: Siloed approaches to AI development often lead to unintended consequences and ethical lapses. By fostering open communication and shared

ownership across functions, organizations can proactively identify and mitigate ethical risks throughout the AI lifecycle.

- **Ethical skills and knowledge must be cultivated**: Comprehensive training programs that develop both technical understanding and ethical reasoning capabilities are essential for empowering marketing teams to navigate the complexities of AI responsibly.

  Why it matters: As AI becomes increasingly central to marketing, it's not enough for teams to know how to use these tools—they must also deeply understand the ethical implications. Investing in robust, ongoing ethics education ensures that ethical considerations are baked into every stage of the marketing process.

- **A learning mindset drives continuous improvement**: Organizations with strong ethical AI cultures embrace continuous learning—they encourage knowledge sharing, view failures as growth opportunities, and reward ongoing skill development.

  Why it matters: In a field as dynamic as AI, static, one-and-done approaches to ethics quickly become outdated. By cultivating a learning culture, organizations ensure their ethical practices remain relevant and responsive to new challenges and insights. This adaptability is key to long-term success in responsible AI innovation.

Food for Thought

1 How well do your current performance metrics and incentive structures encourage continuous learning, knowledge sharing, and ethical behavior around AI? What specific changes could better align them with your ethical AI goals?

2 As a leader, how do you visibly model continuous learning and a growth mindset when it comes to AI ethics? What's one way you could further emphasize the importance of ongoing ethical skill development for your team?

3 How might you proactively create space for teams to discuss potential risks, failure modes, or unintended consequences of AI systems in your specific marketing context before issues arise?

4 If your organization experienced a major AI ethics lapse, how well would your current culture and practices support transparent, accountable, and trust-building responses? What key changes could increase your resilience to such a crisis?

References

Accenture (2023) The Art of AI Maturity: Advancing from Practice to Performance, www.accenture.com/us-en/insights/artificial-intelligence/ai-maturity-and-transformation (archived at https://perma.cc/B2FN-KUUT)

Adams, E, Video interview by Nicole M. Alexander, January 15, 2024

AI Risk Repository (2024) *What Are the Risks from Artificial Intelligence? A Comprehensive Repository*, Massachusetts Institute of Technology, airisk.mit.edu (archived at https://perma.cc/K36N-VZJ2)

Bannos-Ryback, S, Video interview by Nicole M. Alexander, October 18, 2024

Collins, B, Video interview by Nicole M. Alexander, November 24, 2024

Columbia Climate School (2023) AI's Growing Carbon Footprint, June 9, news.climate.columbia.edu/2023/06/09/ais-growing-carbon-footprint/ (archived at https://perma.cc/K4T7-2ATW)

Deloitte (2023) *The State of AI in Marketing: Global Survey Insights,* www2.deloitte.com/us/en/insights/focus/cognitive-technologies/state-of-ai-and-intelligent-automation-in-business-survey.html (archived at https://perma.cc/8ZD2-MNP9)

Edelman (2023) *2023 Edelman Trust Barometer*, www.edelman.com/trust/2023/trust-barometer (archived at https://perma.cc/3PPD-4PDW)

Foy, K (2023) *New tools are available to help reduce the energy that AI models devour,* MIT News, https://news.mit.edu/2023/new-tools-available-reduce-energy-that-ai-models-devour-1005 (archived at https://perma.cc/PJL7-T5WH)

Gopinath, M, Video interview by Nicole M. Alexander, October 18, 2024

Greenly (2024) The Environmental Impact of Artificial Intelligence, greenly.earth/en-gb/leaf-media/data-stories/the-environmental-impact-of-artificial-intelligence (archived at https://perma.cc/92BP-E893)

ICO (n.d.) How Do We Ensure Lawfulness in AI? ico.org.uk/for-organisations/uk-gdpr-guidance-and-resources/artificial-intelligence/guidance-on-ai-and-data-protection/how-do-we-ensure-lawfulness-in-ai/ (archived at https://perma.cc/VG9Z-QNQ5)

Intel (2024) *Responsible AI: Designing AI to benefit society*, www.intel.com/content/www/us/en/artificial-intelligence/responsible-ai.html (archived at https://perma.cc/8KEB-3QMZ)

McKinsey & Company (2023) The State of AI in 2023: Generative AI's Breakout Year, August 1, www.mckinsey.com/capabilities/quantumblack/our-insights/the-state-of-ai-in-2023-generative-ais-breakout-year (archived at https://perma.cc/H644-ECXC)

MIT Sloan Management Review and Boston Consulting Group (2024) Learning to Manage Uncertainty with AI, *MIT Sloan Management Review*, sloanreview.mit.edu/projects/learning-to-manage-uncertainty-with-ai (archived at https://perma.cc/5PW7-LG2Y)

Partnership on AI (2024) *PAI's Guidance for Safe Foundation Model Deployment: A Framework for Collective Action*, partnershiponai.org/ modeldeployment (archived at https://perma.cc/5CK4-HR2Z)

Renieris, E M, Kiron, D, and Mills, S (2022) *To be a responsible AI leader, focus on being responsible*, MIT Sloan Management Review and Boston Consulting Group, https://sloanreview.mit.edu/projects/to-be-a-responsible-ai-leader-focus-on-being-responsible/ (archived at https://perma.cc/9XSN-CRCY)

Salesforce (2023) Business Adopting AI Risk a 'Trust Gap' with Customers – Saleforce Report, August 28, www.salesforce.com/news/stories/customer-engagement-research-2023/ (archived at https://perma.cc/Y8W7-DMFL)

Shevlin, H, Video interview by Nicole M. Alexander, November 22, 2024

World Economic Forum (2021a) *Responsible Use of Technology: The Microsoft Case Study*, www3.weforum.org/docs/WEF_Responsible_Use_of_Technology_2021.pdf (archived at https://perma.cc/25VK-293L)

World Economic Forum (2021b) 4 Lessons on Designing Responsible, Ethical Tech: Microsoft Case Study, *World Economic Forum*, www.weforum.org/stories/2021/02/4-lessons-from-microsoft-on-designing-responsible-ethical-tech (archived at https://perma.cc/GF5G-8BH8)

Conclusion: A Call to Action for Ethical Leadership

As we conclude this exploration of ethical AI in marketing, one truth stands clear: The path forward lies in collaboration, continuous learning, and an unwavering commitment to human-centric values. The insights, strategies, and frameworks provided in this book lay a strong foundation for navigating the complexities of AI-driven marketing. But the real power to shape an ethical future rests with you— the marketers, innovators, and leaders who will bring these principles to life.

Throughout this book, we've seen how AI is transforming marketing, from personalized experiences to targeted campaigns and content creation. The potential benefits are immense—enhanced efficiency, innovation, and consumer engagement. Yet, these opportunities come with significant ethical challenges around privacy, fairness, transparency, and accountability.

To meet these challenges head-on, we began in Part I by laying the ethical groundwork: defining key principles for responsible AI, exploring human-centered design, and examining the evolving role of marketers in an AI-driven world. These chapters emphasized the importance of placing human values at the center of AI strategies, providing a moral compass to guide marketing innovation.

In Part II, we moved from theory to practice, offering concrete frameworks to operationalize these ethical principles. The P.A.C.T. Framework introduced in Chapter 5 provided a practical approach for embedding ethics into every stage of the AI lifecycle—from data collection and algorithm design to deployment and ongoing monitoring. We addressed real-world challenges like balancing personalization with privacy, ensuring fairness in targeting, and maintaining transparency in AI-driven interactions.

Part III delved into the critical role of consumer trust and perception, exploring how cultural, regional, and industry-specific factors shape attitudes toward AI. We offered strategies for building trust through transparency, control, and value alignment, alongside the governance frameworks needed for accountability and compliance.

Finally, Part IV focused on preparing for the future—helping organizations cultivate an ethical AI culture rooted in continuous learning, experimentation, and stakeholder collaboration. We examined adaptive strategies for staying ahead of technological and regulatory shifts and encouraged readers to embrace their roles as ethical leaders and change agents.

Throughout these pages, we've heard from pioneering thinkers and practitioners—from leaders at Ally Financial, Adobe, Ipsos, Dataiku, COLLINS, and OSF Healthcare, to renowned academics and ethical AI pioneers like Dr. Henry Shevlin and Dr. Elizabeth M. Adams. Their insights illuminated the challenges and opportunities of ethical AI and demonstrated the transformative potential of human-centered innovation.

Now, the most important voice remains your own. The true test of these principles lies in how you, the reader, will apply them in your work. Whether you're refining a new personalization engine, launching an AI-powered campaign, or reimagining your organization's data practices, every decision represents an opportunity to champion ethical, human-centric AI.

As you embark on this journey, remember: You're part of a vibrant community of professionals committed to responsible innovation. The path ahead will undoubtedly present challenges, but by staying grounded in values like empathy, fairness, transparency, and accountability—and by embracing continuous learning and collaboration—you have the power not just to navigate these challenges, but to lead the way forward.

The future of marketing—and the lives it touches—will be shaped by the choices we make and the standards we uphold. Let us choose to put human flourishing at the center of our work. Let us be bold in our experimentation, but always guided by a moral compass and a commitment to well-being. Remember the world we imagined in the introduction, where your coffee shop anticipates your every need? Let's ensure that the world is built on trust, transparency, and respect for individual autonomy.

In this AI-driven era, marketers have a profound opportunity and responsibility to wield technology in service of human values. The journey toward ethical AI is not one we can undertake alone—it will require ongoing dialogue, collaboration, and shared commitment. As AI continues to evolve, maintaining the balance between innovation and ethics—as we've explored throughout this book—will require vigilance, adaptation, and lifelong learning. Together, we can shape a future where innovation and ethics, creativity and responsibility go hand in hand—a future where marketing doesn't just sell products but serves people.

Let the journey toward ethical AI in marketing begin today, with you.

GLOSSARY

Accountability: The principle that individuals and organizations are responsible for the actions and decisions of their AI systems. In the context of governance, accountability ensures that there are clear roles and escalation paths for identifying, reporting, and addressing ethical issues.

Adaptive foresight: The organizational capability to maintain a clear long-term vision while adjusting tactical approaches as technology and ethical expectations evolve, enabling more effective strategic planning in AI marketing.

Adaptive governance: A flexible, evolving approach to AI oversight that adjusts to regulatory changes, technological advancements, and consumer expectations.

Adaptive oversight systems: Dynamic monitoring and control mechanisms that evolve alongside AI capabilities to maintain ethical standards while enabling innovation.

Advanced cognitive architectures: AI systems designed to emulate human-like understanding, including natural language comprehension, emotional state recognition, and analogical reasoning.

AI agents: Autonomous systems that perceive their environment, make decisions, and take actions to achieve specific goals, often enhancing customer engagement.

AI literacy: The foundational understanding of artificial intelligence principles, capabilities, risks, and limitations necessary for ethical implementation.

Algorithmic auditing: The process of evaluating AI models to detect and mitigate biases, ensuring fair and equitable outcomes in marketing practices.

Algorithmic bias: The systematic and repeatable errors in AI decision-making that result in unfair outcomes, often reflecting societal biases present in the training data.

Algorithmic impact assessment (AIA): A structured evaluation of an AI system's potential ethical, social, and legal effects, conducted before deployment or at critical development stages. AIAs help identify and mitigate biases, privacy risks, and other adverse outcomes associated with AI-driven marketing tools.

Ambient intelligence: The seamless integration of AI into everyday environments, enabling devices and systems to interact intelligently without user intervention.

Artificial intelligence ethics: The study and implementation of moral principles in AI development and application to ensure responsible use in marketing.

Augmented intelligence: A human-centered approach to AI that focuses on enhancing, rather than replacing, human capabilities in decision-making and customer engagement.

Automation: The use of AI-driven systems to perform tasks with minimal human intervention, improving efficiency and scalability in marketing.

Bias mitigation: Techniques used to identify and reduce biases in AI models to promote fairness and inclusivity in marketing campaigns.

Big data: Large sets of structured and unstructured data that AI systems analyze to derive insights, predict behaviors, and optimize marketing strategies.

Bio-digital convergence: The integration of biological and digital systems to enhance human capabilities and interactions.

Biomimetic AI systems: AI systems that mimic principles from biology, such as natural selection and neural structures, to create adaptive and efficient solutions.

Blameless postmortems: Structured analysis sessions that examine AI ethics incidents or near-misses without assigning individual blame, instead focusing on identifying systemic issues and opportunities for improvement in organizational processes and practices.

Blockchain-based authentication: A technology that records AI-generated content and data usage securely, ensuring transparency and traceability in marketing.

Brand trust: Consumer confidence in a company's ethical practices, particularly in AI-driven marketing initiatives.

Change management: Strategies and processes organizations use to guide employees through cultural and behavioral transformations, particularly in adopting ethical AI practices.

Chatbot: An AI-powered virtual assistant that interacts with users in real time to provide customer support, answer inquiries, and enhance engagement.

Cognitive trust indicators: Related to a consumer's understanding of AI systems, including how well they comprehend the AI's functionality, limitations, and benefits. Clear explanations and transparency in AI processes enhance cognitive trust.

Consent mechanisms: Tools and policies that ensure consumers actively opt in to data collection and AI-driven personalization, reinforcing their autonomy.

Consumer autonomy: The right of individuals to control how their personal data is used in AI-driven marketing, ensuring they have the ability to opt out or modify AI-driven recommendations.

Consumer trust: The confidence consumers have in a brand's ethical use of AI, data privacy, and transparency in marketing practices.

Consumer trust index: A metric used to gauge consumer sentiment, confidence, and perceived fairness of AI-driven marketing strategies. Tracking trust levels over time allows organizations to understand how their governance practices influence consumer attitudes and loyalty.

Content authenticity initiative (CAI): A system for tracking and verifying the provenance of digital content, establishing transparency standards for AI-generated materials.

Contextual privacy: The notion that privacy expectations vary based on the context and perceived value of data sharing. Offering tailored privacy options aligned with the specific nature of each interaction helps build trust.

Conversational AI: AI-powered chatbots and virtual assistants that use natural language processing to interact with consumers in a human-like manner.

Cross-platform integration: The practice of maintaining consistent ethical standards across different software platforms while adapting to specific use case requirements.

Cultural integration: The process of embedding ethical principles and governance practices into the everyday culture of an organization. Cultural integration ensures that responsible AI use is not perceived as a regulatory burden but as a shared value guiding decision-making at every level.

Customer experience: The overall perception and interaction a consumer has with a brand, influenced by AI-driven personalization and engagement strategies.

Data diversity: Ensuring AI training datasets represent a wide range of demographics, behaviors, and preferences to reduce bias and improve inclusivity.

Data ethics: The moral obligations companies have when collecting, processing, and utilizing consumer data for AI-driven marketing.

Data portability: The ability of consumers to access, download, and transfer their personal data, reinforcing their control over AI-driven personalization.

Data privacy: The ethical and legal responsibility of companies to protect consumer data from unauthorized use, breaches, or exploitation.

Data silos: Isolated sets of data stored separately across different departments or platforms, limiting AI's ability to provide a comprehensive, ethical, and unbiased analysis.

Data transparency: The practice of clearly communicating how consumer data is collected, stored, and used in AI-driven marketing, fostering trust and regulatory compliance.

Deep learning: A subset of machine learning involving neural networks with multiple layers that enable AI to process large datasets and recognize complex patterns.

Deepfake: AI-generated synthetic media that can manipulate videos, images, or audio, often raising ethical concerns in marketing and misinformation.

Demographic parity: A fairness criterion wherein AI-driven recommendations, ads, or other marketing outputs are equitably distributed across different demographic groups. Monitoring demographic parity helps organizations avoid discriminatory outcomes and maintain inclusive engagement strategies.

Differential privacy: A data protection technique that allows AI models to analyze trends and patterns without revealing individual user information, enhancing privacy in marketing analytics.

Digital nutrition labels: Transparent documentation that clearly communicates how AI systems use and process data, similar to food nutrition labels.

Distributed responsibility: The practice of embedding ethical accountability across all levels of an organization rather than centralizing it within a single department or team.

Edge computing: A distributed computing paradigm where data processing occurs closer to the source of data generation, enabling faster and more secure interactions.

Emotional AI (affective computing): AI systems designed to recognize, interpret, and respond to human emotions, often used in personalized marketing.

Empathetic AI: AI systems designed to recognize and respond to human emotions, ensuring interactions are contextually appropriate and emotionally intelligent.

Escalation paths: Formal mechanisms, such as anonymous reporting tools, structured feedback processes, or ethics committees, for raising and addressing ethical concerns.

Escalation protocols: Pre-defined procedures for alerting key stakeholders when potential ethical concerns, biases, or compliance issues arise. These protocols ensure that problems are promptly identified, investigated, and resolved, preventing them from being overlooked or ignored.

Ethical AI: The development and use of AI technologies in ways that prioritize fairness, transparency, accountability, and respect for human rights.

Ethical geo-targeting: The practice of tailoring AI-driven marketing strategies to local norms and values while avoiding discriminatory or exploitative targeting.

Ethical impact assessments: Evaluations conducted before launching AI-driven marketing campaigns to ensure compliance with ethical standards.

Ethical infrastructure: The foundational systems, processes, and organizational capabilities that enable consistent ethical AI practices at scale.

Ethical innovation portfolio: A balanced collection of AI marketing initiatives spanning different time horizons and risk levels while maintaining strong ethical alignment throughout all projects and implementations.

Ethical interoperability: The ability to maintain ethical properties (like ownership rights and provenance) as content and data move between different systems and platforms.

Ethical microtargeting: A privacy-conscious approach to targeted advertising that ensures consumer segmentation respects ethical considerations and avoids manipulation.

Ethical moat: A sustainable competitive advantage built on deep stakeholder trust and demonstrated ethical leadership in AI marketing practices, which proves more durable than purely technical differentiators.

Ethical momentum: The compounding positive effect that occurs when organizations consistently implement ethical practices, creating a foundation for further advances.

Ethical network effects: The increasing value of ethical practices as more organizations adopt them, creating industry-wide standards and expectations.

Ethical scaling principles: Guidelines for maintaining ethical standards while expanding AI implementations across different use cases and user populations.

Ethical stage-gating: A process where AI marketing initiatives must clear increasingly stringent ethical reviews as they expand in scope and impact, ensuring consistent ethical oversight during scaling.

Ethics ambassadors: Designated individuals within teams who serve as liaisons between operational staff and oversight committees. Ethics ambassadors promote accountability, raise awareness of ethical guidelines, and help incorporate ethical considerations into daily workflows.

Ethics-by-design workshops: Interactive sessions that involve consumers, marketers, data scientists, and other stakeholders in shaping the ethical dimensions of AI tools before they are fully implemented. These workshops help align product features and communication strategies with end-user values and expectations.

Explainability coverage: A metric that assesses what proportion of an organization's AI models are accompanied by accessible documentation, visualizations, or methods enabling non-technical stakeholders to understand how decisions are made. High explainability coverage improves transparency and trust.

Explainable AI (XAI): The AI system that is able to provide understandable and interpretable explanations for its decisions and recommendations, increasing consumer trust.

Fairness (in AI): The principle of designing AI systems that provide equitable outcomes and do not disproportionately disadvantage any particular group.

Fairness audits: Regular assessments of AI-driven marketing models to detect and correct biases affecting different consumer groups.

Fairness constraints: Technical adjustments or constraints applied to AI models to ensure that outputs meet predefined fairness criteria. Fairness constraints prevent certain demographic groups from being consistently favored or disadvantaged by AI-driven marketing applications.

Federated learning: A privacy-preserving AI training method where data remains decentralized, reducing the risks associated with centralized data collection.

Filter bubble: A phenomenon where AI-driven personalization limits the diversity of content or perspectives presented to users, reinforcing existing preferences.

Foundation models: Large-scale AI models trained on extensive datasets, capable of performing a wide range of language and image-related tasks.

General Data Protection Regulation (GDPR): A European Union regulation that governs data protection and privacy, impacting AI-driven marketing strategies.

Generative AI: AI systems capable of creating original content, such as text, images, videos, and music, based on learned patterns from existing data.

Granular consent: Allowing consumers to specify how their data is used, offering options beyond a simple opt-in or opt-out.

Human-AI collaboration: A design approach in which AI is used to assist and enhance human decision-making rather than replacing human roles in marketing.

Human-centered AI (HCAI): AI systems designed to enhance human creativity, decision-making, and autonomy rather than replacing them, ensuring ethical marketing practices.

Human-in-the-loop (HITL): An AI approach that integrates human oversight into AI decision-making processes to prevent biases and errors.

Hyper-personalization: The use of AI to deliver highly customized marketing messages, recommendations, and content based on real-time consumer data.

Inclusion (in AI): Ensuring that AI systems and marketing strategies consider diverse consumer needs, preventing discrimination and underrepresentation.

Inference privacy: The protection of personal information that AI systems might deduce from seemingly innocuous data points, requiring special consideration in marketing applications.

Internal audits: Regular, systematic reviews of AI models, data handling practices, and compliance measures conducted by an organization's internal teams. Internal audits verify that ethical standards and regulatory obligations are upheld throughout the AI lifecycle.

Kantian approach: A deontological framework that prioritizes universal ethical principles and respect for human dignity in AI-driven marketing strategies, based on the ideas of Immanuel Kant.

Legal compliance: Ensuring AI-driven marketing adheres to global regulations like GDPR and CCPA to avoid legal risks.

Machine learning (ML): A subset of AI that enables systems to learn from data, identify patterns, and make decisions without explicit programming.

Martech stack: A collection of marketing technologies, including AI-driven analytics, CRM systems, and automation tools, used to optimize marketing operations.

Model cards: Standardized documentation templates providing information about a model's purpose, data sources, performance metrics, intended uses, and known limitations. Model cards enhance transparency, help external stakeholders understand an AI model's capabilities, and support informed decision-making.

Natural language processing (NLP): An AI technology that enables machines to understand, interpret, and respond to human language, used in chatbots and voice assistants.

Non-manipulative AI: AI-driven marketing practices that respect consumer autonomy and do not exploit psychological vulnerabilities.

Oversight committee: A group responsible for reviewing AI-driven marketing strategies to ensure ethical alignment and regulatory compliance.

Personalization boundaries: Ethical guidelines ensuring AI-driven personalization does not overstep into intrusive or manipulative territory.

Predictive analytics: AI-driven techniques that analyze past consumer behaviors to anticipate future actions, improving targeted marketing strategies.

Programmatic advertising: AI-powered automated buying and placement of digital ads, optimizing real-time ad targeting.

Progressive customization: A trust-building approach where AI capabilities and personalization increase gradually as users demonstrate comfort and engagement.

Progressive disclosure: A carefully sequenced approach to sharing information about AI systems that helps consumers build understanding and confidence over time, supporting stronger trust relationships.

Psychological safety: A workplace environment where employees feel safe voicing ethical concerns without fear of retaliation or negative consequences.

Quantum computing: A field of computing that utilizes quantum-mechanical phenomena, such as superposition and entanglement, to perform computations much faster than classical computers for certain problems.

Real-time contextual awareness: AI's capability to analyze current events, consumer sentiment, and trends to adjust marketing strategies dynamically.

Recommender system: An AI-driven tool that suggests products, content, or services based on user preferences, behaviors, and interactions.

Regulatory governance: Policies and frameworks that ensure AI-driven marketing aligns with legal and ethical standards.

Regulatory intelligence: The organizational capability to track, anticipate, and prepare for changes in AI regulations, enabling proactive rather than reactive compliance approaches in marketing.

Sandbox: Controlled environment where organizations can test new AI marketing initiatives with real consumers while maintaining strict ethical oversight, enabling rapid learning and iteration without compromising ethical standards.

Sentiment analysis: AI-based analysis of consumer opinions, emotions, and attitudes derived from text, social media, or reviews to refine marketing strategies.

Stakeholder alignment: The practice of finding common ethical ground among different stakeholder groups (creators, enterprise customers, end users) to drive collective value.

Stakeholder-centric AI: AI marketing strategies that consider the interests of all affected groups, including consumers, regulators, and society at large.

Sustainable AI architecture: An approach to AI system design that optimizes for both performance and environmental impact, considering factors like energy efficiency and resource utilization in marketing applications.

Synthetic data: Artificially generated data that mimics real-world datasets, used to train AI models while preserving consumer privacy.

Synthetic media: AI-generated content, such as virtual influencers, deepfake videos, or photorealistic images, used in marketing and media.

Transparency (in AI): The practice of openly communicating AI decision-making processes, limitations, and trade-offs to stakeholders, including customers and employees.

Transparency paradox: The challenge of providing sufficient information to build trust without overwhelming or disengaging consumers. Tailoring the depth of disclosures to the interaction type helps manage this balance.

Trust (in AI): The confidence consumers have in AI-driven marketing decisions based on the system's fairness, transparency, and reliability.

Trust indicators: Actions taken by consumers, such as engagement frequency, data-sharing preferences, and feature usage, that provide insights into trust levels in AI marketing systems.

Trust Measurement Framework (TMF): A framework for assessing consumer trust in AI marketing systems. TMF encompasses behavioral, emotional, and cognitive dimensions to provide a holistic view of trust dynamics.

Trust velocity metrics: Measurements that track not just current trust levels but the rate and direction of trust development over time in AI marketing initiatives, providing insight into the effectiveness of ethical practices.

Trust-aware interfaces: User interaction systems that adapt based on demonstrated trust levels and engagement history.

Utilitarian: A framework emphasizing AI marketing strategies that maximize overall consumer benefit while minimizing harm.

Value exchange mechanisms: Systems that ensure fair compensation and recognition for contributors to AI training data and generated content.

Virtue ethics (in AI): The application of ethical principles inspired by Aristotle's philosophy, ensuring AI systems align with moral character and brand values.

Whistleblower risks (in AI): The potential consequences faced by employees or researchers who expose unethical AI practices within organizations.

Zero-trust security: A cybersecurity approach requiring continuous verification for all systems, users, and devices, even within an organization's network.

Postscript

Ethical AI marketing isn't a destination but a continuous practice. It asks us to lead with intention, question convenience, and design with care. My hope is that this book helps spark deeper conversations and more deliberate choices in how we innovate, connect, and build trust.

If you'd like to stay in touch or share how this work resonates with you, I'd love to hear from you. You can find me on Instagram and BlueSky: **@nikimari.**

Nicole M. Alexander

INDEX

Note: Page numbers in *italics* refer to figures and tables.

Looking for another book?

Explore our award-winning
books from global business
experts in Marketing and Sales

Scan the code to browse

www.koganpage.com/marketing

More from kogan page

ISBN: 9781398622333

ISBN: 9781398615700

ISBN: 9780749483395

www.koganpage.com